3

Grammar Connection

STRUCTURE THROUGH CONTENT

SERIES EDITORS

Marianne Celce-Murcia

M. E. Sokolik

Karen Carlisi

HEINLE
CENGAGE Learning

Australia • Brazil • Japan • Korea • Mexico • Singapore • Spain • United Kingdom • United States

HEINLE
CENGAGE Learning™

Grammar Connection 3:
    Structure Through Content
Karen Carlisi

**Series Editors: Marianne Celce-Murcia,
M. E. Sokolik**

Publisher: Sherrise Roehr

Consulting Editor: James W. Brown

Director of Content Development: Anita Raducanu

Acquisitions Editor, Academic ESL: Tom Jefferies

Senior Development Editor: Michael Ryall

Assistant Editor: Sara Spader

Editorial Assistant: Katherine Reilly

Director of Product Marketing: Amy Mabley

Executive Marketing Manager: Jim McDonough

Senior Field Marketing Manager: Donna Lee Kennedy

Product Marketing Manager: Katie Kelley

Senior Production Project Manager:
    Maryellen Eschmann-Killeen

Manufacturing Buyer: Betsy Donaghey

Production Project Manager: Chrystie Hopkins

Production Services: InContext Publishing Partners

Index: Alexandra Nickerson

Cover and Interior Design: Linda Beaupre

Cover Image: © Harold Sund/The Image Bank/
    Getty Images

Credits appear on page 320, which constitutes
a continuation of the copyright page.

For permission to use material from this text
or product, submit all requests online at
cengage.com/permissions
Further permissions questions can be emailed to
permissionrequest@cengage.com

Library of Congress Control Number: 2007924642

ISBN 13: 978-1-4130-0840-1

ISBN 10: 1-4130-0840-2

International Student Edition

ISBN 13: 978-1-4130-1754-0

ISBN 10: 1-4130-1754-1

Heinle
25 Thomson Place
Boston, MA 02210
USA

Cengage Learning is a leading provider of customized
learning solutions with office locations around the
globe, including Singapore, the United Kingdom,
Australia, Mexico, Brazil, and Japan. Locate our local
office at: **international.cengage.com/region**

Cengage Learning products are represented in
Canada by Nelson Education, Ltd.

Visit Heinle online at **elt.heinle.com**

Visit our corporate website at **cengage.com**

Printed in the United States of America.
3 4 5 6 7 8 9 10 — 11 10 09 08

Using language grammatically and being able to communicate authentically are important goals for students. My grammar research suggests that students' mastery of grammar improves when they interpret and produce grammar in meaningful contexts at the discourse level. *Grammar Connection* connects learners to academic success, allowing them to reach their goals and master the grammar.

— Marianne Celce-Murcia

"Connections" is probably the most useful concept in any instructor's vocabulary. To help students connect what they are learning to the rest of their lives is the most important task I fulfill as an instructor. *Grammar Connection* lets instructors and students find those connections. The series connects grammar to reading, writing, and speaking. It also connects students with the ability to function academically, to use the Internet for interesting research, and to collaborate with others on projects and presentations.   — M. E. Sokolik

Dear Instructor,

With experience in language teaching, teacher training, and research, we created *Grammar Connection* to be uniquely relevant for academically and professionally oriented courses and students. Every lesson in the series deals with academic content to help students become familiar with the language of college and the university and to feel more comfortable in all of their courses, not just English.

While academic content provides the context for this series, our goal is for the learner to go well beyond sentence-level exercises in order to use grammar as a resource for comprehending and producing academic discourse. Students move from shorter, more controlled exercises to longer, more self-directed, authentic ones. Taking a multi-skills approach, *Grammar Connection* includes essential grammar that students need to know at each level. Concise lessons allow instructors to use the material easily in any classroom situation.

We hope that you and your students find our approach to the teaching and learning of grammar for academic and professional purposes in *Grammar Connection* effective and innovative.

Marianne Celce-Murcia   *M. E. Sokolik*
Series Editor   Series Editor

Welcome to
Grammar Connection

■ **What is *Grammar Connection*?**

Grammar Connection is a five-level grammar series that integrates content with grammar instruction in an engaging format to prepare students for future academic and professional success.

■ **What is the content?**

The content in ***Grammar Connection*** is drawn from various academic disciplines: sociology, psychology, medical sciences, computer science, communications, biology, engineering, business, and the social sciences.

■ **Why does *Grammar Connection* incorporate content into the lessons?**

The content is used to provide high-interest contexts for exploring the grammar. The charts and exercises are contextualized with the content in each lesson. Learning content is not the focus of ***Grammar Connection***—it sets the scene for learning grammar.

■ **Is *Grammar Connection* "discourse-based"?**

Yes. With ***Grammar Connection,*** learners go beyond sentence-level exercises in order to use grammar as a resource for comprehending and producing academic discourse. These discourses include conversations, narratives, and exposition.

■ **Does *Grammar Connection* include communicative practice?**

Yes. ***Grammar Connection*** takes a multi-skills approach. The series includes listening activities as well as texts for reading, and the production tasks elicit both spoken and written output via pair or group work tasks.

■ **Why are the lessons shorter than in other books?**

Concise lessons allow instructors to use the material easily in any classroom situation. For example, one part of a lesson could be covered in a 50-minute period, allowing instructors with shorter class times to feel a sense of completion. Alternatively, a single lesson could fit into a longer, multi-skills class period. For longer, grammar-focused classes, more than one lesson could be covered.

■ **Does *Grammar Connection* include opportunities for students to review the grammar?**

Yes. A Review section is included after every five lessons. These tests can also be used by instructors to measure student understanding of the grammar taught. In addition, there are practice exercises in the Workbook and on the website (elt.thomson.com/grammarconnection).

■ **Does *Grammar Connection* assist students in learning new vocabulary?**

Yes. The Content Vocabulary section in each lesson of ***Grammar Connection*** incorporates academic vocabulary building and journaling. In Book 1 this takes a picture dictionary approach. In later books words from the Academic Word List are used. This, along with the content focus, ensures that students expand their vocabulary along with their grammatical capability.

Grammar Connection is organized into thirty concise lessons, each containing two or three parts of connected grammar points. Every lesson follows a unique pedagogical approach.

A **picture-based vocabulary** section in lower levels familiarizes students with the content-based academic vocabulary that is used in the lesson. At higher levels, students are introduced to words from the **Academic Word List.**

The grammar in each lesson is **contextualized** with topics from different **academic disciplines.**

Thought-provoking **discussion questions** activate students' knowledge of the content area. The questions can also be used as **diagnostic tests** to assess students' mastery of the grammar before it is taught.

An integrated **audio program** allows students to listen to the content readings and dialogues.

Content readings and dialogues present the grammar in a meaningful and interesting way.

Contextualized **grammar charts** provide **easy-to-understand** clear explanations of grammar form as well as notes on usage.

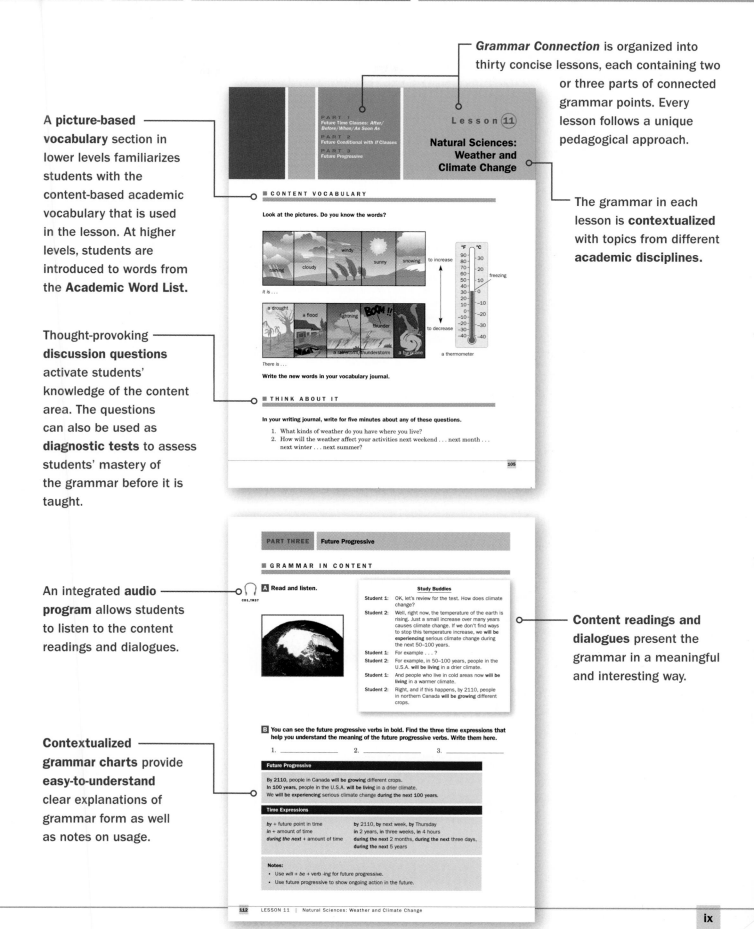

PART 1
Future Time Clauses: *After/Before/When/As Soon As*
PART 2
Future Conditional with *If* Clauses
PART 3
Future Progressive

Lesson 11

Natural Sciences: Weather and Climate Change

■ CONTENT VOCABULARY

Look at the pictures. Do you know the words?

raining   cloudy   windy   sunny   snowing   to increase

°F °C   freezing   to decrease

It is . . .

a drought   a flood   lightning   BOOM!!   thunder   a rainstorm/thunderstorm   a hurricane   a thermometer

There is . . .

Write the new words in your vocabulary journal.

■ THINK ABOUT IT

In your writing journal, write for five minutes about any of these questions.

1. What kinds of weather do you have where you live?
2. How will the weather affect your activities next weekend . . . next month . . . next winter . . . next summer?

105

PART THREE   Future Progressive

■ GRAMMAR IN CONTENT

A Read and listen.

CD1, TR37

Study Buddies

Student 1: OK, let's review for the test. How does climate change?

Student 2: Well, right now, the temperature of the earth is rising. Just a small increase over many years causes climate change. If we don't find ways to stop this temperature increase, we **will be experiencing** serious climate change during the next 50–100 years.

Student 1: For example . . . ?

Student 2: For example, in 50–100 years, people in the U.S.A. **will be living** in a drier climate.

Student 1: And people who live in cold areas now **will be living** in a warmer climate.

Student 2: Right, and if this happens, by 2110, people in northern Canada **will be growing** different crops.

B You can see the future progressive verbs in bold. Find the three time expressions that help you understand the meaning of the future progressive verbs. Write them here.

1. _____   2. _____   3. _____

Future Progressive

By 2110, people in Canada **will be growing** different crops.
In 100 years, people in the U.S.A. **will be living** in a drier climate.
We will be experiencing serious climate change during the next 100 years.

Time Expressions

by + future point in time	by 2110, by next week, by Thursday
in + amount of time	in 2 years, in three weeks, in 4 hours
during the next + amount of time	during the next 2 months, during the next three days, during the next 5 years

Notes:
• Use *will* + *be* + verb *-ing* for future progressive.
• Use future progressive to show ongoing action in the future.

Students move from a **variety** of controlled exercises to more self-directed ones enabling students to become comfortable using the grammar.

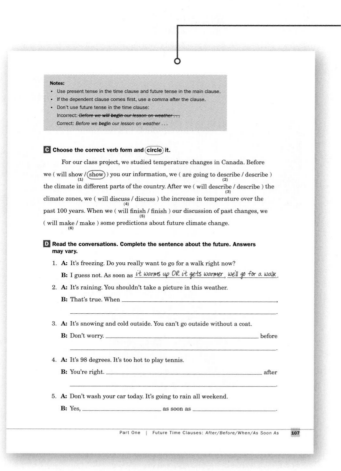

Notes:
• Use present tense in the time clause and future tense in the main clause.
• If the dependent clause comes first, use a comma after the clause.
• Don't use future tense in the time clause:
  Incorrect: ~~Before we will begin our lesson on weather . . .~~
  Correct: Before we **begin** our lesson on weather . . .

C Choose the correct verb form and ⊙circle it.

For our class project, we studied temperature changes in Canada. Before we (will show / ⊙show) you our information, we (are going to describe / describe)
_(1)_ _(2)_
the climate in different parts of the country. After we (will describe / describe) the
_(3)_
climate zones, we (will discuss / discuss) the increase in temperature over the
_(4)_
past 100 years. When we (will finish / finish) our discussion of past changes, we
_(5)_
(will make / make) some predictions about future climate change.
_(6)_

D Read the conversations. Complete the sentence about the future. Answers may vary.

1. **A:** It's freezing. Do you really want to go for a walk right now?
   B: I guess not. As soon as _it warms up OR it gets warmer_, _we'll go for a walk_.

2. **A:** It's raining. You shouldn't take a picture in this weather.
   B: That's true. When _____.
   _____

3. **A:** It's snowing and cold outside. You can't go outside without a coat.
   B: Don't worry. _____ before
   _____

4. **A:** It's 98 degrees. It's too hot to play tennis.
   B: You're right. _____ after
   _____

5. **A:** Don't wash your car today. It's going to rain all weekend.
   B: Yes, _____ as soon as _____.

Part One | Future Time Clauses: After/Before/When/As Soon As **107**

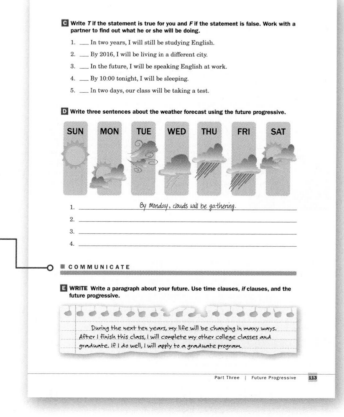

C Write *T* if the statement is true for you and *F* if the statement is false. Work with a partner to find out what he or she will be doing.

1. ___ In two years, I will still be studying English.
2. ___ By 2016, I will be living in a different city.
3. ___ In the future, I will be speaking English at work.
4. ___ By 10:00 tonight, I will be sleeping.
5. ___ In two days, our class will be taking a test.

D Write three sentences about the weather forecast using the future progressive.

| SUN | MON | TUE | WED | THU | FRI | SAT |

1. _____ By Monday, clouds will be gathering. _____
2. _____
3. _____
4. _____

■ **COMMUNICATE**

E WRITE Write a paragraph about your future. Use time clauses, *if* clauses, and the future progressive.

During the next ten years, my life will be changing in many ways.
After I finish this class, I will complete my other college classes and
graduate. If I do well, I will apply to a graduate program.

Part Three | Future Progressive **113**

Communicate sections allow students to speak or write about their thoughts and experiences.

At the end of each lesson, students are encouraged to put together the **grammar and vocabulary** from the lesson in a productive way.

Interesting projects allow students to put newly learned grammatical forms and vocabulary to use in ways that encourage additional independent reading, **research,** and/or communication. Many of these activities are group activities, further requiring students to put their language skills to work.

Internet activities encourage students to connect the grammar with online resources.

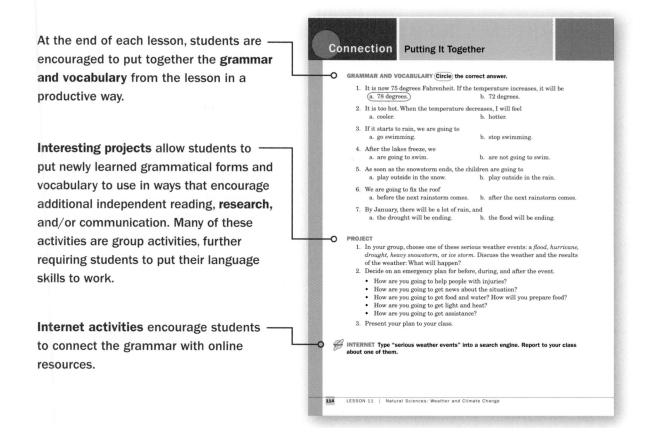

Connection   Putting It Together

GRAMMAR AND VOCABULARY Circle the correct answer.

1. It is now 75 degrees Fahrenheit. If the temperature increases, it will be
   a. 78 degrees.   b. 72 degrees.
2. It is too hot. When the temperature decreases, I will feel
   a. cooler.   b. hotter.
3. If it starts to rain, we are going to
   a. go swimming.   b. stop swimming.
4. After the lakes freeze, we
   a. are going to swim.   b. are not going to swim.
5. As soon as the snowstorm ends, the children are going to
   a. play outside in the snow.   b. play outside in the rain.
6. We are going to fix the roof
   a. before the next rainstorm comes.   b. after the next rainstorm comes.
7. By January, there will be a lot of rain, and
   a. the drought will be ending.   b. the flood will be ending.

PROJECT

1. In your group, choose one of these serious weather events: a *flood, hurricane, drought, heavy snowstorm,* or *ice storm.* Discuss the weather and the results of the weather: What will happen?
2. Decide on an emergency plan for before, during, and after the event.
   - How are you going to help people with injuries?
   - How are you going to get news about the situation?
   - How are you going to get food and water? How will you prepare food?
   - How are you going to get light and heat?
   - How are you going to get assistance?
3. Present your plan to your class.

INTERNET Type "serious weather events" into a search engine. Report to your class about one of them.

A **Review** section after every five lessons helps assess and reinforce language learning.

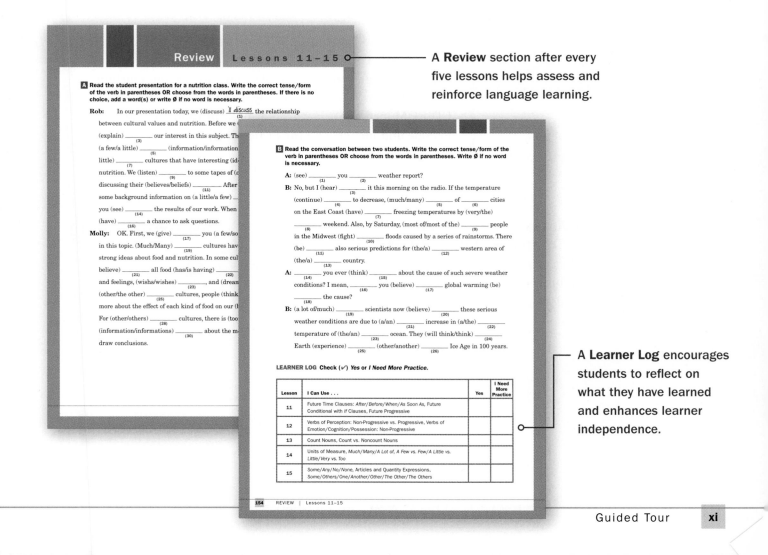

Review   Lessons 11–15

A Read the student presentation for a nutrition class. Write the correct tense/form of the verb in parentheses OR choose from the words in parentheses. If there is no choice, add a word(s) or write Ø if no word is necessary.

Rob: In our presentation today, we (discuss) *'ll discuss* the relationship
(1)
between cultural values and nutrition. Before we (
(explain) _____ our interest in this subject. Th
(3)
(a few/a little) _____ (information/information
(5)
little) _____ cultures that have interesting (id
(7)
nutrition. We (listen) _____ to some tapes of (g
(9)
discussing their (believes/beliefs) _____. After
(11)
some background information on (a little/a few) ____
you (see) _____ the results of our work. When
(14)
(have) _____ a chance to ask questions.
(16)

Molly: OK. First, we (give) _____ you (a few/so
(17)
in this topic. (Much/Many) _____ cultures hav
(19)
strong ideas about food and nutrition. In some cul
believe) _____ all food (has/is having) _____
(21)   (22)
and feelings, (wishs/wishes) _____, and (dream
(23)
(other/the other) _____ cultures, people (think
(25)
more about the effect of each kind of food on our (l
For (other/others) _____ cultures, there is (too
(28)
(information/informations) _____ about the m
(30)
draw conclusions.

B Read the conversation between two students. Write the correct tense/form of the verb in parentheses OR choose from the words in parentheses. Write Ø if no word is necessary.

A: (see) _____ you _____ weather report?
         (1)   (2)
B: No, but I (hear) _____ it this morning on the radio. If the temperature
                      (3)
(continue) _____ to decrease, (much/many) _____ of _____ cities
          (4)   (5)   (6)
on the East Coast (have) _____ freezing temperatures by (very/the)
                          (7)
_____ weekend. Also, by Saturday, (most of/most of the) _____ people
(8)   (9)
in the Midwest (fight) _____ floods caused by a series of rainstorms. There
                       (10)
(be) _____ also serious predictions for (the/a) _____ western area of
    (11)   (12)
(the/a) _____ country.
        (13)
A: _____ you ever (think) _____ about the cause of such severe weather
       (14)   (15)
conditions? I mean, _____ you (believe) _____ global warming (be)
                    (16)   (17)
_____ the cause?
(18)
B: (a lot of/much) _____ scientists now (believe) _____ these serious
                       (19)   (20)
weather conditions are due to (a/an) _____ increase in (a/the) _____
                                      (21)   (22)
temperature of (the/an) _____ ocean. They (will think/think) _____
                        (23)   (24)
Earth (experience) _____ (other/another) _____ Ice Age in 100 years.
                   (25)   (26)

LEARNER LOG Check (✓) *Yes* or *I Need More Practice.*

Lesson	I Can Use . . .	Yes	I Need More Practice
11	Future Time Clauses: After/Before/When/As Soon As, Future Conditional with If Clauses, Future Progressive		
12	Verbs of Perception: Non-Progressive vs. Progressive, Verbs of Emotion/Cognition/Possession: Non-Progressive		
13	Count Nouns, Count vs. Noncount Nouns		
14	Units of Measure, Much/Many/A Lot of, A Few vs. Few/A Little vs. Little/Very vs. Too		
15	Some/Any/No/None, Articles and Quantity Expressions, Some/Others/One/Another/Other/The Other/The Others		

A **Learner Log** encourages students to reflect on what they have learned and enhances learner independence.

Supplements

■ Audio Program

Audio CDs and Audio Tapes allow students to listen to every reading in the book to build listening skills and fluency.

■ Workbook

The Workbooks review and practice all the grammar points in the Student Book. In addition each workbook includes six Writing Tutorials and vocabulary expansion exercises.

■ Website

Features additional grammar practice activities, vocabulary test items, and other resources: elt.heinle.com/grammarconnection.

■ Annotated Teacher's Edition with Presentation Tool CD-ROM

Offers comprehensive lesson planning advice and teaching tips, as well as a full answer key. The Presentation Tool CD-ROM includes a PowerPoint presentation for selected lessons and includes all the grammar charts from the book.

■ Assessment CD-ROM with *ExamView*® Test Generator

The customizable generator features lesson, review, mid-term, and term-end assessment items to monitor student progress.

Grammar Connection is based on scientific research on the most effective means of teaching grammar to adult learners of English.

■ Discourse-based Grammar

Research by Celce-Murcia and Olshtain (2000) suggests that learners should go beyond sentence-level exercises in order to use grammar as a resource for comprehending and producing academic discourse. *Grammar Connection* lets students move from controlled exercises to more self-expressive and self-directed ones.

■ Communicative Grammar

Research shows that communicative exercises should complement traditional exercises (Comeau, 1987; Herschensohn, 1988). *Grammar Connection* balances effective controlled activities, such as fill-in-the-blanks, with meaningful interactive exercises.

■ Learner-centered Content

Van Duzer (1999) emphasizes that research on adult English language learners shows that "learners should read texts that meet their needs and are interesting." In *Grammar Connection* the content readings are carefully selected and adapted to be both high-interest and relevant to the needs of learners.

■ Vocabulary Development

A number of recent studies have shown the effectiveness of helping English language learners develop independent skills in vocabulary development (Nation, 1990, 2001; Nist & Simpson, 2001; Schmitt, 2000). In *Grammar Connection,* care has been taken to introduce useful academic vocabulary, based in part on Coxhead's (2000) work.

■ Using Background Knowledge

Because research shows that background knowledge facilitates comprehension (Eskey, 1997), each lesson of *Grammar Connection* opens with a "Think About It" section related to the lesson theme.

■ Student Interaction

Learning is enhanced when students work with each other to co-construct knowledge (Grennon-Brooks & Brooks, 1993; Sutherland & Bonwell, 1996). *Grammar Connection* includes many pair and group work exercises as well as interactive projects.

■ References

Celce-Murcia, M., & Olshtain, E. (2000). *Discourse and Context in Language Teaching.* **New York: Cambridge University Press.**

Comeau, R. Interactive Oral Grammar Exercises. **In W. M. Rivers (Ed.),** *Interactive Language Teaching* **(57–69). Cambridge: Cambridge University Press, 1987.**

Coxhead, A. (2000). "A New Academic Word List." *TESOL Quarterly,* **34 (2), 213–238.**

Eskey, D. (1997). "Models of Reading and the ESOL Student." *Focus on Basics 1 (B),* **9–11.**

Grennon Brooks, J., & Brooks, M. G. (1993). *In Search of Understanding: The Case for Constructivist Classrooms.* **Alexandria, VA: Association for Supervision and Curriculum Development.**

Herschensohn, J. (1988). "Linguistic Accuracy of Textbook Grammar." *Modern Language Journal 72(4),* **409–414.**

Nation, I. S. P. (2001). *Learning Vocabulary in Another Language.* **New York: Cambridge University Press.**

Nation, I. S. P. (1990). *Teaching and Learning Vocabulary.* **Boston: Thomson Heinle.**

Nist, S. L., & Simpson, M. L. (2001). *Developing Vocabulary for College Thinking.* **Boston: Allyn & Bacon.**

Schmitt, N. (2000). *Vocabulary in Language Teaching.* **New York: Cambridge University Press.**

Sutherland, T. E., & Bonwell, C. C. (Eds.). (1996). "Using Active Learning in College Classes: A Range of Options for Faculty." *New Directions for Teaching and Learning, Number 67,* **Fall 1996. San Francisco, CA: Jossey-Bass Publishers.**

VanDuzer, C. (1999). "Reading and the Adult Language Learner." *ERIC Digest.* **Washington, D.C.: National Center for ESL Literacy Education.**

Acknowledgments

I would like to thank the Thomson team, especially Tom Jefferies for his encouragement, guidance, patience, and sense of humor, as well as my editor, Charlotte Sturdy, for her hard work, support, and grounded sense of our students.

This book is dedicated to Howard, Rose, and Nathan, whose love, support, and sense of reality kept me going.

— *Karen Carlisi*

The author, series editors, and publisher wish to thank the following people for their contributions:

Susan Alexandre
Trimble Technical High School
Fort Worth, TX

Joan Amore
Triton College
River Grove, IL

Cally Andriotis-Williams
Newcomers High School
Long Island City, NY

Ana Maria Cepero
Miami Dade College
Miami, FL

Jacqueline Cunningham
Harold Washington College
Chicago, IL

Kathleen Flynn
Glendale Community College
Glendale, CA

Sally Gearhart
Santa Rosa Junior College
Santa Rosa, CA

Janet Harclerode
Santa Monica College
Santa Monica, CA

Carolyn Ho
North Harris College
Houston, TX

Eugenia Krimmel
Lititz, PA

Dana Liebowitz
Palm Beach Central High
  School
Wellington, FL

Shirley Lundblade
Mt. San Antonio College
Walnut, CA

Craig Machado
Norwalk Community College
Norwalk, CT

Myo Myint
Mission College
Santa Clara, CA

Myra Redman
Miami Dade College
Miami, FL

Eric Rosenbaum
BEGIN Managed Programs
New York, NY

Marilyn Santos
Valencia Community College
Valencia, FL

Laura Sicola
University of Pennsylvania
Philadelphia, PA

Barbara Smith-Palinkas
University of South Florida
Tampa, FL

Kathy Sucher
Santa Monica College
Santa Monica, CA

Patricia Turner
San Diego City College
San Diego, CA

America Vasquez
Miami Dade College, Inter-
  American Campus
Miami, FL

Tracy von Mulaski
El Paso Community College
El Paso, TX

Jane Wang
Mt. San Antonio College
Walnut, CA

Lucy Watel
City College of Chicago - Harry
  S. Truman College
Chicago, IL

Donald Weasenforth
Collin County Community
  College
Plano, TX

PART 1
Simple Present Tense:
Statements/Questions/Short
Answers

PART 2
Adverbs of Frequency

Lesson ①

Academic Success: The First Week of Class

■ CONTENT VOCABULARY

Look at the pictures. Do you know the words?

Syllabus
English 1A
MWF 11:00–11:50

Assignments:
Paper #1 – Due on 10/5
Paper #2 – Due on 11/26
Final Project – Due on 12/6

a syllabus

a planner

a study buddy

a textbook

There are three important ideas. The first is. . .

to participate in class

to take notes

a lecture

Write the new words in your vocabulary journal.

■ THINK ABOUT IT

In your writing journal, write for five minutes about this question.
What are the habits of a successful student?

■ GRAMMAR IN CONTENT

A **Read and listen.**

CD1,TR1

regular: every day

punctual: on time

revisions: changes and corrections
in writing

Academic Success

    Is there a secret to academic success? Do successful students have specific habits? A 2005 study answers these questions and discusses the habits of successful students. For example, a successful student **reviews** the syllabus and **uses** a daily planner. Successful students **don't waste** time. They **don't watch** TV or **play** video games for many hours in the evenings. Successful students also **work** with a "study buddy." The study buddy **spends** time with his/her friend on homework and test preparation. In addition, successful students **register** early for classes, **participate** in class, and **communicate** with the professor. They **have** regular, punctual attendance. A successful student also **uses** the college library, **visits** the tutoring center, and **makes** revisions on written work. The research **shows** that successful college students **are** punctual, efficient, and hard-working.

B **Look at the verbs in the reading above.**

1. The present tense verbs are in **bold.** Circle the subject of each present tense verb.

2. Underline the verbs with an *-s* ending. How are the subjects of these verbs different? Write a rule for the use of the *-s* ending:

_____

Simple Present Tense Regular Verbs				
Affirmative		**Negative**		
Subject	**Verb**	**Subject**	***Do/Does + Not***	**Verb**
I/You/We/They	read.	I/You/We/They	do not	write.
He/She/It	reads.	He/She/It	does not	write.
Be				
Subject	**Verb**	**Subject**	***Be + Not***	
I	am	I	am not (I'm not)	
You/We/They	are late.	You	are not (aren't OR You're not)	early.
He/She/It	is	He/She/It	is not (isn't)	

Yes/No Questions			Short Answers		
Do	**Subject**	**Verb**	**Yes/No**	**Subject**	**Do**
Do	I/you/we/they	read?	Yes, No,	I/you/we/they	do. don't.
Does	he/she/it		Yes, No,	he/she/it	does. doesn't.

Be	**Subject**		**Yes/No**	**Subject**	**Be**
Am	I	late?	Yes, No,	you	are. aren't.
Are	you (singular) we/you/they		Yes, No,	I	am. am not.
			Yes, No,	we/you/they	are. aren't.
Is	he/she/it		Yes, No,	he/she/it	is. isn't.

Notes:

- After *he/she/it,* change **have** to **has.**
- The following contractions are used for *be:* **I'm/He's/She's/It's/You're/We're/They're.** Do not use contractions with affirmative short answers:

  Incorrect: ~~Yes, I'm. Yes, she's.~~

- **Spelling**
   1. Add **-s** after verbs that end in consonants or vowel + **y**: *runs, says.*
   2. Add **-es** after **s, ss, sh, ch, x**: *pushes, misses.*
   3. If the verb ends in consonant + **y**, change the **y** to **i** and add **-es**: *tries, cries.*
   4. Add **-es** after *go* and *do* when *he/she/it* is the subject: *goes, does.*
- **Pronunciation**
   1. Voiceless consonants + s = /s/, as in *hits*
   2. Voiced consonants + s OR Vowels + s OR y + s = /z/, as in *needs, does, pays, studies*
   3. ss, sh, ch, x + es = /iz/, as in *misses*
   4. says = /sez/

C **Fill the blanks with the correct form of the verb. Use a contraction if possible.**

Susan (be) ___is___ a successful student. She (work) ___works___ hard in class
(1)   (2)

and she (study) ___studies___ hard outside of class. She (not/talk) ___Do not talk___ to her
(3)   (4)

friends or (use) ___uses___ her cell phone during class. She (listen) ___listen___ to the
(5)   (6)

professor and (take) ___taking___ notes. At the beginning of the semester, she (read)
(7)

___read___ the syllabus carefully, and she (write) ___writes___ the important dates in
(8)   (9)

her planner. When her teacher (return) ___return___ her assignments, Susan (correct)
(10)

___corrected___ her mistakes and (revise) ___revised___ her compositions.
(11)   (12)

D **Write a simple present tense *yes/no* question for each conversation.**

1. **Q:** ___Is a successful language student hard-working?___

   A: Yes, that's right. A successful language student is hard-working.

2. **Q:** ___Are Rica and Jenny hard working language students___

   A: Yes, Rica and Jenny are hard-working language students.

3. **Q:** ___Does Rica practices new grammatical structures after class.___

   A: Yes, she does. Rica practices new grammatical structures after class.

4. **Q:** ___Does Jenny writes a journal about her daily learning experiences.___

   A: Yes, she does. Jenny writes a journal about her daily learning experiences.

5. **Q:** ___Do Rica and Jenny go to the student learning center every day___

   A: Yes, they do. Jenny and Rica go to the Student Learning Center every day.

6. **Q:** ___Does Jenny changes her plans when she needs to study___

   A: Yes, she does. Jenny changes her plans when she needs to study.

7. **Q:** ___Is Rica arranges her schedule with regular study hours___

   A: Yes, Rica arranges her schedule with regular study hours.

8. **Q:** ___Is Jenny Rica's study buddy. Are they study for test together.___

   A: Yes, Jenny is Rica's study buddy. They study for tests together.

■ COMMUNICATE

E **WRITE** Choose two friends or classmates: one successful student and one unsuccessful student. Describe the habits of each person.

> My friend Howard is a very successful student. He studies hard and does all of his homework. He has two study buddies, and he works with them in the library. He gets As on his assignments and tests. My other friend, Martin, is not a very successful student. He comes late to class and he doesn't complete all of his homework. He doesn't practice his English outside of class. He gets Cs and Ds on his tests and assignments.

PART TWO	Adverbs of Frequency

■ GRAMMAR IN CONTENT

CD1,TR2

A **Read and listen.**

The First Day of Class

Professor: OK. Class meets every Monday and Wednesday from 10:00 to 11:30, and we don't meet on Fridays.

Student 1: Do we ever have a break during class?

Professor: No, we don't. We have too much work, so we rarely have a break. Remember, we always begin class punctually at 10:00 and end at 11:30. Every other week, you write an in-class essay, and every Tuesday, class begins with a short quiz.

Student 2: How often do you assign homework?

Professor: I usually assign homework at the end of each class. And I never accept late homework.

Student 3: Does class ever end early?

Professor: Hardly ever. But sometimes students leave class early after finishing a test.

to assign: teacher gives students work to do

B Look again at the reading passage on page 5. The expressions of frequency are in bold. They answer the question "How often?" Find the words with the same meaning as those below and write them.

1. on Tuesdays: _short quiz_

2. almost never: _class ends early._

3. every Friday: _we don't meet._

4. most of the time: _you writing easy_

5. at any time: _No break during class._

Adverbs of Frequency

Frequency	Words	Examples/Notes
100% 0%	always almost always usually, generally often sometimes hardly ever, rarely, seldom never	Use frequency words to answer the question *Do you ever . . .?* Q: Do you ever study in the library? A: Sometimes. I **always** study there **before a big test**.

Notes:

• The adverb of frequency usually comes before the main verb but after the *be* verb. Example: *She **always uses** a planner. She **is always** punctual.*

• Change the word order for negative adverbs (**seldom, rarely, hardly ever**) if they come at the beginning of the sentence. Example: *She **rarely** sees a tutor. **Rarely** does she see a tutor.*

Frequency Expressions

on Mondays/Tuesdays/Wednesdays, etc. **every** day/Tuesday/week/semester/summer **every other** day/week/Thursday **during** the day/week/semester **in** the spring/summer/fall/winter **in** the morning/afternoon/evening **once/twice/three times** a day/week/month; **once in a while**	Use these frequency expressions to answer the questions *How often . . .?* or *When . . .?* Q: **How often** do you see a tutor? A: **Every Friday** in the Writing Center. Q: **When** do you write your essays? A: I write them **on Fridays**.

C Look at the chart below. Write one question and answer about each student. Use *"Does (name) ever . . .?"* in each question. Use a frequency word in your answer.

Habits	Frequency of Habit (% of Time)			
	Eva	Jim	Maria	Bill
reviews the syllabus	100%	80%	50%	5%
uses a planner	100%	85%	20%	0%
reads the textbook	100%	90%	50%	10%
works with a "study buddy"	90%	80%	50%	0%
studies for exams	90%	85%	60%	0%
participates in class	100%	80%	70%	5%
takes notes during class	100%	80%	5%	5%

1. Eva

   Q: _____ Does Eva ever use a planner? _____

   A: _____ Yes, she does. She always uses a planner. _____

2. Jim

   Q: _____ Does Jim read the textbook? _____

   A: _____ Yes, he does. Jim does read the textbook. _____

3. Maria

   Q: _____ Does Maria takes notes during class? _____

   A: _____ No, she does not. Maria does not takes notes during class. _____

4. Bill

   Q: _____ Does Bill ever studies for exams? _____

   A: _____ No, he does not studie for exams. _____

D Look at Susan's academic planner. Write four questions and answers about her schedule. In each question, use *"How often does Susan . . .?"* Use frequency expressions in your answers (i.e. use plural instead of singular nouns).

September

Sun	Mon	Tues	Wed	Thur	Fri	Sat
check syllabus	1 7:00– library	2 3:00– meet tutor	3 4:00– library	4	5 1:00 meet study buddy	6
7	8 7:00– library	9 3:00– meet tutor	10 4:00– library	11	12 1:00 meet study buddy	13
14 check syllabus	15 7:00– library	16 3:00– meet tutor	17 4:00– library	18	19 1:00 meet study buddy	20
21	22 7:00– library	23	24 4:00– library	25	26 1:00 meet study buddy	27 write paper
28 write paper check syllabus	29 7:00– library	30 3:00– meet tutor	4:00– library			

1. **Q:** How often does Susan go to the library?
   A: She goes to the library every Monday and Wednesday.

2. **Q:** _____
   A: _____

3. **Q:** _____
   A: _____

4. **Q:** _____
   A: _____

5. **Q:** _____
   A: _____

E (Circle) **the correct verb and frequency adverb.**

The students in Professor Martin's class ((have) / has) different study habits.
(1)

For example, Ewa is a C student. She (never / usually) doesn't (review / reviews)
(2)   (3)

important ideas in her textbook. Jeong is a B student. She (seldom / often)
(4)

(miss / misses) class and (hardly ever / usually) (work / works) with a study
(5)   (6)   (7)

buddy. Anita is a D student. She only (use / uses) her daily planner for test dates.
(8)

She (never / rarely) (look / looks) at her planner, and she doesn't (take / takes)
(9)   (10)   (11)

notes in class. Anita (isn't / doesn't) a successful student. She (often / hardly ever)
(12)   (13)

(receives / doesn't receive) low grades.
(14)

F **Look at the underlined verb in the first sentence. Write the correct form of that verb in the second sentence. Then practice reading both sentences with a partner. Help correct your partner's pronunciation if necessary.**

1. I never <u>miss</u> class. She always _____misses_____ class.

2. I always <u>use</u> a daily planner. She rarely _____ a daily planner.

3. I always <u>pay</u> attention in class. She hardly ever _____ attention in class.

4. I usually <u>take</u> notes during class. She never _____ notes during class.

5. I often <u>participate</u> in class. She seldom _____ in class.

6. I sometimes <u>review</u> the syllabus. She rarely _____ the syllabus.

◼ **C O M M U N I C A T E**

G **PAIR WORK Look at the charts on pages 7 and 8 (Exercises C and D). Take turns asking questions about the students and their habits. Use the information in the charts to answer the questions.**

| Does Maria ever review the syllabus? | | Sometimes she reviews it. |

| How often does Susan check her syllabus? | | Every other Sunday. |

H PAIR WORK Are you a successful student? Discuss your study habits with a partner. Ask the questions below. Use frequency adverbs (words and phrases). Your partner will take notes and report to the class. Take turns asking questions and taking notes.

1. How often do you review your syllabus or notes?
2. Do you ever use a planner? If not, how do you remember important dates?
3. Do you ever work with a "study buddy"? How often do you meet? (If you do not have a "study buddy," how often do you think study buddies *should* meet?)
4. Do you have regular study hours? What are your study hours?
5. Do you read your textbook? Why/Why not?
6. How often do you take notes in class?

Connection | Putting It Together

GRAMMAR AND VOCABULARY Write a paragraph, Describe the regular activities and rules of your English class or another class. Describe your habits as a student in the class. Use the syllabus for information, if you have one.

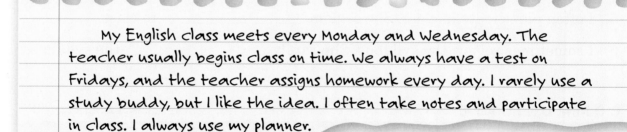

My English class meets every Monday and Wednesday. The teacher usually begins class on time. We always have a test on Fridays, and the teacher assigns homework every day. I rarely use a study buddy, but I like the idea. I often take notes and participate in class. I always use my planner.

PROJECT What makes a successful student? Interview a teacher or a student from another class. Take notes during the interview. Meet with your group to list all of the information you got from the interview.

INTERNET Go to a college website and find an example of a syllabus. Tell your class about the subject, the schedule, and the rules.

Academic Success: Registration and Choosing Classes

■ CONTENT VOCABULARY

Look at the pictures. Do you know the words?

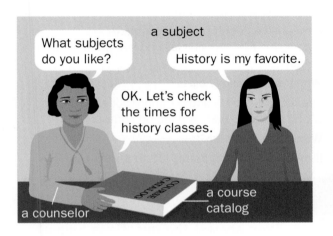

Write the new words in your vocabulary journal.

■ THINK ABOUT IT

When you go to see an academic counselor to plan your schedule, what questions do you ask? What questions does the counselor ask you? Make two lists of questions.

■ GRAMMAR IN CONTENT

A **Read and listen.**

CD1,TR3

units: a measure or value for an American college class, e.g., 1 class = 3 units

to register: sign up for classes

Appointment with a Counselor

Counselor: OK, Serge, you need 12 units. With your English test score, you can register for an academic class this semester. **What subjects do you like?**

Serge: I like health and biology. **Why do I need 12 units?**

Counselor: That is the requirement for full-time students. Here's a biology class, and there's no prerequisite. There are also a few health classes still open.

Serge: **What does *prerequisite* mean?**

Counselor: It means you don't need to complete any classes before this one. **Which class do you prefer, health or biology?**

Serge: **When is the biology class?**

Counselor: The lecture is on Mondays and Wednesdays from 11:30 to 3:00. There's a lab on Fridays.

Serge: **What time is the lab?**

Counselor: It meets on Fridays from 9:00 to 11:00 A.M.

B **Look at the questions in the reading passage. Then answer the questions below.**

1. The *wh-* questions are in **bold.** How many of the questions have *be* as the main verb? _____ *Tree*

2. What is the location of *be* in those questions?
   _____ *at last and first* _____

3. How many of the questions have other verbs as the main verb?
   _____ *Tree* _____

4. What is the position of *do* in those questions?
   _____ *In middle* _____

Type 1: **Wh + Aux + Subject + Verb**	**When does** the class **begin?** **What does** *prerequisite* **mean?** **Why do** I **need** 12 units?
Type 2: **Wh + Be + Subject**	**When is** the class? **Where are** the students? **How is** your class?
Type 3: **Who/What = Subject** When the subject of the question is **who** or **what,** the verb takes the -s ending.	**What** happens at registration? **Who** teaches that class?
Type 4: **What/Which + Noun = Subject** Use **what** to ask a general question. Use **which** to ask about specific members of a set.	**What class** meets in this room? **Which teacher** is Mr. Sanchez?
Type 5: **Which one = Subject** Use **one** after **which** in place of a noun if the reference and meaning are clear.	**Which one** has a lab, biology or health? A: Do you want a morning or afternoon class? B: **Which one** has fewer students?

Notes:
- Don't forget the auxiliary. INCORRECT: ~~When the class begins?~~ CORRECT: *When **does** the class begin?*
- When the verb is *be* (Type 2), it agrees with the subject noun following *be*.

C **Read the answer. Write a *wh-* question. Use any *wh-* question word only once.**

1. **Q:** _____ *Where does the class meet?* _____

   A: The class meets in Room C-204.

2. **Q:** ___ When I can register class es? _____

   A: You can register in July.

3. **Q:** ___ which Professor teaches the lab? _____

   A: Professor James teaches the lab.

4. **Q:** ___ What is a requirement? _____

   A: *Requirement* means you must do something.

5. **Q:** ___ which Semenster she does like? _____

   A: She likes the fall semester.

D For each conversation, fill one blank with *what* and the other with *which.*

1. **A:** _*what*_ class do you have at 10:00 on Fridays?

   B: Tennis, but it's too hard for me. I want to drop it.

   A: _*which*_ physical education class do you want to add?

   B: Swimming.

2. **A:** _*Which*_ subjects are interesting to you?

   B: Well, I have a music class right now, and I really like it.

   A: _*what*_ music class is it?

   B: Music Appreciation.

3. **A:** _*What*_ English class are you in this semester, 400 or 100?

   B: I'm in 100. _*which*_ classes are you taking?

   A: Anthropology and Biology.

4. **A:** _*What*_ hours do you like for your classes?

   B: I like all of my classes in the afternoon. _*Which*_ hours do *you* think are better for class: morning, afternoon, or evening?

   A: Morning hours are better for me.

■ **COMMUNICATE**

E **PAIR WORK** Look at the following schedule for college English classes. Your partner will look at the schedule on page 299. Ask and answer questions to complete the schedule. Use *who, when, where, what, which,* and *which one(s).*

What is the course number for English 400?

Let's see. I have course number 2137. Reed is the instructor.

Student A

Course #	Class	Days	Time	Location	Instructor
	Engl 400		8:00–9:20 AM	R-228	
2139		MWF		V-201	Santos
2245	Engl 100		1:00–2:20 PM		Najpul
3186	Engl 1A	TTh	2:00–3:30 PM	C-165	
	Engl 1A	TTh		R-354	Oleksy

F GROUP WORK Ask your partner about his/her favorite subject. Ask as many questions as you can to get more information.

What subject do you like?

History.

Why do you like it?

Because I learn about the past.

Which historical period is interesting to you?

I like ancient Greek and Roman history.

Then, join with two other pairs (make a group of 6) and share what you learned about your partner. Take turns.

PART TWO	Tag Questions

■ GRAMMAR IN CONTENT

CD1,TR4

A Read and listen.

Preparing for Registration

Serge: Hey, Jahi, registration opens this week, **doesn't it?**

Jahi: Yeah, it does.

Serge: You have a lot of experience with registration, **don't you?**

Jahi: Yeah, this is my fourth semester here. I always select early morning classes, so I have the afternoons free. This is your second semester, **isn't it?**

Serge: That's right, and I got help from a counselor the first time. What happens at registration? I don't have a lot of choices as a new student, **do I?**

Jahi: It's not that bad, **is it?** If you read the course catalog and talk to a counselor, you understand the courses and requirements better. Then you're in a good position to make choices. I also register online. That way I don't have to wait in line at the Administration Building. You aren't worried about this whole registration thing, **are you?**

Serge: No, not really, I just want a good schedule.

B **Reread the dialog on page 15. See how it uses tag questions.**

1. The questions in **bold** are tag questions. For each one, draw an arrow from the verb in the tag question to the main verb. Then draw an arrow from the pronoun in the tag question to the noun in the main sentence.

    Example: Hey, Jahi, registration opens this week, doesn't it?

2. Look at all of your arrows.

    a. Write a rule about the main verb and tag questions.
       (Hint: Use the words *positive* and *negative* in your rule.)

       _____

    b. Write a rule about the pronoun in the tag question and the main subject.
       (Hint: Use the words *singular* and *plural* in your rule.)

       _____

Tag Questions

Question	Answer
Registration **opens** this week, **doesn't it?**	Yes, it does. / No, it doesn't.
You **have** experience with this, **don't you?**	Yes, I do. / No, I don't.
This **is** your second quarter, **isn't it?**	Yes, it is. / No, it isn't.
I **don't have** a lot of choices, **do I?**	Yes, you do. / No, you don't.
You **aren't** worried about this, **are you?**	Yes, I am. / No, I'm not.

Notes:

- If the main verb is not *be,* use the auxiliary *do* in the tag question.
- If the main verb is positive, the tag question is negative. If the main verb is negative, the tag question is positive.
- When you write, use a comma before the tag question.
- Use a pronoun in the tag question to refer back to the subject of the main sentence/clause.

C Add a tag question.

Pilar: Hey, Cara, registration opens today at 8:00 in the morning,

_____*doesn't it*_____?
(1)

Cara: That's right. There are so many subjects to choose from,

_____*doesn't it*___?
(2)

Pilar: There sure are. I have to read the course catalog and make the

right choices. Listen, if I'm a full-time student, I need 12 units,

_____*Do not I*___?
(3)

Cara: Yes, you do. You don't read the course catalog every semester,

_____*Don't you*___?
(4)

Pilar: Yeah, I do. It really helps.

Cara: Counselors help too, _____*doesn't they*___?
(5)

Pilar: Yeah, they do, but I don't always have time to see a counselor. You don't

like to select classes without a counselor, _____*Don't you*___?
(6)

Cara: No, I don't. I see a counselor every semester. I always go with Ravi two

weeks before registration.

Pilar: He has enough units to graduate in the spring, _____*Doesn't he*___?
(7)

Cara: Yes, he does. That's because he always gets help from his counselor.

Pilar: A lot of students register for their classes online, _____*Don't they*___?
(8)

Cara: They sure do.

D Use the information from the course catalog. Use the verb and complete the question. Then write the answer.

COLLEGE OFFICES AND SERVICES

OFFICE	LOCATION	PHONE
Bookstore	U-248	617-7156
Counseling	R-156	617-7248
Financial Aid	R-158	617-7346
Health Services	V-105	617-3155
Library (Info)	LL-117	617-3876
Records	R-215	617-7235
Registration	R-205	617-7312
Testing Center	D-315	617-3076
Writing Center	C-341	617-3586

1. Health Services (be) _____ isn't _____ in U-247, _____ is it? _____
   _____ No, it isn't. It's in V-105. _____

2. If I need help with my writing, I (go) _____ have to go _____ to D-315,
   _____ don't? _____
   _____ No, it isn't. It's in C-341. _____

3. If I don't know the library hours, I (call) _____ have to call _____ 617-3876,
   _____ Isn't it? _____
   _____ Yes, It is. _____

4. The bookstore (be) _____ isn't _____ in the R building, _____ is it? _____
   _____ No, it isn't, It's in V-248 Building. _____

5. The Testing Center and the Writing Center (be) _____ Aren't _____ in the
   same building, _____ Are they? _____
   _____ No, they Aren't. _____

E Listen to the tag question. (Circle) the correct answer about yourself.

CD1,TR5

1. (a. Yes, I do.)   b. No, I don't.   c. Yes, I am.   d. No, I'm not.

2. a. Yes, it is.   b. No, it isn't.   c. Yes, it does.   d. No, it doesn't.

3. a. Yes, they do.   b. No, they don't.   c. Yes, they are.   d. No, they aren't.

4. a. Yes, I have.   b. No, I haven't.   c. Yes, I do.   d. No, I don't.

5. a. Yes, I do.   b. No, I don't.   c. Yes, I am.   d. No, I'm not.

6. a. Yes, it is.   b. No, it isn't.   c. Yes, it does.   d. No, it doesn't.

▪ COMMUNICATE

F **PAIR WORK** Use the course catalog page in Exercise D. Take turns. Ask your partner tag questions. Use affirmative and negative questions. Your partner will answer and give correct information.

If I want to get help with my writing, I go to D-315, don't I?

No, you don't. That's the Testing Center. The Writing Center is in C-341.

G **WRITE** Step 1: Write three *wh-* questions and two tag questions to ask a student or teacher about college, for example, "Why is the first day of class important?" "Which science classes are interesting?" "You write a lot of papers in college, don't you?" "It's helpful to meet with a counselor, isn't it?"

1. _____?

2. _____?

3. _____?

4. _____?

5. _____?

Step 2: Interview two students at your college or at a school near you. If you cannot find a college student to interview, interview a friend or family member who has been to college or, if possible, interview a teacher at your school.

Step 3: Write a paragraph about your interview.

GRAMMAR AND VOCABULARY Complete and answer the questions.

1. What _____does_____ a counselor do?

   ____She helps students with academic plans and schedules.____

2. ___What___ kind of information ___is___ a course catalog have?

   ____It have all the Course with Cdit____

3. ___when___ is your next appointment with a counselor?

   ____It's next monday on 9:00 AM.____

4. ___Which___ subject do you like better, science or math?

   ____I like math batter then Science.____

5. A counselor selects your classes for you, ___Isn't he___?

   ____Yes, it is,____

PROJECT Learn about your school. Get information about a college service or office and share the information with your class.

1. Divide into groups. Your teacher will assign to each group in your class one of the following offices and services: Library/Health Services/Registration/Counseling/Bookstore/Testing Center/Writing Center.
2. In your group, write eight to ten questions about your topic. Use *wh-* questions and tag questions.
3. Before your next class, go to the office at your college and ask your questions or get the information online.
4. Come back to your group and report your information. All group members take notes.
5. Form new groups with one student from each of the first groups. Each student in the new group will have information about a different place.
6. Take turns. The students in your new group will ask you questions about your place. Answer their questions with the information you have.

 INTERNET Look up a class for one of your favorite subjects on an online course catalog. Read the description of the class and take notes. Report what you learned to your classmates.

Nursing:
Illness and Injury

■ CONTENT VOCABULARY

Look at the pictures. Do you know the words?

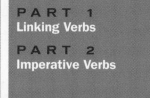

an illness – flu

to get a shot

an allergy – to sneeze

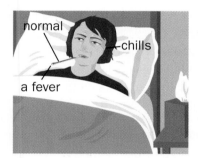

a rash – itchy

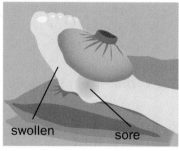

an injury – sprained ankle

an injury – burn

Write the new words in your vocabulary journal.

■ THINK ABOUT IT

In your writing journal, write for five minutes about this question.
What do you think are the most common health problems of college students? How do you feel when you have a cold or the flu?

■ GRAMMAR IN CONTENT

CD1,TR6

A Read and listen.

Health Lesson Review

Professor: OK class, let's review our lesson on colds and flu. When I describe the symptoms, you tell me the illness—cold or flu. OK Tania. You have a runny nose. Food **tastes** and **smells** strange.

Tania: I have a cold.

Professor: Good. Leo, Ali has a bad headache and serious body aches. He **stays** at home and **remains** in bed all week. He **is** very ill. When he goes to the doctor, he says he **feels** terrible.

Leo: It's the flu because usually we don't have body aches with a cold.

Professor: Right. OK Wang, two students go to the College Health Center in December because they don't feel well. They **appear** very weak and tired to the nurse.

Wang: I think it's the flu because we don't **become** that weak and tired with a cold.

symptoms: signs of illness   **aches:** pains in body

B In the dialog above, the linking verbs are in bold. Find the words that follow the verbs. Write them here.

1. Food tastes and smells ___Cold___

2. He stays ___at home___

3. He remains ___in bed___

4. He is ___very ill.___

5. He feels ___terrible___

6. They appear ___very weak.___

7. We don't become ___weak and tired___

How many are adjectives? ___ How many are prepositional phrases? ___

Linking Verbs

Be

Be + Adjective	I **am** ill.
Be + Noun	You **are** a patient.
Be + Prepositional Phrase	He **is** in the hospital.

Other Linking Verbs

Perception (Verb + Adjective) feel look smell sound taste seem appear	Food **tastes** and **smells** strange. He **feels** terrible. He **doesn't look** healthy. They **appear** weak and tired.
State (Verb + Prepositional Phrase) stay lie remain rest stand	He **stays** in bed when he has the flu. I **lie** in the dark when I have a headache.
Change-of-State (Verb + Adjective) become get grow	We **don't become** so weak and tired. When you **get** very ill, you **grow** weak.

Notes:
- A linking verb connects the subject to a noun, adjective, or prepositional phrase. Linking verbs do not have direct objects.
- Use an adjective after *look,* but not after *look like.* Incorrect: ~~He looks like pale.~~ Correct: *He looks pale. He looks like a sick person.*
- We also use nouns after *become,* for example, *She is becoming a nurse.*
- Use *get* + noun to show changes in state of health, for example, *get well/ better, get a cold, get a headache, get a stomachache.*

C **Fill in the blanks with the affirmative or negative form of a linking verb.**

Salim is in his third year of college. He works very hard because he takes five courses each semester and has a job at the library. At the end of the week, he always ____**looks**____ pale and tired. If he eats healthy food, he _____
(1)   (2)
strong, and he _____ sick all the time. However, this is difficult with
(3)
such a heavy schedule. Every winter, Salim _____ very ill with the
(4)
flu, and this year is no different. He has a fever, so he _____hot, and
(5)
his body aches. Food _____ good. Also, he has a bad headache, so his
(6)
roommate's music _____ loud. Because he has a sore throat, he gargles
(7)
with salt water every two hours. It _____ good, but it helps. When he
(8)
has the flu, he needs to _____ for at least a week.
(9)

D Add a linking verb and other words to help the nursing students ask yes-no questions. Once you have written the questions, write a short answer. Follow the example.

| taste | look | lie | ~~appear~~ | smell | sound | stay |

1. face/pale/sick

   Does your face appear pale when you're sick? Yes, it does.

2. voice/hoarse/sore throat

   Does your voice sound hoarse when you're sore throat? Yes, it is.

3. in the dark/headache

   Do you lie in the dark when you're headache? Yes, I do.

4. food/strange/cold

   Does your food taste strange when you've cold? Yes, I have.

5. at home/flu

   Do you stay at home when you've flu? Yes, I do.

6. anything/stuffy nose

   Do you smell anything when you've stuffy nose? Yes, I do.

7. eyes/red/allergies

   Does your eyes looks red when you have allergies? Yes, I does.

E Listen to the interview about college students' health. Check the problems that you hear.

Symptoms	Cold	Flu	Depression	Allergies
appear tired and pale		✔		
have chills and body aches		✓		
feel weak		✓		
have a fever	✓			
life seems hopeless			✓	
become nauseous			✓	
can't taste or smell	✓			
eyes look red				✓
runny nose and sneezing	✓			
sore throat				✓

■ COMMUNICATE

F **PAIR WORK** Describe an illness or injury. Your partner will ask a question. Then your partner will guess the illness or injury. Use linking verbs and the new vocabulary.

> My ankle feels sore and it looks swollen.
>
> Yeah, it hurts a lot.

> Does it hurt when you walk on it?
>
> Well, I think it is sprained.

PART TWO	Imperative Verbs

■ GRAMMAR IN CONTENT

A **Read and listen.**

CD1, TR8

College Health Services ✚

October–December Is Cold and Flu Season. Know the Difference!

The symptoms of a cold are stuffy nose, sore throat, and sneezing.

<u>If you have a cold:</u>
* **Drink** plenty of fluids.
* **Don't sneeze** or **breathe** on others.
* **Wash** your hands frequently.

The symptoms of the flu are body aches, fever, headache, sore throat, and cough.

<u>When you get the flu:</u>
* **Take** your temperature.
* **See** a doctor.
* **Rest** in bed.

fluids: water, juice, etc.

B **In the e-bulletin shown on page 25, the imperative verbs are in bold. Look at each verb and answer these questions.**

1. What is the subject of an imperative verb? _____

2. What form of the verb do we use for the imperative? _____

Imperative Verbs	
Forms	
Affirmative	**Negative**
Wash your hands.	**Don't sneeze** on other people.
Drink plenty of fluids.	Please **don't come** to work.
Uses	

Advice:	**Drink** plenty of fluids.	**Don't drink** a lot of soda.
Instructions:	**Take** two pills at bedtime.	**Don't take** the pills without food.
Warnings:	**Take** care of yourself!	**Don't stay** up too late.
Orders:	**Stay** home!	**Don't get** out of bed for three days.
Polite requests:	Please **cover** your mouth.	**Don't cough** on me, please.

Imperative with Introductory *When* and *If* Clauses

When you have the flu, **remain** at home.	If you get sick, **don't go** to work.
When you don't feel well, **stay** in bed.	If you don't get better, **see** a doctor.

Notes:
- The subject of an imperative is *you,* but we usually leave it out.
- Use the base form of the verb for imperatives.
- To make imperatives general, use introductory *when* and *if* clauses.

C Complete each sentence with an affirmative or a negative imperative.

1. If you get a cold, _____ *drink plenty of fluids.* _____

2. When you have a burn, _____

3. If you feel tired, _____

4. When you have a stomachache, _____

5. If your temperature doesn't seem normal, _____

6. If you get a serious injury, _____

D Work with a partner. Write the nurse's response for each health problem. Use an imperative verb.

1. **Student:** I have the chills.

   Nurse: _____ *Lie in bed under a warm blanket* _____.

2. **Student:** My head feels hot.

   Nurse: _____ Lie in bed under a A.C. _____.

3. **Student:** I think I have a rash.

   Nurse: _____.

4. **Student:** I sprained my ankle.

   Nurse: _____.

5. **Student:** I have a sore throat.

   Nurse: _____.

6. **Student:** I have a headache.

   Nurse: _____.

7. **Student:** Ahhhhchooo!

   Nurse: _____.

8. **Student:** I have the flu.

   Nurse: _____.

E Listen to the nurse talking to new college students about their health. Check DO or DON'T.

	DO	DON'T		DO	DON'T
be careful about your health	✔		drink 6–8 glasses of water	✓	
keep a good diet	✓		eat nuts or fruit for a snack	✓	
go to bed at the same time every night	✓		exercise every day	✓	
get 6–7 hours of sleep every night	✓		when the flu season comes, wash your hands	✓	
eat foods with fat and sugar for energy	✓		cover your mouth if you cough	✓	
drink coffee or tea for energy		✓	call a nurse if you have questions	✓	
drink 6–8 glasses of soda		✓	call the information line if you have questions		✓

F **WRITE** Write a paragraph about helping someone with one of the illnesses. Describe a home remedy if you know one. Use some *if* and *when* clauses to introduce instructions, advice, warnings, and polite requests. Use the methods suggested here or choose your own.

Headache: sleep/meditation/darkness/quiet/massage
Sore throat: salt water/lemon and honey/hot drinks
Sprained ankle: ice/X-ray/no walking
Cold: fluids/chicken soup/steam/nose spray
Flu: shot (to prevent)/sleep/fluids/medicine/no work or school
Burn: cold water/milk/vitamin C/aloe

Many people get headaches and they always take medicine for the headache. However, if you don't like medicine, there are other methods you can use. First, if you get a headache, go to a quiet place and meditate. Sit in a chair or lie on your bed. Relax your whole body and begin deep, slow breathing. Feel the pain in your head. Don't push against the pain; just relax and feel it. Second, if you are at home, lie in the darkness and remain there until your headache gets better. Third, if the headache is in one spot on your head, press one or more fingers against that spot on your head. Relax the rest of your body, but hold that pressure on the spot for a few minutes.

GRAMMAR AND VOCABULARY Complete each sentence with an imperative.

1. When you have the flu, _____

2. If you have a sprained ankle, _____

3. When you have a rash, _____

4. If you have a fever, _____

5. When you have a sore throat, _____

PROJECT Depression is a common health problem with college students. Read the list of symptoms for depression. What helps? What doesn't help? With your group, choose one of the following: (1) Write a script for the College Health Services Hotline. (2) Write a script for a teaching video. (3) Make a poster for the College Health Center. Include the information about the symptoms. Use imperative verbs to give advice, warnings, and instructions to students and to the friends and family of a student with depression.

Symptoms	Things that help	Things that don't help
insomnia	emotional support	guilt, shame, or blame
loss of appetite	talking and listening	alcohol
low energy	time to rest	isolation
negative thoughts	information	too much advice
alcohol or drug abuse	counseling	lack of support

 INTERNET Go to a college website. Search for the Health Services. Prepare to report to your class about these questions: Where is it? What services do they provide? When are they open? What other helpful information do they give?

Social Sciences: Child Development

■ CONTENT VOCABULARY

Look at the pictures. Do you know the words?

to repeat words

to dress herself

to feed herself

to put on/tie shoes

Mental and Linguistic Development

Write the new words in your vocabulary journal.

■ THINK ABOUT IT

In your writing journal, write for five minutes about this question.

What are you able to do now that you couldn't do when you were two years old?

■ GRAMMAR IN CONTENT

CD1,TR10

A **Read and listen.**

an **observation:** watch; look at for a purpose

Preparing for the Observation

Professor:	Before we go to the Child Care Center tomorrow, let's review what we know about toddlers. Some toddlers **can't walk** alone yet, and some **are able to walk** with help. Many toddlers **can walk** and even run and climb. Tomorrow, you will see a few toddlers at 11 months. They **can walk**, but they **aren't able to run** or **climb** yet. One of them, Johnny, **couldn't crawl** when he was eight months, but he **could stand up**. So he **will** probably **be able to run** when he's 23 months.
Student:	**Can** toddlers **throw** a ball?
Professor:	Yes, they**'re able to throw**, but they **can't catch** yet.
Student:	When **will** they **be able to catch** a ball?
Professor:	They**'ll be able to catch** when they're three.

B **Look at the dialog. Find the modal verbs and phrases in bold and write the time above the verb: *Pr* for present time; *Pa* for past time; *F* for future time.**

Present and Past Ability: *Can/Could/Be Able To*

Present	Past
She **can (can't)** walk.	She **could (couldn't)** walk.
Can you throw a ball?	**Could** you throw a ball?

Present, Past, and Future Ability: *Be Able To*

Present	Past	Future
I **am (not) able to** sing.	I **was (not) able to** sing.	They **will (not) be able to** sit.
You **are (not) able to** run.	They **were (not) able to** run.	
He **is (not) able to** catch.	She **was (not) able to** catch.	
Are they **able to** catch?	**Were** they **able to** run?	**Will** they **be able to** sit?
When **are** they **able to** catch?	*When* **was** she **able to** run?	*When* **will** he **be able to** sit?

Notes:

- The modals *can, could,* and *will* do not change when the pronoun changes.
- For *be able to,* change *be* to agree with the pronoun and the tense: Present: I **am**; You/We/They **are**; He/She/It **is**; Past: I /He/She/It **was**; You/We/They **were**.

C Fill in the blank with something true. Use *can/could* and *be able to.*

1. I (talk) __couldn't talk__ when I was an infant, but I (cry) __could cry__ .

2. I (run) __couldn't ran__ when I was a baby, but I __could run__ now.

3. At the age of two, I (turn) __can turn__ the pages of a book, but I (read) __couldn't read__.

4. When I was three, I (read) __couldn't read__ and I (write) __couldn't write__ either.

5. At seven months, I (sit up) __can sit up__, but I (stand up) __couldn't stand__.

D Fill in the blanks with a correct form of *can/could/be able to* and the verb.

Madhu: Hey, Kateri! How was your observation at the Child Development Center?

Kateri: It was good. I saw the preschoolers playing. You know, the two-year-olds (catch) __couldn't catch__ (1) a ball, but the three-year-olds __could__ (2). The three-year-olds (bounce) __couldn't bounce__ (3) a ball, but the four-year-olds __could__ (4). The three-year-olds (put) __can put__ (5) on their shoes, but they (tie) __couldn't tie__ (6) them.

Madhu: _____ (7) the five-year-olds (tie) _____ (8) their shoes?

Kateri: No, they __couldn't__ (9). Children (tie) __are tie__ (10) their shoes when they're six years old.

Madhu: What about speech? _____ (11) the children (repeat) _____ (12) sentences?

Kateri: Well, you know, the two-year-olds (say) _____ (13) a sentence with more than three to five words, for example, "I want my ball." But all the four-year-olds (speak) _____ (14) in longer sentences.

🎧 **E** Listen and fill in the blanks. Then practice pronouncing the sentences.

CD1,TR11

1. **A.** Lisa _____*can*_____ write paragraphs.

   B. Lisa _____*Can*_____ write essays.

2. **A.** A year ago, Sergio _____*Could*_____ read a newspaper.

   B. A year ago, Sergio _____*Could*_____ only read his language textbook.

3. **A.** Last year, she _____*Could*_____ understand the people in England.

   B. This year, she _____*Can*_____ understand the people in America either.

4. **A.** In two years, I _____*Can*_____ speak English better.

   B. In two years, I _____*Can*_____ speak English perfectly.

F Correct the errors. There are six errors.

Alisa's Baby Diary

Two months

Alisa looked in my eyes today. Two months ago, she ~~can't~~ *couldn't*

do this, so I am very happy that now she ~~could~~ *can*. In two more

months, she can be able to control her head and lifting her

chest. It is so exciting to see her develop. In August, she

can't couldn't be able to lift her head or body, but in four more

months, she will be able to sit up. After that she can stand up.

G PAIR WORK Discuss these questions with your partner. Compare past and present times/events.

What were you able to do when you were six years old?

When I was six, I was able to run very fast, but I can't do that now.

1. What can a toddler do that an infant can't do?
2. What is an adult able to do that a child is not able to do?
3. What can you do now that you couldn't do when you were five?
4. What were you able to do when you were 16 that you can't do now?
5. What couldn't you do when you were 12 that you could do when you were 18?
6. What can you do now that you won't be able to do when you're 90?
7. When your English skills improve, what will you be able to do that you can't do now?

PART TWO	Reflexive and Reciprocal Pronouns

■ GRAMMAR IN CONTENT

CD1,TR12

A Read and listen.

Min's Observation Report

Today I had a very interesting observation at the Child Development Center. The environment was very good for young children. There were puzzles and balls, so the children could play **by themselves** or with **one another**. I observed the physical and mental development of two children. One was a two-and-a-half-year-old girl, Li. She could feed **herself** and walk **by herself**, but she wasn't able to do a puzzle **by herself**. I also observed a three-year-old boy, Nate. I think he **enjoyed himself**. He could climb **by himself**, and he and Li could play ball with **each other**. Nate was even able to **dress himself**. At the end of the day, he put on his coat and hat before going outside. He could put his shoes on, but he couldn't tie his shoes **by himself**. His language development was good. When I **introduced myself**, he could say, "hello" and repeat my name.

an environment: the objects, feeling, and people around you in a place

B In the reading on page 35, find the reflexive and reciprocal pronouns in bold. For each one, circle the pronoun and draw an arrow from the pronoun to the subject(s).

Example: . . . the children could play by (themselves) . . .

Reflexive and Reciprocal Pronouns

Reflexive Pronouns		
I	myself	
You	yourself	**Li** could feed **herself.**
He	himself	The children could play **by themselves.**
She	herself	
It	itself	
We	ourselves	
You	yourselves	
They	themselves	
Reciprocal Pronouns		Li played with Nate, and Nate played with Li. Nate and Li
We/You/They	each other/	played with **each other.**
	one another	The children in the class played with **one another.**

Notes:

• Use a reflexive pronoun when the subject and object refer to the same person or people.

• Use *by* or *for* before the reflexive pronoun to mean "alone" or "without help."

• These verbs are often followed by reflexive pronouns: *wash, dress, introduce, enjoy, take care of, hurt, behave, teach.*

• Use *each other* for two people or for informal contexts with two or more; use *one another* for formal contexts involving more than two people.

• Don't confuse the meaning of reflexive and reciprocal pronouns, for example, *We **introduced** ourselves to the class.* (I introduced myself. She introduced herself.) *We **introduced each other** to the class.* (I introduced her, and she introduced me.)

C Look at Min's report on page 35. Write *T* for True and *F* for False. Discuss why.

1. __T__ Li couldn't play alone with puzzles.

2. __F__ Li could not eat alone.

3. __F__ Li needed help when she walked.

4. __T__ Nate and Li played together.

5. __F__ Nate needed help when he got dressed.

6. __T__ Nate could tie his shoes by himself.

D Read Carolina's observation notes. Fill in the blanks with *can, could* or the correct tense of *be able to,* a reflexive pronoun, or a reciprocal pronoun.

Yesterday I observed Budi, a two-year-old boy, and Jamie, a three-year-old boy. Jamie _____couldn't_____ (1) play ball by _____himself_____ (2), but Budi _____could_____ (3). Budi and Jamie _____are_____ (4) play with _____themselves_____ (5). Budi rolled the ball to Jamie, and Jamie _____couldn't_____ (6) push it back to Budi. During lunch, they both _____ (7) feed _____ (8). At the end of the day, Budi wanted to tie his shoes, but he _____couldn't_____ (9). I said: "When I was two, I _____couldn't_____ (10) tie my shoes by _____myself_____ (11) either. You _____can_____ (12) tie your shoes by _____yourselves_____ (13) when you are six."

E Using the given words, write a sentence about the child's ability.

Example: Miki/three years old/feed with a fork or spoon

When Miki was three years old, she could feed herself with a fork or spoon.

1. Jahi/18 months old/walk

   When Jahi was eighteen months old, he could walk by himself.

2. Sarah and Jenny/four years old/dress

   When Sarah and Jenney were four years old, they could dress themselves.

3. Lali/two years old/tie shoes

   When Lali was two years old, she couldn't tie shoes by herself.

4. Mara/five years old/brush teeth

   When Mara was five years old, she could brush her teeth by herself.

5. Jose and Andrew/four years old/wash hands

   When Jose and Andrew were four years old, they could wash their hand by themselves.

F Fill in the blanks in Tara's report. Use modals and reflexive pronouns.

My observation at the Child Care Center was very interesting. I spent most

of the day with Lali and Marco. Marco is three and Lali is five. They played with

_____each other_____ in the morning. First, Lali helped Marco put a puzzle together
        (1)

because Marco ____couldn't____ do it by ____himself____. Then, they looked at
                    (2)   (3)

a book. They ____couldn't____ read by ____themselves____, so they just looked at
                (4)   (5)

each page and talked to ____each other____ about the pictures. Later, Marco wanted
                              (6)

to cut pictures out of magazines, and Lali said, "Marco, you ____couldn't____ do
                                                                  (7)

that by ____yourself____. I'll help you."
            (8)

■ **C O M M U N I C A T E**

G **WRITE** Write about your progress in English. Compare your abilities past and
present. Use reflexive pronouns.

Connection | Putting It Together

GRAMMAR AND VOCABULARY Observe and write a report.

1. Observe a child you know, or go to a public place, for example a park or a
   shopping mall.
2. Take notes on the child's behavior and language.
3. Write a short report about your observation but do not include the child's age.
4. Read your report to your classmates. They will try to guess the child's age.

PROJECT Interview a student and ask the student to compare his/her past and
present abilities in using English. Summarize the interview for your class.

 INTERNET Choose an age for a child, for example, a two-year-old or a four-year-old.
Type this question into the search engine: *What can a (two-year-old) do?* Report to
your classmates.

PART 1
Present Progressive:
Statements/Questions/Short
Answers

PART 2
Simple Present vs. Present
Progressive

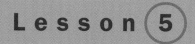

Lesson 5

Academic Success: Balancing School and Work

■ CONTENT VOCABULARY

Look at the Financial Aid page of the Wilson College website below. Do you know the words?

WILSON COLLEGE

Classes/Academic Programs | Apply & Register | Student Services | **Financial Aid** | Library

Application steps:

Step 1: Complete the forms.

Step 2: Collect the important papers.

Step 3: Send the application by the **deadline:** March 16.

Before you complete the application, gather the following information:

1. What are your costs?

Tuition = ? **Fees** = ? Housing = ? Food = ? **Expenses** = ?

2. Are you working? Are you earning any **income**?

3. Do you have any other financial support, for example, your parents, any scholarships?

4. What is the best kind of **aid** for you, for example, **loan**, **grant**, **work-study**?

Write the new words (in bold) in your vocabulary journal.

■ THINK ABOUT IT

In your writing journal, write for five minutes about any of these questions.

How are you paying for school? Are you working? If yes, where do you work? Are you receiving any financial aid? How did you get this aid?

■ GRAMMAR IN CONTENT

A Read and listen.

CD1,TR13

Discussion with a Financial Aid Counselor

Counselor:	OK Sonja, I'm ready for you. How can I help you today?
Sonja:	Well, I'm seeking financial aid. At present, I'm not receiving any grants or loans. My parents are paying my tuition and fees, but I'm not getting money for food and expenses.
Counselor:	I see. Well, you know we do have a work-study program. Many students pay for their expenses through work-study. Are you working at all right now?
Sonja:	No, I'm not.
Counselor:	Are you taking twelve units this semester?
Sonja:	Yes, I am.
Counselor:	Well, that's good. You need to have twelve units for work-study. You know, the library is looking for student workers now, and the Writing Center is also hiring.
Sonja:	That sounds good. Thanks. You've been very helpful.

seeking: looking for

hiring: taking new workers

B Look at the dialog above. Notice the present progressive verbs in bold. The action of the verbs is going on in the present. Circle four time expressions that show this present ongoing action.

Present Progressive Tense					
Affirmative			**Negative**		
Subject	*Be*	**Verb** *-ing*	**Subject**	*Be* + Not	**Verb** *-ing*
I	am		I	am not OR I'm not	
You/We/They	are	working.	You/We/They	are not OR aren't OR (you)'re not	studying.
He/She/It	is		He/She/It	is not OR isn't OR (she)'s not	

Present Progressive Tense

Yes/No Questions

Be	Subject	Verb -ing
Am	I	
Are	you/we/they	working?
Is	he/she/it	

Short Answers

Yes/No	Subject	Be (+ Not)
Yes, No,	I	am. (I) am not. OR (I)'m not.
Yes, No,	you/we/they	are. aren't. OR (we)'re not.
Yes, No,	he/she/it	is. isn't. OR (she)'s not.

Wh- Questions

Wh-	Be	Subject	Verb -ing
Where	is	Mei	working?
What	are	Padma and Mei	doing?

Notes:

Spelling rules:

Most verbs add -ing (going, seeing, eating). However, if the verb ends in

1. *ie*	change *ie* → *y*	add *-ing*	(*tie* → *tying*)
2. consonant + *e*	drop e	add *-ing*	(*make* → *making*)
3. vowel + consonant	double the consonant	add *-ing*	(*stop* → *stopping*)
			(*offer* → *offering*)*

*(When a verb has 2 or more syllables with the last syllable unstressed, just add -*ing*.)

C **Look at the pictures. Fill in each blank with the correct form of an appropriate verb from the box. Create short answers with _be_ as necessary.**

check out
~~work~~
~~give~~
sell

1. _____*Is*_____ Marisa ____*working*____ at the library? Yes, she is. She ____*is giving*____ Andrew directions.

2. _____*Is*_____ Padma ___*selling*___ Mei a book? No, she ___*is not*___. She ___*is checking out*___ a book for Mei.

make
schedule
study
work

3. _____*Are*_____ Ron and Tuti ___*working*___ in the library today? No, they ___*Aren't*___. They ___*are*___ in the Financial Aid office.

4. _____*Is*_____ Tuti ___*Scheduling*___ an appointment for Jeung? Yes, she ___*is makeing*___. She ___*is studies*___ the appointment time on the computer.

5. ___Is___ Wang _shoping_ at the grocery store? No, she ___isn't___.

   She _is getting_ some books in the bookstore.

6. ___Are___ Wang and Malik _buying_ books? Yes, they

   ___Are___. Maria and Stephen _are helping_ them.

D **Listen and fill in the blanks in the following conversation between Padma and Mei.**

CD1,TR14

M: Padma, how ___is___ your semester ___going___?
(1) (2)

P: It _is going_ well, Mei. I ___have___ three classes, and I ___am___
(3) (4) (5)
here in the library. How about you?

M: Yeah, I ___am___ really busy, too. I _'m takeing_ four classes this
(6) (7)
semester, and I ___am___ in the cafeteria. It's a difficult schedule, but I
(8)
am doing it. ___Is___ Jin here today?
(9) (10)

P: Yes, she ___is___. She ___is___ books on the shelves—right over
(11) (12)
there.

M: We ___saw___ a video for our health class. I ___have___ some problems
(13) (14)
with it, so I need to talk to her.

P: Oh really? What is the video about?

M: Well, the topic is drugs. In the video, we ___saw___ the bad effects of drugs.
(15)

E **PAIR WORK** Work with a partner. Write five questions about the three pictures in Part 1C, on pages 42–43. Then take turns with your classmates asking and answering questions.

What is Mei doing?

She's checking out a book.

F **OBSERVE AND WRITE** Go to a busy place at your school, for example, the library, the cafeteria, or the administration building. Sit and observe the activities and write a short summary of what people are doing.

PART TWO	Simple Present vs. Present Progressive

■ G R A M M A R   I N   C O N T E N T

CD1,TR15

A Read and listen.

Work-Study

College students often need financial assistance and support. The cost of education is high and students have many expenses. It is difficult to balance work and school, but college students sometimes have no choice.

Many colleges and universities offer work-study programs for their students. In these programs, students work in the college library, cafeteria, or in department offices. These jobs help students pay for their tuition and expenses.

This year, Sean is studying at a two-year college. He is taking twelve units, and he is working five hours per week in the school library. However, he does not earn enough money from this job. Right now he is also making some extra income at a second job. On Tuesday and Thursday evenings, he works at a restaurant near the college. Sean's schedule is very busy and he usually gets only five to six hours of sleep every night. Somehow Sean is finding a way to balance school and work.

to earn: get money for work

B Underline the present progressive verbs in the reading on the prior page and (circle) the simple present verbs. Work with a partner to explain the difference.

Simple Present vs. Present Progressive	
Simple Present	**Present Progressive**
• General Truth/Statement of Fact: *The school **offers** financial aid.* • Habitual or Repeated Activity: *Maria **works** on Tuesdays.* • Longer/Permanent Activity: *Raji **lives** in an apartment.*	• Action in Progress at This General Time: *The library **is offering** work-study jobs.* • Activity in Progress at This Time: *Maria **is working** in the library today.* • Shorter/Temporary Activity: *Susan **is living** in an apartment right now.* (This may change soon.)
Time Expressions	
usually, always, sometimes, seldom on Mondays/Tuesdays in spring/summer every day/week/semester/summer every other day/week/Thursday during the day/week/semester	now right now at present today this week/month/semester

Note:
• Be careful not to confuse simple present with present progressive:
  Incorrect: *I do my homework right now.*   Correct: *I'm doing my homework right now.*
  Incorrect: *I'm knowing the answer.*   Correct: *I know the answer.*

C Fill in the blanks with the simple present or present progressive form of the verb. Use the affirmative or negative as needed.

1. (hire) The Learning Center _____*hires*_____ new student workers every semester. They _____*have*_____ five new cashiers this semester.

2. (meet) The Financial Aid counselor _____*meets*_____ with students on Monday, Wednesday, and Friday. She __*is working*__ with three students today.

3. (conduct) The Writing Center tutors _____*conducts*_____ seminars this week. They _____*have*_____ workshops and seminars every other week.

4. (sit) The student worker in the Languages Office _____sits_____ at the desk during the day. She _____'s not_____ at the desk today because she is sick.

5. (help) Lisa _____helps_____ students in the bookstore. This week, she _____helped_____ a lot of students find their textbooks.

D Use the verbs to complete the dialogs. Use the simple present and the present progressive form of each verb.

~~work~~   pay   answer   apply

1. **A:** _____Does_____ Padma _____work_____ in the library on Tuesdays and Thursdays?

   B: Yes, she _____does_____, but this week she _____working_____ on Friday also.

2. **A:** _____Does_____ Stephen _____pay_____ for his tuition this year?

   B: No, he _____does not_____. His parents _____paying_____ for his tuition every year.

3. **A:** _____Does_____ Mrs. Santos _____answer_____ questions at the Financial Aid office today?

   B: Yes, she _____does_____, but usually she _____answers the_____ questions at the Registration Desk.

4. **A:** _____Does_____ Taisha _____apply_____ for a work-study job every semester?

   B: Yes, she _____does_____. This semester she _____applying_____ for a job at the Writing Center.

E **Editing Practice: Find the verb tense errors in the e-mail message below, and correct them. There are eleven errors.**

Hi Maria!

    It's very late on Thursday night, and I ~~study~~ *am studying* for a test. My roommate is sleep and I'm taking a

little break. Everything is going well at school, but I am very tired every day. I am often awake

late in the evenings. I don't usually go to bed until 2 a.m. Sometimes I'm finishing my work

early, and I go to bed at midnight.

    During the day, I am working at the library for a few hours after my classes. I sitting at the

circulation desk and helping students to check out their books. I am always enjoy this job

because I meet people and learning about books.

    I like my job, but I am find it very difficult to balance school and work. I rarely have time to

rest. How about you? Are you enjoy school? Are you also have a job?

Take care,

Padma

■ COMMUNICATE

F **PAIR WORK Discuss your study/work/family schedule with your partner. Ask your partner questions. Use contrasting time expressions in your answers.**

What do you do in the evenings?

I usually cook dinner for my family every evening, but this semester I am working at the library in the evenings.

1. usually/right now
2. every semester/this semester
3. every day/today
4. rarely/this month
5. every week/this week
6. usually/today

GRAMMAR AND VOCABULARY Choose from the vocabulary below to fill in the blanks. Use the correct form of the verbs.

work-study	tuition	earn	receive	apply
income	expenses	hire	fees	~~financial~~

This semester, Jun is applying for __financial__ aid at Wilson College. Many
(1)
students __receive__ this kind of support. Jun needs help because her parents are
(2)
not paying her __tuition__ or __expenses__ , and her __fees__ are high. Right now,
(3)   (4)   (5)
she is not __earning__ any __income__ , so in addition to the aid, she is applying for
(6)   (7)
a __work-study__ job at the college bookstore. They __hire__ student workers right
(8)   (9)
now. She has classes on Mondays and Wednesdays, so she __is applying__ for hours on
(10)
Tuesdays and Thursdays.

Write a paragraph about your work-study situation. Include the grammar and vocabulary from the lesson. Think about these questions to help you write your paragraph.

- Do you work hard to balance work and school or school and other activities?
- What is your study schedule? How often do you have classes? When do you study?
- How do you pay for school? Do you have a job? What are your work hours?

PROJECT **Create a survey.**

1. With your classmates, write questions for conducting a survey on work-study. (for example, Are you taking classes now? Do you have a job?)
2. Ask five to ten people to complete your survey.
3. Compare the results of your survey with the results from the classmates in your group.
4. Write a summary paragraph about the results from your group.

 INTERNET **Find a university or college website. Get information about the financial aid process at the school. Report to the class.**

A Susan is interviewing her neighbor for a child development class assignment. Write the correct tense/form of the verb in parentheses OR choose from the words in parentheses. If there is no choice, think of a word or words to add.

Susan: Hi, Mrs. Burton, ___do___ you (have) ___have___ a few minutes?
(1)   (2)

Mrs. B: Yes, Susan, ___come___ in. The baby (sleep) ___is in sleep___, so I (make)
(3)   (4)

___am makeing___ some appointments. She (need) ___needs___ a flu shot,
(5)   (6)

and tomorrow ___is___ the deadline for free shots. I (write)
(7)

___am writeing___ the appointment in my planner now, so I won't forget.
(8)

Susan: Sadie ___is___ eighteen months old now, ___Isn't___ she?
(9)   (10)

Mrs. B: Yes, she ___is___.
(11)

Susan: I (write) ___'m writeing___ a paper for my child development class, and I
(12)

have to interview the parent of a toddler.

Mrs. B: Oh, really? That (seem) ___seems___ interesting. So you (have)
(13)

___have any___ some questions for me, ___to help___ you?
(14)   (15)

Susan: Yes, I ___do___. You (not/be) ___aren't___ busy, ___are___ you?
(16)   (17)   (18)

Mrs. B: No, no. Go ahead. (ask) ___ask___ the first question.
(19)

Susan: OK. How often (take) ___you take___ Sadie to the Child Care Center?
(20)

Mrs. B: Let's see. Every week I (work) ___am working___ on Monday, Wednesday,
(21)

and Friday, so she (spend) ___is spending___ those mornings at the Center.
(22)

Susan: How (she likes/does she like) ___is___ it there?
(23)

Mrs. B: She (look) ___is looking___ (happy/happiness) ___happy___ when I (pick)
(24)   (25)

___pick___ her up.
(26)

Susan: ___Does___ she ever (cry) ___cry___ when you (leave)
(27)   (28)

___leave___ her in the morning?
(29)

Mrs. B: Umm. Well, hardly (ever/never) ___ever___ (she does/does she)
(30)

___she does___ cry when I (leave) ___leave___ her, but (ever/sometimes)
(31)   (32)

___Sometimes___ she (cry) ___cries___ when I (pick) ___am picking___ her up.
(33)   (34)   (35)

B Write the correct tense/form of the verb in parentheses OR choose from the words in parentheses.

This semester, Jenny (work/is working) *is working* (1) at the university Writing Center. She (have/has) *has* (2) a work-study position as a student assistant. She (receives/are receive) *receives* (3) financial aid, and her parents also (give/giving) *give* (4) her some support with tuition and fees. However, she (feels/feeling) *feeling* (5) good about working because the extra income (helps/is help) *helps* (6) her with living expenses.

Today is Thursday, so Jenny (tutors/is tutor) *tutors* (7) for three hours. Every Tuesday and Thursday, she (is arriving/arrives) *arrives* (8) at 4:00 pm and (is leaving/leaves) *leaves* (9) at 7:00 pm. Seldom (she arrives/does she arrive) *she arrives* (10) late because if she (is/will be) *will be* (11) late, the students (becoming/become) *become* (12) a little angry. They need her help with their papers. They (can't/aren't) *aren't* (13) able to solve all of the problems with their papers by (each other/themselves) *themselves* (14).

LEARNER LOG Check (✔) *Yes* or *I Need More Practice.*

Lesson	I Can Use . . .	Yes	I Need More Practice
1	Simple Present Tense, Adverbs of Frequency	✓	
2	*Wh-* Questions, Tag Questions	✓	
3	Linking Verbs, Imperative Verbs	✓	
4	*Can/Could/Be Able to,* Reflexive and Reciprocal Pronouns	✓	
5	Present Progressive Tense, Simple Present Tense vs. Present Progressive Tense	✓	

PART 1
Phrasal Verbs: Transitive/
Separable

PART 2
Phrasal Verbs: Transitive/
Inseparable

PART 3
Phrasal Verbs: Intransitive/
Inseparable

Lesson 6

**English:
Reading and Writing
Assignments**

CONTENT VOCABULARY

Look at the pictures. Do you know the words?

a discussion

an assignment

an outline

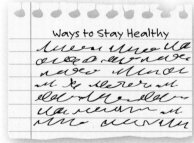

a draft

a due date

Write the new words in your vocabulary journal.

THINK ABOUT IT

In your writing journal, write for five minutes about this question.
What are some good tips for English reading and writing assignments?

■ GRAMMAR IN CONTENT

A Read and listen to the professor talking to the class.

CD1,TR16

Writing Assignment Tips

OK now, before I give you the first writing assignment, I want to **point out** some useful tips. When I hand out the assignment, **read** it **over** a few times and try to **figure out** the topic, the focus, and the main ideas. This kind of analysis is very important. If there is a word you don't understand, **look up** the definition in your English dictionary. Then, **look over** your notes from our readings and discussions and begin to **write down** your ideas. **Start out with** some brainstorming or a quickwrite. Don't **put** it **off.** Just **think through** the issues and questions about the topic. If you want to read more about your topic, **check out** a book from the library, or **look** it **up** on the Internet. Then, write an outline and your first draft. Be sure to **turn in** your first draft by the due date, and I will **hand** it **back** by the following week. Sometimes when I **give** your paper **back,** I ask you to **do** it **over.** That way, if you do very poorly, you have a chance to improve.

B Look at the reading. Choose five phrasal verbs in bold. Write the verb, particle, and object in the order you find it. Label each (V) for verb; (P) for particle; (O) for object.

1. _point (V)_ _out (P)_ _some useful tips (O)_
2. _read_ _over_ _figure out_
3. _look over_ _write down_ _ideas_
4. _start out_ _brainstorming_ _quickwrite_
5. _check out_ _books_ _write_

Phrasal Verbs: Transitive/Separable (TS)

Form			Common Phrasal Verbs (TS) in Academic Situations
verb **Look**	*particle* **up**	*object (noun)* the definition.	**point out**—show; explain **read over/read through**—review **hand out**—give to group, e.g., class
verb **Look**	*object (noun)* the definition	*particle* **up.**	**figure out**—try to understand; solve **look up**—find information, e.g., definition
verb **Look**	*object (pronoun)* it	*particle* **up.**	**write down**—write on paper **start out (with)**—begin
verb **Figure**	*particle* **out**	*object (noun)* the topic.	**look over**—review **put off**—do later **think through**—think carefully and deeply
verb **Figure**	*object (noun)* the topic	*particle* **out.**	**turn in/hand in**—give teacher assignment **hand back/give back**—teacher returns paper/ test/assignment
verb **Figure**	*object (pronoun)* it	*particle* **out.**	**do over**—write again, revise

Notes:

- Phrasal verbs have a verb followed by a particle that may in turn be followed by a preposition.
- If *transitive,* the verb has an object.
- If *separable,* a noun or pronoun object can come between the verb and the particle.
- Don't put the pronoun after the two-word verb: Incorrect: ~~Look up it.~~   Correct: *Look it up.*

C First, underline the phrasal verb in the first sentence and (circle) the object. Then, do the following to complete the second sentence: Separate the phrasal verb. Change the noun to a pronoun. Use the simple present form of the verb.

1. I'd like to <u>point out</u> (some useful tips.) After I ____*point them out*____, we will practice.

2. OK. I'm handing out the assignment now. After I ____*hand them out*____, please read it carefully.

3. Read over the questions about the reading. After you ____*read over it*____, begin to think and brainstorm.

4. If there is a word you don't know, look up the definition. After you ____*find the definition*____ in your dictionary, write it in your vocabulary journal.

5. I always write down my first ideas in a quickwrite. If I
_____Write them down_____, it's a good start because I have something on paper.

6. Don't put off the writing until you feel good about it. When you
_____Write them out_____, it becomes more and more difficult to begin.

7. I try to think through the main issue. When I _____am brainstorming_____, I write a better paper.

8. Always hand in your assignments by the due date. When you don't
_____hand them_____ on time, your grade will be lower.

D **Fill in the blanks with the correct particle for the phrasal verb. If necessary, look at the list of common academic phrasal verbs in the chart on page 53.**

1. **A:** Hey Ravi, do we need to do our assignment _____over_____ when we get it
   (1)
   _____back_____?
   (2)

   B: I'm not sure. I think we do if the teacher hands it _____back_____ with a note.
   (3)

2. **A:** How do you learn new words?

   B: I look them _____out_____ in the dictionary and write the definition _____of the word_____
   (4)   (5)
   in my vocabulary notebook.

   A: Really? When I start _____do_____ reading an assignment, first I try to
   (6)
   figure _____out_____ the meaning of the words that I don't know.
   (7)

3. **A:** In my paper, I'm pointing _____do_____ one important issue, but I need to
   (8)
   think it _____over_____ before I write.
   (9)

   B: That sounds right. Do you ever check books _____out_____ of the library to
   (10)
   help you with such issues?

   A: Sometimes, but usually I just read _____do_____ the class notes and the
   (11)
   readings.

E **PAIR WORK** Ask your partner a question. Use one of the phrasal verbs in the box. Your partner will answer with the phrasal verb and a pronoun.

> Do you always look words up in the dictionary if you don't know them?

> No, I don't. Sometimes I look them up, but sometimes I guess the meaning and continue to read.

write down	start out	look over	put off	hand in
read over	read through	hand out	figure out	look up

PART TWO	Phrasal Verbs: Transitive/Inseparable

■ GRAMMAR IN CONTENT

CD1,TR17

A **Read and listen.**

The Reading Assignment

Shan: Hey, Inas, what are you **working on**?

Inas: Oh, I'm **going over** the reading assignment and **thinking about** the questions. I want to be ready for the class discussion tomorrow. I'm **coming across** some difficult ideas in this reading.

Shan: Yeah, me too. It's taking a long time to **get through** it. I hope the professor doesn't **call on** me during the discussion. I always get nervous and **leave out** important ideas, or I lose my focus while I'm speaking.

Inas: I know. That's why I'm **working through** the ideas now. I'm trying to **find out** the deeper meaning. She likes that kind of analysis.

Shan: Yeah, I think you're right. Also, when I do that, **I end up with** a better understanding of the ideas, and then I don't get so nervous during the discussion.

B **Find the phrasal verbs in the dialog above. Underline the object of each phrasal verb in bold. Are any of the objects between the verb and the particle?**
___ yes ⌞ no

Phrasal Verbs: Transitive/Inseparable (TI)

Form			Common Academic Phrasal Verbs (TI)
verb I'm **going**	*particle* **over**	*object (noun)* the reading.	**to work on**—work with a specific focus **to go over**—review **to get through**—complete **to come across**—see; meet; find; discover **to call on**—teacher chooses a student **to leave out**—forget; omit **to work through**—think until you understand **to find out**—solve; discover **to end up with**—have at the end of something
object (wh- question) What	*verb* are you **working**	*particle* **on?**	
verb I'm **thinking**	*particle* **about**	*object* it.	
verb I **end**	*particle* **up with**	*object* a better grade.	

Notes:

- If inseparable, the object must not come between the verb and preposition:

  Incorrect: ~~I'm going the reading over.~~   Correct: *I'm going over the reading.*

- In *wh-* questions, ***what*** is the object.

- Some phrasal verbs can have a particle and a preposition, for example, end *up with.*

C **Fill in the blanks with one of the phrasal verbs from the box.**

go over	~~work on~~	get through	call on	leave out
work through	end up with	come across		

Today, Naja is ___working on___ a story for her English class. She is
            (1)

following the steps to prepare for class discussion. She always ___ending up with___
                                                                              (2)

a good understanding if she follows these steps. First, she thinks about the

title. Today, it's "Frankenstein." She doesn't know the meaning of this title, but

she ___come across___ that name all the time. Usually it means "monster."
         (3)

She can ___get through___ the real meaning when she reads the story. Next,
              (4)

she always ___goes over___ the difficult vocabulary. If she understands
                (5)

the words, she can ___work through___ the story faster. Then, she reads it
                          (6)

again, and ___call on___ the discussion questions. The professor always
               (7)

___goes over___ her, so she doesn't want to ___leave out___ any important
        (8)   (9)

ideas.

D Part 1: Match the phrasal verb on the left with a phrasal verb on the right with a similar meaning. Write the letter on the line. Do not choose the same verb.

1. _d_ work through   a. look over

2. _c_ read over   b. hand back

3. _f_ turn in   c. read over

4. _b_ give back   d. think through

5. _a_ go over   e. find out

6. _e_ come across   f. hand in

Part 2: Choose three of the pairs and write a short dialog for each pair.

■ COMMUNICATE

E **PAIR WORK** Take turns. Use the words to ask your partner a question. Your partner will answer with one or more phrasal verbs from the box.

How long do you usually spend on a writing assignment?

I usually work on an assignment for a few days. First, I go over the questions carefully. Then I think about my topic.

work through	get through	call on	end up with	come across
leave out	go over	find out	work on	

1. How long/spend/on a writing assignment?
2. How/study/for a test?
3. Do/ever/forget/important ideas/when/write?
4. What/do/when/find/words/don't know?
5. What grade/want/at the end/of the semester?
6. Do/have/any tips/for completing/this level?
7. How/feel/when/the teacher/chooses/you/to speak/during class?
8. What thoughts/have/during a test?
9. What kind/problems/like/to solve?
10. How long/take/do/a reading assignment?

■ GRAMMAR IN CONTENT

A Read and listen.

CD1,TR18

A Difficult Reading Assignment

Just remember, this next assignment is very difficult, so try to **get ahead** if you can. We will do two chapters in each class, so if you **get behind**, just follow the discussion and take notes. Then, **catch up** before the next class. If you want to see me for extra help, you can **sign up** for my office hours. Or if you have a difficult time, work with your study buddy. Just don't **give up**. **Go on** with the reading, and do your best.

B Look at the reading. Can you find any objects for the phrasal verbs in bold?

___ yes ___ no

Phrasal Verbs: Intransitive/Inseparable (II)

Form				Common Academic Phrasal Verbs (II)
	verb	*particle*		**to get ahead**—work ahead of schedule
Try to	**get**	**ahead**	if you can.	**to get behind**—work behind schedule
				to keep up—stay on schedule
verb	*particle*			**to catch up (with)**—no longer behind schedule
Catch	**up**		before the next class.	**to sign up**—add your name to a list
				to give up—stop working; feel hopeless
				to go on—continue

Notes:

• If *intransitive,* there is no object, and the phrasal verb is never separated:

Incorrect: ~~I'm catching it up.~~   Correct: *I'm catching up.*

Incorrect: ~~I'm getting the reading ahead.~~   Correct: *I'm getting ahead in the reading.*

• There is often a prepositional phrase or a clause after an intransitive verb, for example, Go on *with the reading.*

C Listen to the question. Choose the correct answer.

1. a. Well, I'm getting them behind because they're a little difficult.
   (b.) Well, I'm getting behind because they're a little difficult.

2. a. I'm signing on for tutoring in the Writing Center.
   (b.) I'm signing up for tutoring in the Writing Center.

3. (a.) I like to get ahead with the reading assignments.
   b. I like to keep up with the reading assignments.

4. (a.) My schedule is just too busy. I can't go on like this.
   b. My schedule is just too busy. I can't go it on like this.

5. a. I was sick last week, so I'm giving up on my assignments.
   (b.) I was sick last week, so I'm catching up with my assignments.

6. a. Oh, you know, I have a lot of assignments, but I'm keeping them up.
   (b.) Oh, you know, I have a lot of assignments, but I'm keeping up.

D Correct the errors in the e-mail. There are six errors.

Dear Professor Johnson,

I would like to sign up for an appointment with you. I am getting ahead with the reading assignments, and I need to talk to you about this. I don't like to go behind, but my schedule at work is very busy right now. I have so much reading to do, and I don't know if I can catch it. I like this class, and I don't want to give up it, but I'm having a hard time. When I talk to you, I hope you can help me. I really want to go with the class.

Thank you,

Mirka Milowska

■ COMMUNICATE

E PAIR/GROUP WORK Each pair or small group will have one of the following groups of verbs. Write a short skit using the verbs and act it out for the class.

1. get ahead/do over/find out
2. get behind/come across/work on
3. catch up (with)/sign up/turn in
4. go on/leave out/put off

5. call on/give up/write down
6. think about/go over/look up
7. hand out/figure out/point out

GRAMMAR AND VOCABULARY Write a letter to a friend or family member. Tell them about your experience in English class. Use the phrasal verbs and vocabulary from this chapter.

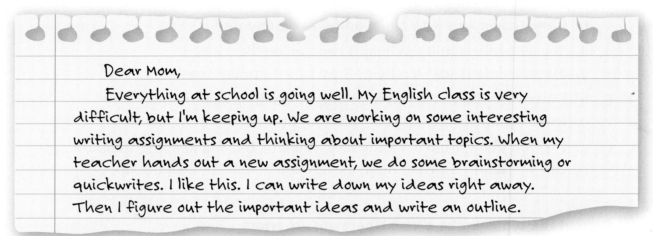

> Dear Mom,
>
> Everything at school is going well. My English class is very difficult, but I'm keeping up. We are working on some interesting writing assignments and thinking about important topics. When my teacher hands out a new assignment, we do some brainstorming or quickwrites. I like this. I can write down my ideas right away. Then I figure out the important ideas and write an outline.

PROJECT Work with your group to create and design a tip sheet for the future students of the class you are in now. Use the phrasal verbs and vocabulary from this lesson. Give the students tips about the class. Help them to work well and succeed in the class. Share your tip sheet with the class.

 INTERNET What is an OWL? Type OWL into a search engine and find out. How does an OWL help students with reading and writing assignments? Report to your class on three ways an OWL can help you.

PART 1
Simple Past: Statements/
Questions/Short Answers;
Common Irregular Past Forms

PART 2
Simple Past Time Expressions:
Words/Phrases/Clauses

L e s s o n ⑦

Music History:
Great Composers

■ CONTENT VOCABULARY

Look at the pictures. Do you know the words?

a composer

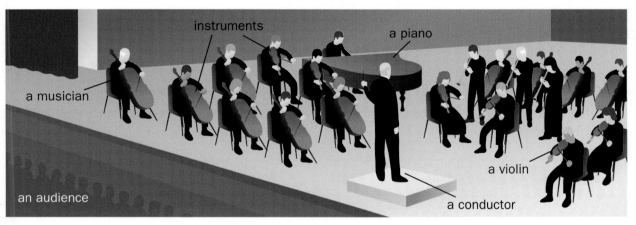

instruments

a piano

a musician

a violin

an audience

a conductor

a concert

Write the new words in your vocabulary journal.

■ THINK ABOUT IT

In your writing journal, write for five minutes about any of these questions.
Did you study music, play an instrument, or sing when you were a child? Did you have music lessons at school? Did any of your family or friends study music or play instruments? What kind of music was it? What did you/they play/sing?

■ GRAMMAR IN CONTENT

A Read and listen.

CD1,TR20

Mozart

Wolfgang Amadeus Mozart **was** a great composer. He **was** born on January 27, 1756, in Salzburg, Austria. His father **was** a composer and author of books about music. He **taught** Mozart about music. Mozart **was** only three years old when he **began** his lessons. His father quickly **saw** that Mozart **had** a lot of talent. It **took** Mozart 30 minutes to learn his first piece of music. When Mozart **was** six years old, he **wrote** five pieces for the piano. He **composed** his first symphony when he **was** eight years old.

Mozart **traveled** through Europe several times. He often **gave** concerts with his older sister, Nannerl. They **played** piano together for these concerts. People **were** surprised by their talent, but they **didn't show** their appreciation with money. During his life, Mozart **created** six hundred pieces of music, but he **didn't earn** very much money. He **died** poor on December 5, 1791, at the age of 35. After he died, he became famous for his musical talent.

a symphony: a long piece of music with three or four parts

famous: very popular; well-known

a talent: natural ability

B In the reading, look at the past tense verbs in bold. What is the present tense form of these verbs? Write both forms in the chart. Place a check if the verb has a regular past form.

Present	Past	Reg.?	Present	Past	Reg.?
is	was				

Simple Past

Affirmative Statements

Subject	Verb
I/You/We/They He/She/It	played.

Negative Statements

Subject	*Did* + Not	Verb
I/You/We/They He/She/It	did not (didn't)	work.

Questions

Did	Subject	Verb
Did	I/you/we they/he/ she/it	play?

Short Answers

	Subject	
Yes,	I/you/we	did.
No,	they/he/ she/it	didn't.

Wh-	*Did*	Subject	Verb
When	did	I/you/we they/he/ she/it	play?

Be

Affirmative Statements

Subject	Verb	Adj./Noun
I/He/She/It	was	famous.
You/We/They	were	musicians.

Negative Statements

Subject	*Be* + Not	Adj./Noun
I	was not (wasn't)	a musician. famous.
You/We/They	were not (weren't)	
He/She/It	was not (wasn't)	

Questions

Be	Subject	Adj./Noun
Was	I/he/ she/it	famous?
Were	we/you/ they	musicians?

Short Answers

	Subject	
Yes,	I/he/she/it	was.
No,		wasn't.
Yes,	we/you/they	were.
No,		weren't.

Wh-	*Be*	Subject	Adj./Noun
When	was	I/he/she/it	famous?
Where	were	you/we/they	musicians?

Notes:

- **Spelling:** Add *-ed* to most regular verbs. If the verb ends in

1. consonant + **y**	change the **y → i**	add **-ed**	(carry → carried)
2. consonant + **e**		add **-d**	(live → lived)
3. vowel + consonant	double the consonant	add **-ed**	(stop → stopped)
(except **w** or **x**)			(fix → fixed)
(except 2 or more syllables, last syllable unstressed)			(travel → traveled)

- **Pronunciation of** *-ed:*

    (1) Pronounce as /t/ after voiceless consonants (except *t*) *(stopped).*

    (2) Pronounce as /d/ after vowels and voiced consonants except *d (played, composed).*

    (3) Pronounce as /ɪd/ after /t/ and /d/ *(needed, waited).*

Common Irregular Past Forms

become-became	give-gave	meet-met
come-came	go-went	pay-paid
begin-began	hear-heard	read-read
buy-bought	keep-kept	see-saw
cost-cost	lead-led	teach-taught
fight-fought	make-made	write-wrote

- Study more irregular past verb forms on page 308 in the appendix.

C **Use the past tense of the verb to write a question. Use the reading about Mozart on page 62 to answer each question. Use the verb in your answer.**

Example: (be)

   Q: _____*Was*_____ Mozart born in 1752?

   A: _____*No, he wasn't. He was born in 1756.*_____

1. **Q:** (teach) _____ Mozart's sister _____ Mozart about music?

    A: _____

2. **Q:** (begin) _____ Mozart _____ his music lessons when he was six?

    A: _____

3. **Q:** (see) What _____ Mozart's father _____ ?

    A: _____

4. **Q:** (write) When _____ Mozart _____ five pieces for the piano?

   A: _____

5. **Q:** (give) _____ Mozart always _____ concerts in Europe alone?

   A: _____

6. **Q:** (create) _____ Mozart _____ a lot of music?

   A: _____

7. **Q:** (die) When _____ Mozart _____ ?

   A: _____

D **Use the past tense of the irregular verb to fill the blanks.**

Mozart (be) ___was___ a great composer. He (write) _____ music and
          (1)   **(2)**

(meet) _____ many famous musicians. But during his life, Mozart (have)
      (3)

_____ trouble with money and health. His father (teach) _____ him to play
(4)   **(5)**

music when he was very young and he (make) _____ a concert schedule for
                                       (6)

Mozart to travel all over Europe. When people (hear) _____ his music, they loved
                                       (7)

it, but his father (keep) _____ the money for himself. Later, when Mozart was
                (8)

older and people (pay) _____ him for his compositions and performances, he
                (9)

(spend) _____ all of the money. Mozart had a very heavy performance schedule.
      (10)

The traveling was difficult, and Europe was very cold. Mozart (become) _____
                                       (11)

tired on these trips and the schedule (cost) _____ Mozart his health. He (fight)
                                (12)

_____ many illnesses during his life and (die) _____ at an early age.
(13)   **(14)**

■ COMMUNICATE

E **PAIR WORK** Use the words to ask your partner: When you were young . . .? Your partner will answer: No, I didn't, but I . . . OR Yes, I did. I . . .

> When you were young, did you play the piano?

> No, I didn't, but I played the violin.

> Yes, I did. I played for eight years. How about you? Did you play the piano when you were young?

1. play/an instrument
2. hear/great composers
3. go/to any concerts
4. learn/about Mozart
5. see/talented musicians
6. study/music/in school
7. take/piano lessons
8. have/talent for music

PART TWO	Simple Past Time Expressions: Words/Phrases/Clauses

■ GRAMMAR IN CONTENT

CD1, TR21

A **Read and listen.**

A Class Discussion about Beethoven

Professor: So, as you can see, Beethoven was another great composer.

Student 1: Excuse me, Professor, did Beethoven know Mozart?

Professor: No, he didn't. He wanted to study with Mozart, but Mozart died **before Beethoven went to Vienna.** So he studied with Haydn.

Student 2: Was Haydn a good composer?

Professor: Yes, he was an excellent composer. **After Beethoven arrived in Vienna,** they met and began their work together.

Student 3: When did Beethoven lose his hearing?

Professor: He became completely deaf **in 1818.** However, he knew he had a problem long **before 1818,** and **when he began to lose his hearing in 1801,** he felt sad and lost.

Student 4: Did he write any more music **after 1818?**

Professor: Yes, in fact, he wrote music **until he got sick in 1826.** He also kept "conversation books" about his music **from 1802 to 1825.** He used them for communicating with his friends about his music **after he began to lose his hearing.**

deaf: unable to hear

B In the reading on the prior page, the past time expressions are in bold.

1. Underline the time **clauses.** How many did you find? ___

2. (Circle) the time **phrases.** How many did you find? ___

3. Discuss the difference between the clauses and phrases.

Simple Past Time Expressions: Words/Phrases/Clauses

Words/Phrases

before/after/until + date	He **knew** he had a problem **before 1818.**
yesterday	I **went** to a concert **yesterday.**
last (night/week/month/year/summer)	They **heard** a symphony **last night.**
in (+ date)	He **died** suddenly **in 1827.**
from (+ date) to (+ date)	He **wrote** music **from 1762 to 1791.**

Clauses

Examples	Meaning
Before he died, he was not famous.	First he died. Then he became famous.
People bought his music **after he died.**	First he died. Then people bought his music.
He wrote music **until he got sick.**	First he wrote music. He got sick. Then he didn't write music.
When he died, his music became famous.	First he died. Then he became famous.

Note:

If the time clause comes first in the sentence, use a comma after the clause.

C Write *T* for True or *F* for False.

1. _T_ First Beethoven went to Vienna. Then he worked with Haydn.

2. ___ First Beethoven went to Vienna. Then Mozart died.

3. ___ First Beethoven began to lose his hearing. Then he felt sad and lost.

4. ___ First he became deaf. Then he knew he had a problem.

D Write about the concert. Combine the sentence on the left and the sentence on the right. Use time clauses.

First	Then
The musicians took their seats.	The audience became quiet.
The audience turned off their cell phones.	The concert began.
The orchestra sat.	The conductor came out, and they stood up.
The orchestra prepared their instruments.	They played the first note.
The orchestra played the last note.	The audience showed appreciation.
The audience waited.	The conductor left the stage and they left.
The concert was over.	The audience felt happy.

1. _____ *After the musicians took their seats, the audience became quiet.* _____

2. _____

3. _____

4. _____

5. _____

6. _____

7. _____

E First read the ten facts about Beethoven's life. Guess the order of events. Write the numbers on the left. The first one is done for you. Then listen and write the correct order. Listen a third time and write the dates on the right.

CD1,TR22

___ He returned to Vienna. _____

___ His father gave him lessons. _____

___ He traveled to Vienna. _____

_1_ Beethoven was born in Bonn. _____

___ He wrote his first music. _____

___ His mother got sick. _____

___ His father decided to teach him. _____

___ He gave his first concert. _____

___ He returned to Bonn. _____

___ He had his first concert in Vienna. _____

F **SPELLING AND PRONUNCIATION** Write the past tense of the word. Then work with a partner to practice the pronunciation.

1. stop _stopped_

2. need _____

3. play _____

4. raise _____

5. wait _____

6. offer _____

7. change _____

8. work _____

■ **C O M M U N I C A T E**

G **PAIR WORK** Beethoven was deaf, so he kept a conversation book. When he became deaf, he communicated with his friends this way. It was a conversation in writing. Write a conversation book with your partner. Begin the conversation with a question in the past tense. Your partner will write an answer. Then your partner will write a question for you. Have an interesting conversation!

Beethoven: What did you think about my last piece of music?

Friend: I heard it a few weeks ago. It was wonderful. I really liked it.

Sanji: What did you do last weekend?

Elisa: I studied for my exam and worked at the library.
Then I went to a concert.

Sanji: How did you like the concert?

GRAMMAR AND VOCABULARY Use the information about Beethoven in Exercises A and E to write a paragraph about his life. Use the time expressions you have learned in this lesson.

PROJECT Learn about other great composers.

1. In a group of four, choose another great composer, such as Bach, Haydn, Liszt, Mahler, or Chopin. You may also choose another composer that you know.
2. Assign a different time from the composer's life for each student: birth–10 years old; 10–20 years old; 20–30 years old; 30–death.
3. Find at least two pieces of important information about your topic.
4. Each member of the group should report the information to the other members. Everyone should take notes, so each has complete information.
5. Leave your group. Form a new group with one member from each of the other groups.
6. Teach the new group about your composers.

 INTERNET Type "concerts in (your city)" into your search engine. Find information about a past concert (last week/last month, etc.). Report to your class: Who played? What time did the concert begin? Where was the concert? Did the audience like the concert?

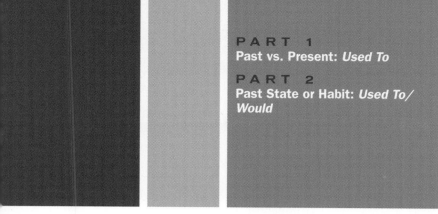

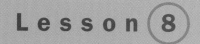
Lesson 8

Sociology: Urban History

■ CONTENT VOCABULARY

Look at the pictures. Do you know the words?

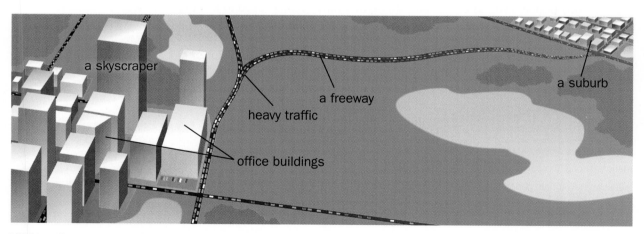

a neighborhood

Write the new words in your vocabulary journal.

■ THINK ABOUT IT

Choose a place you know well (for example, your native town, village, or city). How do you think life in that place was different 200 years ago? In your writing journal, write for five minutes about the place you chose.

■ GRAMMAR IN CONTENT

A Read and listen.

CD1,TR23

History of City Life

The cities of the past were very different from the cities of today. For example, in the Middle Ages (600–1500), the cities of Europe were small and not very crowded. Farmers **used to live** nearby in the countryside, and they **used to bring** food into the city and sell it. People **used to travel** on foot. The dirt streets were narrow, and there was little traffic. Also, there **used to be** a lot of open space in the center of a city. The cities had markets and gardens in these open spaces. If people lived in the city, their houses were often narrow and tall. They **used to have** their shops on the lower level, and they **used to live** on the upper floor.

With the start of the Industrial Revolution, people started to work in manufacturing jobs in the city, and many people lived in the cities. During this time, people **used to live** in small neighborhoods, **and they used to work** and **live** in the same area. People **didn't use to travel** very far to work. They **used to go** to an open market for their shopping.

Today, cities are huge and crowded, with very little open space. A lot of cities are 30–50 miles across. People live in apartments in the city or in big suburbs far from the city. They drive many miles on freeways or take subways and buses to work in large factories and tall skyscrapers. Now most people shop in large grocery stores and shopping malls.

crowded: many people in a small space

manufacturing: the part of industry that makes things

Industrial Revolution: period beginning in the 1800s when machines changed the way of life

B The words in bold show past states or habits that are different today. Can you find any habits like this in your writing journal? Write two sentences from your journal:

1. _____

2. _____

Past vs. Present: *Used To*

Affirmative Statements

used to + verb	People **used to live** near the countryside. There **used to be** a lot of open space.

Negative Statements

didn't + *use to*	People **didn't use to live** in apartments. There **didn't use to be** skyscrapers.

Yes/No Questions

Did + subject + *use to* + verb	**Did** people **use to live** close to the farms? **Did** there **use to be** a lot of open space?

Wh- Questions

Wh- + *did* + *use to* + verb	Where **did** people **use to live?** How **did** people **use to shop?**

Notes:
- Use -*ed* ending only in affirmative statements.
- Don't confuse *used to* with *be used to*. *Used to* = past habit. *Be used to* = become familiar with a past or present habit. For example, *I **used to live** in the city.* vs. *I **was used to living** in the city.*
- Don't use *was/were* before *used to* for past habit.
  Incorrect: *People ~~were~~ used to live in tall, narrow houses.*
  Correct: *People **used to live** in tall, narrow houses.*

C **Answer the questions about cities today. Write the answer with *used to*. Add information about present and past differences.**

1. **Q:** Do people walk to work on dirt roads?

   A: _No, people used to walk on dirt roads, but now they drive on paved roads._

2. **Q:** Are cities crowded?

   A: _____

3. **Q:** Do cities have a lot of open space?

   A: _____

4. **Q:** Is there a wall around every city?

   A: _____

5. **Q:** Do people buy fresh food from farmers?

   A: _____

6. **Q:** Are there a lot of skyscrapers and factories?

   A: _____

7. **Q:** Is there heavy traffic in most cities?

   A: _____

D Fill in the blanks with the simple past tense of the verb given or with *used to* plus the verb.

Dara: Hi, Li, how (be) _____was_____ your semester in Beijing?
(1)

Li: It was great! You know, I (be) _____ born in Beijing and (live)
(2)

_____ there until I (start) _____ school.
(3)   (4)

Dara: Oh yeah, that's right. Is it very different now?

Li: It sure is. When I was young, I (ride) _____ my bicycle
(5)

everywhere. There are still a lot of bicycles, but I (see) _____ so
(6)

many cars. When I lived in Beijing, there (be/not) _____ as many
(7)

cars and there (be/not) _____ as much traffic. Also, I remember
(8)

I (go) _____ shopping with my mother at the open markets. We
(9)

(buy) _____ everything at those markets. There (be) _____
(10)   (11)

no malls. But during my visit, even my mother (want) _____ to
(12)

shop at the huge mall.

Dara: How about food? (be) _____ that different?
(13)

Li: Well, of course Beijing (be) _____ so full of fast food restaurants
(14)

back then. And we (eat) _____ at small, cheap, and tasty places.
(15)

Many of those places are gone now.

Dara: It sounds like Beijing is changing very quickly.

E Compare the past and the present. Write two sentences. Use *used to* plus a verb in the first sentence and *didn't use to* in the second sentence.

Example: talk on the phone ___*People used to talk in phone booths.*___

___*They didn't use to carry phones in their cars.*___

1. write letters _____

_____

2. shop for food _____

_____

3. travel between countries or distant cities _____

_____

4. eat the main meal _____

_____

■ COMMUNICATE

F **PAIR WORK** Which is better: city life in the past or present? Discuss the topics with your partner. Practice with *used to/didn't use to.*

Example: neighborhoods

There used to be small neighborhoods in my city, and all the neighborhoods were close to the downtown area.

Yeah, my city was the same. People didn't use to drive to the store and they used to know all the neighbors.

1. traffic
2. shopping
3. transportation
4. buildings

■ GRAMMAR IN CONTENT

CD1,TR24

A **Read and listen to Jin's report.**

Study Abroad in Rome

Jin: One day we visited the Forum. In the ancient city of Rome, the Forum was a very busy place. The Forum **used to be** the center of culture, business, and politics in Rome. On most days, it **would be** full of people.

Student 1: What **would** they **do** there?

Jin: The Romans **would go** there to do their shopping, banking, and trading. Also, some people **used to stand** up and **speak** in public about important ideas. The shoppers **would stop** and **listen**. The speaker **wouldn't be afraid** to express strong ideas.

Student 2: Interesting. Did you see or learn about the ancient public baths in the city?

Jin: Yes, we did. As you know, there **used to be** many public baths all over Rome. At one time there were 900. The Romans **used to spend** a lot of time at the baths. They **would go** there early in the morning after they got up, or they **would stop** there after work to rest, read, exercise, and meet friends.

public: open to everyone; not private

to study abroad: spend a semester in another country

B **In the reading above, underline the sentences with *would*. In these sentences, what is the past state or habit?**

Past State or Habit: *Used To/Would*	
Affirmative Statements	
would + simple verb	The Forum **used to be** the center of culture. The Romans **would go** there every day.
Negative Statements	
would + *not* + verb	The speaker **wouldn't be afraid**.
Questions	
Would + subj. + verb *Wh-* + *would* + subj. + verb	**Would** children **go** there? *What* **would** they **do** there?

C Read the sentences about children in ancient Rome. Write two sentences about yourself—the first sentence with *used to/didn't use to* and the second with *would/wouldn't.*

1. Children studied at home with their parents. They didn't go to school.

   <u>   *I didn't use to study at home with my parents.*   </u>

   <u>   *I would go to school to study.*   </u>

2. They didn't go to a school building. They went to a tutor's house for group lessons.

   _____

   _____

3. Children got up very early. They began their school day before sunrise.

   _____

   _____

4. They went home for lunch and rested. Then they stayed at school until late evening.

   _____

   _____

5. Children in ancient Rome studied Latin, Greek, and arithmetic. They used small stones for their arithmetic problems.

   _____

   _____

6. A child in ancient Rome lived in a single-family home or an apartment. Children didn't have to go to visit their grandparents because they lived in the same home.

   _____

   _____

CD1,TR25

D Listen as the sociology professor talks about urban history around the world. (Circle) the correct answer(s).

1. New York
   - (a.) It used to have the name "Big Apple."
   - (b.) It has the name "Big Apple."

2. Moscow
   - a. Ice cream used to be very popular and cheap.
   - b. Ice cream is popular and cheap.

3. Cairo
   - a. Only animals and farmers used to be in the streets.
   - b. Cars didn't use to be in the streets.

4. Jakarta
   - a. The building used to be a museum.
   - b. The building is a museum.

5. Los Angeles
   - a. Water didn't use to be a problem in Los Angeles.
   - b. Water used to be a problem in Los Angeles.

E Correct the errors in Jin's e-mail message. There are eight errors.

Hi Everybody!

Here I am in this wonderful city. There is so much history here, and I'm learning a lot.

                visited
Yesterday, I ~~visit~~ the Forum. The rich Romans use to go there every day. They would be shop and
              ^

meet with their friends. I think they used to having a lot of free time. They also used go to the

public baths and relax. The baths were very popular, and they had many different rooms.

The poor people in Rome didn't used to went to the public baths. They would working all day,

so they wouldn't to have time.

See you soon!

Jin

F PAIR WORK

Part 1: Write five things that you used to do in your city or hometown when you were a child.

1. _____

2. _____

3. _____

4. _____

5. _____

Part 2: Now share your ideas from Part 1. Use the example to practice with your partner.

I used to play kickball every day with my friends.   Where did you use to play?

In the streets of my neighborhood. We would play for many hours. Did you use to play kickball?

GRAMMAR AND VOCABULARY Write about a place you lived in when you were younger. Discuss how that place was different from the place you live in now. Use the grammar and vocabulary from the lesson.

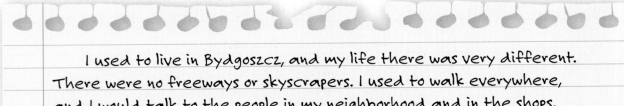

> I used to live in Bydgoszcz, and my life there was very different. There were no freeways or skyscrapers. I used to walk everywhere, and I would talk to the people in my neighborhood and in the shops. I used to shop at the open markets, and I would buy fresh food for dinner each day. Sometimes I would take the streetcar to another part of the city to see my friends.

PROJECT Find someone who was born in the town or city where you live now. The person should be over 50 years old. Interview the person. Ask: "How was (name of place) different when you were a child? How was your life different then?" Report to your classmates.

 INTERNET Look up the history of a city. Choose one topic, such as transportation, population, parks, occupations, or hobbies. Compare the past and present. Report to your class.

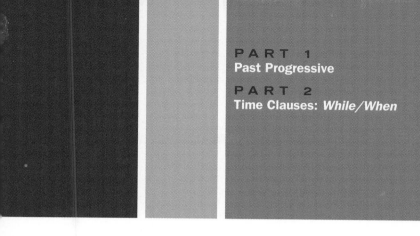

PART 1
Past Progressive

PART 2
Time Clauses: *While/When*

Lesson ⑨

Geology: The Earth and Earthquakes

■ CONTENT VOCABULARY

Look at the pictures. Do you know the words?

Earth

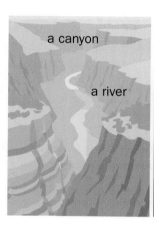

an earthquake

damage

Write the new words in your vocabulary journal.

■ THINK ABOUT IT

In your writing journal, write for five minutes about these questions.

Have you ever been in an earthquake? If you have, what were you doing when the earthquake happened? What did you do when you felt the earthquake? If you haven't been in an earthquake, what do you think people do when an earthquake strikes?

■ GRAMMAR IN CONTENT

CD1,TR26

A **Read and listen.**

The Changing Earth

Geologists study the earth. They try to understand the history of the earth. Geologists discovered that at one time, the earth had only one continent, "Pangaea." During that time, there were many earthquakes and volcanoes. The surface of the earth **was changing**. The changes **were creating** new mountains, canyons, rivers, valleys, and deserts. Geologists used to think that the continents **were moving** across the earth. Now, they believe that Pangaea **was breaking** apart into smaller continents. Two hundred million years later, the continents **were** still **breaking** apart. For example, they think that South America broke apart from Africa. Today the continents look very different. There are still many earthquakes, and the earth is still changing.

a surface: top; covering

B **In the reading above, the verbs in bold show continuing incomplete action in the past. Circle the verbs that show a completed action in the past. Discuss the difference in form and meaning.**

Past Progressive Tense

Affirmative			Negative		
Subject	**Was/Were**	**Verb -ing**	**Subject**	**Was/Were + Not**	**Verb -ing**
I/He/She/It You/We/They	was were	changing.	I/He/She/It You/We/They	was not OR wasn't were not OR weren't	changing.

Yes/No Questions			Short Answers		
Be	**Subject**	**Verb -ing**	**Yes/No**	**Subject**	**Was/Were + Not**
Was	I/he/ she/it	shaking?	Yes, No,	I/he/she/it	was. was not. OR wasn't.
Were	you/ we/they		Yes, No,	you/we/they	were. were not. OR weren't.

Past Progressive Tense

Wh- Questions

Wh-	Was/Were	Subject	Verb -ing
Where	was	it	going?
What	were	they	studying?

Past Progressive vs. Simple Past

Ongoing Incomplete Action = Past Progressive	Completed Action = Simple Past
What **was happening** at that time? Pangaea **was breaking** apart during that time. (The action was not completed.)	What **happened** long ago? Pangaea **broke** apart 200 million years ago. (The action was completed.)

Notes:

- Follow the present progressive spelling rules for adding **-ing** to the main verb (see page 41).
- Past progressive is sometimes used with **still** to show ongoing action, for example, *The continents were **still breaking apart.***

C **Fill in the blanks with the affirmative or negative forms of the past tense or past progressive tense.**

Last weekend I (take) _____*took*_____ my family to the mountains.
(1)

We decided to go on Saturday morning because it (rain) _____ and
(2)

the sun (shine) _____. We (leave) _____ the house
(3)   (4)

at 8:00 and (arrive) _____ at the park at 9:00. By 9:10 we (hike)
(5)

_____ up the mountain. All the way up, we (look) _____
(6)   (7)

down into a beautiful canyon. Suddenly I (feel) _____ something
(8)

strange. For about 30 seconds, the ground (move) _____ under my feet,
(9)

but I (walk) _____. The trees (shake) _____, but the wind
(10)   (11)

(blow) _____. Can you guess what (happen) _____? We
(12)   (13)

(have) _____ an earthquake.
(14)

D **Look at the pictures. Complete the sentences.**

last week

the next day

1. **A:** What _____were_____ you _____doing_____ last week during the
   earthquake?

   B: We _____were hiking_____ in the desert.

   A: _____Were_____ you still _____hiking_____ the next day?

   B: No, we _____weren't_____. We _____were driving_____ home.

2. **A:** What _____ Mario and Adam _____ yesterday
   at 3:00?

   B: They _____.

   A: _____ they still _____ at 4:00?

   B: _____ . They _____.

3. **A:** What _____ Junko _____ yesterday at 3:00?

   B: She _____.

   A: _____ she still _____ at 6:00?

   B: _____. She _____ .

summer   fall

4. **A:** What _____ Gina _____ in the summer?

   B: She _____.

   A: _____ she still _____ in the fall?

   B: _____. She _____.

two weeks ago

last weekend

5. **A:** What _____ Brian and Jenny _____ two weeks ago?

   B: They _____.

   A: _____ they still _____ last weekend?

   B: _____. They _____.

E Listen and check *C* if the action in the sentence is complete. Check *N* if the action is not complete.

CD1,TR27

	C	N
1.	☑	☐
2.	☐	☐
3.	☐	☐
4.	☐	☐
5.	☐	☐
6.	☐	☐

■ **COMMUNICATE**

F **PAIR WORK** Use simple past and past progressive. Ask your partner questions:

"What did you do _____? Where were you? What were you doing _____?"

- yesterday
- yesterday at 12:00 noon
- last weekend
- last Saturday at 4:00
- ten years ago
- this morning at 6:30 AM
- last night
- last night at 10 PM
- in 2002

■ GRAMMAR IN CONTENT

CD1, TR28

A **Read and listen to the blog.**

Karachi Earthquake

October 8, 2005

Two days ago, a major earthquake hit Karachi at 8:50 in the morning. **When** the earthquake **struck**, I **was cooking** breakfast, and my husband **was getting** ready for work. My two children **were** still **sleeping**. Suddenly, the whole house **was shaking**. Pictures **were falling** off the walls, and books **were flying** off the shelves. **When** the shaking **began**, I **stood** in the doorway. My children **sat** under the table. **While** they **were sitting** there, they **were shaking** too! **When** the shaking **stopped**, we **went** outside to see the damage. The bricks **were** still **falling** off the chimney.

Alia

major: serious, very important

B *When* and *while* introduce time clauses (*when/while* + subject + verb).

What verb tense is used with *when?* _____

What verb tense is used with *while?* _____

Time Clauses: *While/When*	
Meaning/Form	**Examples**
Type 1 • Two actions happen at the same time. • Use the past progressive in the time clause and in the main clause.	Time Clause / Main Clause past progressive / past progressive *While* they **were sitting** there, they **were shaking** too!
Type 2 • The first action was already in progress. The second action happened at a specific point during the first action. • Use the past progressive in the time clause and the past tense in the main clause.	Time Clause / Main Clause past progressive / past *While* I **was sleeping**, the earthquake **hit**.

Meaning/Form	Examples

Type 3
- The first action happened and then the second action happened. The first action caused the second action.
- Use the past tense in both clauses.

Time Clause	Main Clause
past	past

When it **stopped,** we **went** outside.

Note:

- Be careful not to mix the past progressive form and the past tense form.

  Incorrect: ~~What were you did while she talked?~~

  Correct: *What* **were** *you* **doing** *while she* **was talking?**

C Review the reading on the Karachi earthquake. Write *T* for True and *F* for False.

1. ___ The children were sleeping when the earthquake hit.

2. ___ While the house was shaking, pictures were falling off the walls.

3. ___ When Alia felt the earthquake, she was standing in the doorway.

4. ___ While her husband was getting ready for work, the earthquake struck.

5. ___ When the earthquake stopped, they stood under the doorway.

6. ___ The bricks were falling off the chimney when they went outside.

D Read the sentence. Then (circle) the letter of the other sentence that has the same meaning.

1. First the earthquake stopped, and then we went outside.
   a. When the earthquake stopped, we went outside.
   b. While the earthquake was stopping, we went outside.

2. We were standing outside, and we felt another shock.
   a. When we stood outside, we felt another shock.
   b. While we were standing outside, we felt another shock.

3. We felt the shock, and then we ran back into the house.
   a. When we felt the shock, we ran back into the house.
   b. While we were feeling the shock, we were running back into the house.

4. My husband was checking the gas line, and I was checking the water pipes.
    a. When my husband checked the gas line, I checked the water pipes.
    b. While my husband was checking the gas line, I was checking the water pipes.

5. I was looking for damage, and I found a lot of broken dishes and glasses.
    a. When I looked for damage, I was finding a lot of broken dishes and glasses.
    b. While I was looking for damage, I found a lot of broken dishes and glasses.

E Correct the 12 errors in the 1989 San Francisco earthquake journal.

> _was sleeping_
> Early yesterday morning I ~~slept~~ very deeply. I was waking up
>
> suddenly when a picture was drop on my head. I quickly ran
>
> under the doorway. The house shook and the dog barked.
>
> I was scream. This continued for 15 seconds. When the
>
> shaking stopped, I was going outside. The buses didn't run
>
> and the telephones didn't working. Everybody talked about
>
> the earthquake. While we were talk, fire trucks were race
>
> by us through the streets to save people.

■ **COMMUNICATE**

F **GROUP WORK** Take turns. Send one student from your group out of the room. The other students in the group will plan activities, such as *read, stand up, look out the window,* etc. When the student returns to the room, some group members will be doing their activities. Others will begin their activity when the student sits down. The student will then move to a new group and report the activities of the first group, e.g., *When I came into the room, Kaisha was writing.*

GRAMMAR AND VOCABULARY Choose one of the places from the list and write a story—true or fictional—about that place and/or an event. Use the grammar and vocabulary from the lesson. Answer these questions in your story: Where/When did it happen? What did she/you see? What was happening while she/you were there? What were other people doing?

- river
- ocean
- valley
- volcano
- islands
- continent
- mountains
- canyon

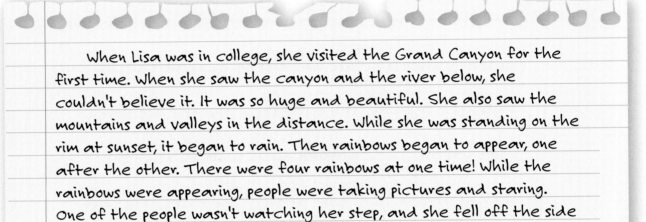

When Lisa was in college, she visited the Grand Canyon for the first time. When she saw the canyon and the river below, she couldn't believe it. It was so huge and beautiful. She also saw the mountains and valleys in the distance. While she was standing on the rim at sunset, it began to rain. Then rainbows began to appear, one after the other. There were four rainbows at one time! While the rainbows were appearing, people were taking pictures and staring. One of the people wasn't watching her step, and she fell off the side of the canyon. Lisa was so scared, but when she looked, she saw that the woman was not hurt.

PROJECT Work with a partner and take turns. Your partner will tell you about a major experience from his/her past, such as an earthquake, accident, or storm. While your partner is speaking, ask questions like these:

Where were you when _____?

What were you doing/thinking/feeling while _____?

What did you do when _____?

Take notes while your partner is speaking. Then write the story of your partner's experience. Your partner will ask you about your experience as well.

 INTERNET Use a search engine to look up "earthquake accounts." Find a story and summarize it to your class.

PART 1
Future—*Be Going To/Will:* Forms

PART 2
Be Going To vs. *Will:* Uses

PART 3
Present Progressive and Simple
Present for Future

L e s s o n ⑩

**Geology:
A Field Trip**

■ CONTENT VOCABULARY

Look at the pictures. Do you know the words?

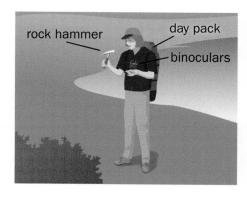
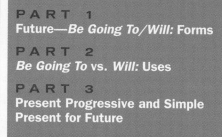
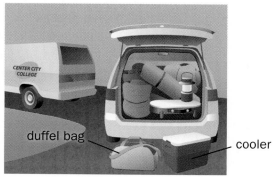

duffel bag

cooler

van

rock hammer

day pack

binoculars

tent

headlamp

rain gear

flashlight

sleeping bag

camping

Write the new words in your vocabulary journal.

■ THINK ABOUT IT

In your writing journal, write for five minutes about these questions.
Imagine the members of the Geology Club are going to take a trip to the Grand
Canyon. They will camp for five nights. What do you think they are going to bring?
What do you think they are going to do?

■ GRAMMAR IN CONTENT

A Read and listen.

CD1,TR29

Grand Canyon Field Trip

Professor: For this year's Geology Club field trip, we**'re going to drive** to the Grand Canyon during spring break. We**'re going to study** the rocks and **learn** about the history of the canyon. We**'ll drive** there in two vans and **spend** seven days in the North Rim region of the canyon. It's the best area for us. But we **won't hike** to the bottom.

Ling: So what **are** we **going to bring? Are** we **going to camp?**

Professor: Yes, You**'re going to pack** rain gear, your headlamp, and your field notebook in a day pack. You**'ll pack** the rest of your clothes and personal things in a duffel bag.

Sasha: **Will** we **take** individual tents?

Professor: No, two people **will share** one tent.

an individual: for one person

a region/area: a part of a larger place

B Look at the dialog. Find four future tense verbs with contractions. Write the contraction and the full form.

	Be Going To	Will
Full Form		
Contraction		

Future Tense—*Be Going To/Will*: Forms

Be Going To

Affirmative			**Negative**		
Subject	*Be Going To*	Verb	Subject	*Be + Not + Going To*	Verb
I	am going to		I	am not going to OR I'm not going to	
You We They	are going to	camp.	You We They	are not going to OR aren't going to OR (you)'re not going to	drive.
He She It	is going to		He She It	is not going to OR isn't going to OR (she)'s not going to	

Will

Affirmative			**Negative**		
Subject	*Will*	Verb	Subject	*Will + Not*	Verb
I/You/We/ They/He/She/It	will	camp.	I/You/We/ They/He/ She/It	will not OR won't	camp.

***Yes/No* Questions**				**Short Answers**		
Be	Subject	*Going To*	Verb	*Yes/No*	Subject	*Be + (not)*
Am	I			Yes, No,	I	am. am not. OR I'm not.
Are	you/we/they	going to	camp?	Yes, No,	you/we/ they	are. aren't. OR (we)'re not.
Is	he/she/it			Yes, No,	he/she/it	is. isn't. OR (she)'s not.

Will	Subject	Verb		*Yes/No*	Subject	*Will + (not)*
Will	I/you/we/ they/he/ she/it	camp?		Yes,	I/you/ we/they/ he/she/it	will.
				No,	I/you/ we/they/ he/she/it	will not. OR won't.

Wh- Questions

Wh-	Be	Subject	Going To	Verb
Where	is	Sasha	going to	camp?
What	are	the students	going to	bring?

Wh-	Will	Subject	Verb	
Where	will	Sasha	camp?	
What	will	the students	bring?	

Notes:

- Don't use **will** before **be going to.**

  Incorrect: ~~She will be going to hike.~~

  Correct: She **is going to** hike. / She **will** hike.

- Common pronunciation of *going to: gonna.*

C **Add the correct future tense form of the verb.**

stay	plan	send	sleep	
talk	bring	give	have	share

Professor: OK. So, we're ___*going to plan*___ the trip during the next few weeks.
(1)

I'll _____ you a list of things to pack, and Barbara is
(2)

_____ you an e-mail a few days before the trip.
(3)

Sasha: _____ we each _____ our own tent?
(4)   (5)

Professor: No, you're not _____ in an individual tent. You'll
(6)

_____ with one other student. We'll _____
(7)   (8)

for five nights and hike some of the trails.

Sasha: What kind of food are we _____ ?
(9)

Professor: I'm _____ about that at our next meeting.
(10)

D Fill in the blanks with *be going to* or *will* and the verb.

1. Lia (study) _is going to study_ geology in college. She (go)

   will go on field trips.

2. My class (take) _____ a field trip next month. We (spend)

   _____ two days in the desert.

3. A few students (give) _____ a speech in our next class. They

   (speak) _____ about the rocks of this area.

4. My parents (go) _____ camping this weekend. They (bring)

   _____ their rain gear.

5. I (visit) _____ the Grand Canyon this year. I (hike)

   _____ to the bottom.

6. The earth (not/be) _____ the same in 100 years. There (be)

   _____ many interesting changes.

E Listen to the two sentences. For each one, check the word you hear.

CD1,TR30

		gonna	going to
1.	a.		
	b.		
2.	a.		
	b.		
3.	a.		
	b.		
4.	a.		
	b.		
5.	a.		
	b.		

F **PAIR WORK** Take turns. Ask your partner about his/her future plans. Follow the example.

take/on the field trip

What are you gonna take on the field trip?

I'm gonna take my rain gear and a flashlight.

- study/before the next test
- do/tomorrow
- go to sleep/tonight
- spend/next vacation

- camp/this year
- buy/today
- watch TV/this weekend
- write a composition/next week

PART TWO	*Be Going To* vs. *Will:* Uses

■ GRAMMAR IN CONTENT

A **Read and listen.**

CD1,TR31

Packing for the Trip

Rashid: Hey, Sanji, when **are** you **going to** pack for the field trip?

Sanji: I'm not sure. **I'm** probably **going to pack** on Thursday morning, so I**'ll get** to bed early Thursday night. Then I **won't wake up** late on Friday.

Rashid: That's a good idea. **I'll drive**, OK? **Will** you **be** ready at 7:00? We can't be late. The buses **will leave** without us.

Sanji: Don't worry. I **won't be** late. This **is going to be** a great trip!

Rashid: You're right. I think it**'ll be** very interesting.

B **Look at the dialog. Number each future tense verb in the conversation (1) plan, (2) prediction, (3) offer, or (4) promise.**

Be Going To vs. Will: Uses

Use	Be Going To	Will
Plans/Intentions	I'm going to pack today.	I'll get to bed early.
Predictions	This is going to be a great trip.	Yes, I think it'll be interesting.
Offers		I'll drive.
Promises		I promise I won't be late.

Notes:

- In general, put **probably** after **will** and before **won't**: *I will probably pack tomorrow. I probably won't pack today.*

- **Be going to** is not usually used for offers and promises. Use **will** instead.

C Fill in the blank with **will** or **be going to** and the verb in parentheses if one is provided. Then discuss if it is a plan, prediction, offer, or promise.

Jose: OK, this is our last meeting before the trip. So today we (plan)

are going to plan the shopping.
    (1)

Sasha: Ling and I (do) _____ the food shopping on Thursday.
                    (2)

Jose: Oh, that's very helpful. Thanks. Now, it (be) _____ cold in
                                    (3)

the canyon at night, so we (need) _____ a lot of hot food.
                    (4)

Sasha: OK. We (buy) _____ soups and hot cereal.
                (5)

Jose: _____ we have enough money for all of the food we need?
        (6)

Ling: Well, it (be) _____ difficult, but don't worry, Sasha and
                    (7)

I have a lot of experience with this. We (make) _____ it
                                    (8)

work.

D Your class is going to take a field trip to the Canadian Rocky Mountains. For each pair of words, write a sentence with a plan and prediction. Use *be going to* and *will.*

1. a pair of binoculars/bring

    I'm going to bring a pair of binoculars, so I'll be able to see the mountains.

2. hiking boots/wear

    _____

3. pocket knife/carry

    _____

4. rain gear/pack

    _____

5. field notebook/use

    _____

6. sweater/bring

    _____

7. rock hammer/use

    _____

E Check the use for each future tense verb that you hear.

CD1,TR32

1. ✔ Plan   ___ Prediction   ___ Offer   ___ Promise

2. ___ Plan   ___ Prediction   ___ Offer   ___ Promise

3. ___ Plan   ___ Prediction   ___ Offer   ___ Promise

4. ___ Plan   ___ Prediction   ___ Offer   ___ Promise

5. ___ Plan   ___ Prediction   ___ Offer   ___ Promise

6.	__ Plan	__ Prediction	__ Offer	__ Promise
7.	__ Plan	__ Prediction	__ Offer	__ Promise
8.	__ Plan	__ Prediction	__ Offer	__ Promise

■ COMMUNICATE

F **PAIR WORK** **Take turns with your partner. Discuss a class field trip to the Grand Canyon. Follow the example.**

> Are you going to pack your field notebook?

> Yes, I am. I'm going to take notes on the hikes, so I'll remember the rocks.

> Do you think we're going to see some interesting rocks?

> Oh yeah. We'll probably see a lot of interesting things.

1. field notebook
2. flashlight
3. rain gear
4. headlamp
5. rock hammer
6. extra socks
7. camera

PART THREE | **Present Progressive and Simple Present for Future**

■ GRAMMAR IN CONTENT

A **Read and listen.**

CD1,TR33

Phone Call Home

Nathan:	Hey, Mom, we**'re going** on a field trip this weekend for my geology class.
Mom:	That sounds interesting. Where **are** you **going**?
Nathan:	We**'re taking** buses down to Baja, Mexico.
Mom:	When **do** you **leave**?
Nathan:	We **meet** at 7:00 am on Friday in the school parking lot, and the buses **leave** at 8:00.

B Look at the dialog. The present progressive and simple present tenses are in bold.

Which time expression tells us that it is about the future? _____

Which time expressions give a schedule? _____

Present Progressive for Future

We're **going** on a field trip **this weekend**. I'm **taking** an extra pair of socks.
We're **leaving** at 8:00 **in the morning**. She's **waking up** at 7:00.

Note:
Use the present progressive tense for near future or sudden plans.
A future time expression is used to show the future.

Simple Present Tense for Future

The buses **leave** at 8:00 AM. We **arrive** at 3:00 PM.
We **have** an orientation at 7:00 the next morning.

Note:
Use the simple present tense for future schedules. Use a time
expression, for example, **tomorrow, in the morning**. Use words that
indicate schedules, for example, **start, finish, begin, end, arrive, leave**.

C Read the sentence about present activity. Add a time expression and any other words to make it a future plan.

1. The bus is leaving. _____ *The bus is leaving at 8:00 in the morning.* _____

2. He is packing. _____

3. We are planning the trip. _____

4. Are you studying? _____

5. What are you doing? _____

D Correct the errors in Sanji's journal. There are eight errors.

We just finished Day 2 in the Grand Canyon. Tomorrow we

will wake

~~waking~~ up early at 6:00 and start our hike at 7:00. Professor

Nelson is going prepare us for the hike at breakfast. He tell us

about the different places we see during the hike. Today,

I forgot my rain gear and I got wet. I will be going to bring it

tomorrow, so I won't be going to get wet again. Tomorrow night,

after our hike, Professor Nelson going to give us a quiz about

the rocks in the Grand Canyon. I think it will easy because

we are learning so much.

■ **COMMUNICATE**

E **PAIR WORK** Student A: Ask your partner about the morning schedule. Student B: Look at page 299. Give your partner information. Then ask about the afternoon schedule.

What are we doing at 7:00?

We're meeting in the parking lot.

Student A

FIELD TRIP SCHEDULE

7:00		2:30	arrive at the Grand Canyon
8:00		3:00	group will set up camp
9:00		5:00	introduction to the park
12:00		6:00	dinner at camp

GRAMMAR AND VOCABULARY Write about a plan for a camping trip to a place that is interesting geologically. Describe the plan. What are you going to take and why? Predict what will happen and how you will feel. Here are some possible places: Baja (Mexico), Yosemite Park (U.S.), Dolomites (Italy), Blue Mountains (Australia), Mount Wuyi (China).

In two years, I'm going to take a trip to Peru. I'm going to spend three weeks in the Andes Mountains hiking and camping. I'll sign up for the trip through a good company, and I'll go with a group of people. We'll have a pack of horses and two guides. It won't be too difficult to hike because I won't have to carry a tent and sleeping bag. I will take my good hiking boots. I will also bring warm clothes, so I won't get cold at night. It is going to be a special experience because I will see many mountains, valleys, rocks, and canyons. I will see many interesting things and learn so much on this trip.

PROJECT Imagine that you are going to take a geology field trip.

1. Choose a place that has interesting rocks, mountains, canyons, etc.
2. Each group member will find information about the area, for example, When is the best time of year to go? How warm is it during the day? How cold is it during the night? What will you see there?
3. Discuss the information with your group, and make a list of things to pack. Discuss what you are going to bring and why.

INTERNET Use a search engine to look up "geology field trip." Choose an interesting trip and report to the class about it.

A Two students are talking about a research paper assignment for their music appreciation class. Write the correct tense/form of the verb in parentheses OR choose from the words in parentheses. If there is no choice, think of a word or words to add.

Katia: Hey, Sam, ___*did*___ (1) you (choose) ___*choose*___ (2) a musician for your research paper?

Sam: Yeah, I (decide) _____ (3) to write about Mahler. Yesterday, I (spend) _____ (4) two hours in the library. When I (looked up him/looked him up) _____ (5), I (find) _____ (6) a lot of interesting information. After I (was reading/read) _____ (7) for awhile, I (was checking/checked) _____ (8) (out/up) _____ (9) a few books. I (wanted/used to want) _____ (10) to get ahead on this assignment because it's (taking/going to take) _____ (11) a lot of time and hard work to complete it by the due date. How about you?

Katia: Well, I (went over/looked up) _____ (12) the assignment, and I (think) _____ (13) about the topic. Finally, I (was deciding/decided) _____ (14) to write about Mozart. I think it will (going to be/be) _____ (15) interesting to do an analysis of his Ninth Symphony. While I (thought/was thinking) _____ (16) about this, I (looked up/looking up) _____ (17) the concert schedule on the Internet. In two weeks there (is/would be) _____ (18) a Mozart concert at the symphony hall, so I'll (figure out/figure up) _____ (19) a way to use that concert in my analysis.

Sam: That sounds good. You know, when I (be) _____ (20) in high school, I (use to/used to) _____ (21) have such a difficult time with writing assignments. I (would/will) _____ (22) wait until the day before the due date to begin, and I (am going to/would) _____ (23) get very poor grades. Now, I know the right way to approach a writing assignment.

B Read the conversation between two students. Write the correct tense/form of the verb in parentheses. Add words if necessary.

Nate: Hey, Jie, you look really tired. (do) _____ you (sleep) _____ last
(1)   (2)
night?

Jie: Not very much. I (go) _____ on a field trip to the Grand Canyon with
(3)
my geology class. We (sleep) _____ in tents, and the other student in
(4)
my tent (sneeze) _____ all night. She (catch) _____ a cold while
(5)   (6)
we (hike) _____ in the rain.
(7)

Nate: Why (do) _____ you (hike) _____ while it (rain) _____?
(8)   (9)   (10)

Jie: Well, it (begin) _____ to rain while we (go) _____ down into the
(11)   (12)
canyon. We (put) _____ on our rain gear, but we still (get) _____
(13)   (14)
quite wet.

Nate: So, what (do) _____ you (do) _____ when you (finish) _____
(15)   (16)   (17)
the hike?

Jie: Well, on our way down, while we (study) _____ the history of the
(18)
canyon, we (write) _____ down all of our questions. When we (arrive)
(19)
_____ at the bottom, we (make) _____ camp and (have) _____
(20)   (21)   (22)
a discussion about our questions. Then we (cook) _____ our dinner
(23)
and (go) _____ to sleep . . . well, some people (sleep) _____.
(24)   (25)

LEARNER LOG Check (✔) *Yes* or *I Need More Practice.*

Lesson	I Can Use . . .	Yes	I Need More Practice
6	Phrasal Verbs: Transitive/Separable and Inseparable, Phrasal Verbs: Intransitive/Inseparable		
7	Simple Past Tense, Simple Past Time Expressions		
8	Past vs. Present: *Used to,* Past State or Habit: *Used to/Would*		
9	Past Progressive Tense, Time Clauses: *While/When*		
10	Future Tense: *Be Going To/Will*—Forms, *Be Going To* vs. *Will:* Uses, Present Progressive and Simple Present for Future		

P A R T 1
Future Time Clauses: *After/*
Before/When/As Soon As

P A R T 2
Future Conditional with *If* **Clauses**

P A R T 3
Future Progressive

L e s s o n (11)

Natural Sciences: Weather and Climate Change

■ CONTENT VOCABULARY

Look at the pictures. Do you know the words?

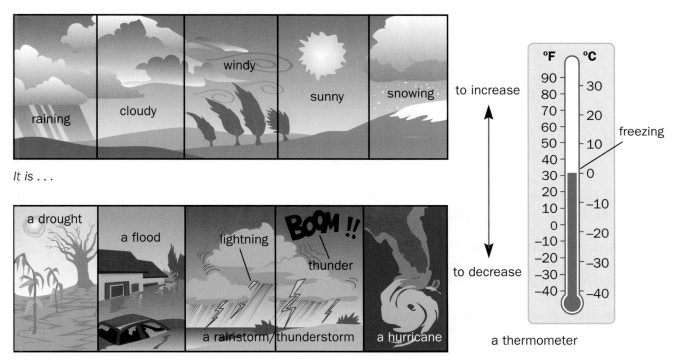

It is . . .

There is . . .

Write the new words in your vocabulary journal.

■ THINK ABOUT IT

In your writing journal, write for five minutes about any of these questions.

1. What kinds of weather do you have where you live?
2. How will the weather affect your activities next weekend . . . next month . . . next winter . . . next summer?

■ GRAMMAR IN CONTENT

A Read and listen.

CD1,TR34

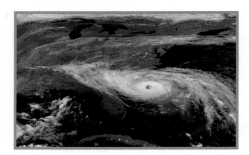

Introduction to Weather and Climate

In this class, we are going to study weather and climate. Weather is the day-to-day changes in temperature, humidity, wind, and pressure in one area. Climate is the type of weather in a larger area over a long period of time. **Before** we **begin** our first lesson on weather, we'll look at the weather today and **think** about it. For example, today it's sunny and dry. This is our weather for today. We **will discuss** climate **after** we **finish** the lessons on weather. We live in Florida, so hurricanes are part of the climate of this area. **As soon as** this dry season **ends**, we'll have our yearly hurricane season. We're going to experience a lot of humidity, wind, and rain **when** the hurricane season **starts**. **When** we finish our lessons on weather and climate, you **will understand** temperature change, hurricanes, droughts, floods, rainstorms, and snowstorms.

humidity: the amount of water in the air

pressure: the weight of the air mass around the earth

B The time words and verb forms for future time are in bold. Circle each time word or expression. Notice that the time words introduce dependent clauses.

What verb tense is used in the dependent clauses? _____

What verb tense is used in the main clauses? _____

Future Time Clauses: *After/Before/When/As Soon As*

Time Clause	Main Clause
Before we **begin** our lesson on weather,	we'll **look** at the weather today.

Time Clause	Main Clause
As soon as this dry season **ends**,	we'll **have** our yearly hurricane season.

Main Clause	Time Clause
We're **going to experience** more humidity	**when** the hurricane season **starts**.

Main Clause	Time Clause
We **will discuss** climate change	**after** we **finish** the lessons on weather.

Notes:
- Use present tense in the time clause and future tense in the main clause.
- If the dependent clause comes first, use a comma after the clause.
- Don't use future tense in the time clause:

  Incorrect: ~~Before we **will begin** our lesson on weather . . .~~

  Correct: *Before we* **begin** *our lesson on weather . . .*

C Choose the correct verb form and (circle) it.

For our class project, we studied temperature changes in Canada. Before we (will show /(show)) you our information, we (are going to describe / describe)
(1)   (2)
the climate in different parts of the country. After we (will describe / describe) the
(3)
climate zones, we (will discuss / discuss) the increase in temperature over the
(4)
past 100 years. When we (will finish / finish) our discussion of past changes, we
(5)
(will make / make) some predictions about future climate change.
(6)

D Read the conversations. Complete the sentence about the future. Answers may vary.

1. **A:** It's freezing. Do you really want to go for a walk right now?

   B: I guess not. As soon as *it warms up OR it gets warmer*, *we'll go for a walk*.

2. **A:** It's raining. You shouldn't take a picture in this weather.

   B: That's true. When _____,

   _____.

3. **A:** It's snowing and cold outside. You can't go outside without a coat.

   B: Don't worry. _____ before

   _____.

4. **A:** It's 98 degrees. It's too hot to play tennis.

   B: You're right. _____ after

   _____.

5. **A:** Don't wash your car today. It's going to rain all weekend.

   B: Yes, _____ as soon as _____.

6. **A:** You're going on a hike in the mountains? The weather report said we're going to have thunder and lightning this afternoon.

   B: Don't worry. _____ before

   _____ .

7. **A:** Are you sure you want to ride your bike now? It's very windy.

   B: Maybe you're right. When _____ ,

   _____ .

■ COMMUNICATE

E **PAIR WORK** Take turns with your partner. Use the words below to ask a question. Add necessary words and use correct verb forms. Answer in a complete sentence with a future time clause.

Example: What classes/take/before/graduate?

 What classes are you going to take before you graduate?

 Before I graduate, I'm going to take biology, English literature, and philosophy.

1. Which English class/take/before/graduate?
2. What/do/as soon as/this class/finish/today?
3. Where/work/when/get/a college degree?
4. How/dress/when/the weather/get/colder (or warmer)?
5. How/life/be different/after/your/English/improve?
6. What/do/before/reach/next birthday?
7. What/study/after/finish/this lesson?
8. Who/see/as soon as/leave/school today?

■ GRAMMAR IN CONTENT

A Read and listen.

CD1,TR35

What's the Difference?

Student 1: I don't understand the difference between weather and climate.

Teacher: Well, you can see changes in the weather every day, and those changes affect you. **If** it **is** cold, you**'ll wear** a sweater or a jacket. **If** it **is** hot and sunny, you **won't wear** a sweater or a jacket. **If** it **looks** like rain, you**'ll take** your umbrella.

Student 2: So we can't see changes in climate?

Teacher: Yes, we can, but not from one day to the next. **If** the temperature of the earth **rises** over some years, we**'re going to see** changes in the climate in many areas. Some areas will be warmer and other areas will get colder. For example, the climate of Europe **will be** much colder **if** we **have** another ice age.

an ice age: a period of thousands of years when Earth becomes very cold and ice covers the northern continents

B Find the five sentences in the dialog that have *if* clauses. Notice that they have a *condition* and a *result*. Write the condition and the result for each sentence below.

	Condition	Result
1.	*if it is cold*	*you'll wear a sweater or a jacket*
2.		
3.		
4.		
5.		

Future Conditional with *If* Clauses

If Clause	Main Clause
If it is cold, you'll wear a sweater or a jacket.

Main Clause	If Clause
You'll wear a sweater or jacket **if** it is cold.

If Clause	Main Clause
If it **looks** like rain, you'll **take** your umbrella.

Main Clause	If Clause
You'll **take** your umbrella **if** it **looks** like rain.

Notes:

- The condition is stated in the *if* clause (dependent clause). The result is stated in the main clause.
- Both clauses are about the future, but use the present tense in the *if* clause:
  Incorrect: ~~If it will be cold,~~ you'll **wear** a sweater or a jacket.
  Correct: *If it **is** cold, you'll **wear** a sweater or a jacket.*
- When the *if* clause comes first, use a comma. When it comes second, omit the comma.

C Read the weather lesson. Fill in the blanks with the present tense or future tense form of the verb.

Right now, it's very dry in the West. If it (not/rain) ___doesn't rain___ (1),
we (have) _____ (2) a drought. However, if these clouds here
(fill) _____ (3) up with enough water, it (rain) _____ (4).
In the South, we're watching this storm system. If the strong wind here
(meet) _____ (5) up with this warm water in the ocean, we (see)
_____ (6) a hurricane. The rivers in that area (flood) _____ (7)
if a hurricane (hit) _____ (8). You know, this type of strong weather
(continue) _____ (9) if we (not/stop) _____ (10) the increase in
the ocean temperature by changing some of our practices.

D Complete each sentence with a condition (*if* clause) or a result (main clause). Add correct punctuation.

1. If clouds become too full with water , it will rain. _____

2. We will have a drought _____

3. If ice fills up the clouds _____

4. If the ocean temperatures rise _____

5. The lakes will freeze _____

6. We are going to have a flood _____

7. If a strong wind meets warm water _____

E Listen and (circle) the sentence with the same meaning.

CD1,TR36

1. a. If you don't take an umbrella, you'll get wet.
   b. If you take an umbrella, you'll get wet.
2. a. If you don't drive carefully, you'll have an accident.
   b. If you drive carefully, you'll have an accident.
3. a. If you stay inside, you won't be safe.
   b. If you stay inside, you'll be safe.
4. a. If you forget your hat and gloves, you won't be warm.
   b. If you forget your hat and gloves, you'll be warm.
5. a. If you get out of the pool, you'll get hurt.
   b. If you stay in the pool, you'll get hurt.
6. a. If you don't wear a hat, you'll get a sunburn.
   b. If you don't wear a hat, you won't get a sunburn.
7. a. If you don't try to use the phone, you'll get a connection.
   b. If you try to use the phone, you won't get a connection.

■ COMMUNICATE

F **WRITE** Step 1: Write four plans or goals you have for the *near* future and three plans or goals you have for the *far* future.

1. _I'm going to play soccer this weekend._
2. _____
3. _____
4. _____
5. _____
6. _____
7. _____

PAIR WORK Step 2: Take turns with your partner. State one of your plans or goals. Your partner will ask you a *"What if?"* question. Answer truthfully. Follow the model.

I'm going to play soccer this weekend.

If it rains, I'll play basketball at the gym.

What are you going to do if it rains?

■ GRAMMAR IN CONTENT

CD1,TR37

A **Read and listen.**

Study Buddies

Student 1:   OK, let's review for the test. How does climate change?

Student 2:   Well, right now, the temperature of the earth is rising. Just a small increase over many years causes climate change. If we don't find ways to stop this temperature increase, we **will be experiencing** serious climate change during the next 50–100 years.

Student 1:   For example . . . ?

Student 2:   For example, in 50–100 years, people in the U.S.A. **will be living** in a drier climate.

Student 1:   And people who live in cold areas now **will be living** in a warmer climate.

Student 2:   Right, and if this happens, by 2110, people in northern Canada **will be growing** different crops.

B **You can see the future progressive verbs in bold. Find the three time expressions that help you understand the meaning of the future progressive verbs. Write them here.**

1. _____   2. _____   3. _____

Future Progressive

By **2110**, people in Canada **will be growing** different crops.
In 100 years, people in the U.S.A. **will be living** in a drier climate.
We **will be experiencing** serious climate change **during the next 100 years**.

Time Expressions

by + future point in time   **by** 2110, **by** next week, **by** Thursday
in + amount of time   **in** 2 years, **in** three weeks, **in** 4 hours
during the next + amount of time   **during the next** 2 months, **during the next** three days,
                                       during the next 5 years

Notes:

• Use *will* + *be* + verb *-ing* for future progressive.
• Use future progressive to show ongoing action in the future.

C Write *T* if the statement is true for you and *F* if the statement is false. Work with a partner to find out what he or she will be doing.

1. ___ In two years, I will still be studying English.

2. ___ By 2016, I will be living in a different city.

3. ___ In the future, I will be speaking English at work.

4. ___ By 10:00 tonight, I will be sleeping.

5. ___ In two days, our class will be taking a test.

D Write three sentences about the weather forecast using the future progressive.

SUN	MON	TUE	WED	THU	FRI	SAT

1. _____ By Monday, clouds will be gathering. _____

2. _____

3. _____

4. _____

■ **COMMUNICATE**

E **WRITE** Write a paragraph about your future. Use time clauses, *if* clauses, and the future progressive.

During the next ten years, my life will be changing in many ways. After I finish this class, I will complete my other college classes and graduate. If I do well, I will apply to a graduate program.

GRAMMAR AND VOCABULARY (Circle) the correct answer.

1. It is now 75 degrees Fahrenheit. If the temperature increases, it will be
   a. 78 degrees.
   b. 72 degrees.

2. It is too hot. When the temperature decreases, I will feel
   a. cooler.
   b. hotter.

3. If it starts to rain, we are going to
   a. go swimming.
   b. stop swimming.

4. After the lakes freeze, we
   a. are going to swim.
   b. are not going to swim.

5. As soon as the snowstorm ends, the children are going to
   a. play outside in the snow.
   b. play outside in the rain.

6. We are going to fix the roof
   a. before the next rainstorm comes.
   b. after the next rainstorm comes.

7. By January, there will be a lot of rain, and
   a. the drought will be ending.
   b. the flood will be ending.

PROJECT

1. In your group, choose one of these serious weather events: a *flood, hurricane, drought, heavy snowstorm,* or *ice storm.* Discuss the weather and the results of the weather: What will happen?

2. Decide on an emergency plan for before, during, and after the event.

   - How are you going to help people with injuries?
   - How are you going to get news about the situation?
   - How are you going to get food and water? How will you prepare food?
   - How are you going to get light and heat?
   - How are you going to get assistance?

3. Present your plan to your class.

 INTERNET Type "serious weather events" into a search engine. Report to your class about one of them.

PART 1
Verbs of Perception: Simple vs. Progressive

PART 2
Stative Verbs of Emotion/ Cognition/Possession

Lesson (12)

Cultural Anthropology: The Quechua of Peru

■ CONTENT VOCABULARY

Look at the pictures. Do you know the words?

values   a belief   a custom   a ritual

a nuclear family   an extended family

Write the new words in your vocabulary journal.

■ THINK ABOUT IT

In your writing journal, write for five minutes about any of these questions.

- What are some beliefs/values/customs/rituals in your culture?
- How close is your nuclear family? Your extended family?

■ GRAMMAR IN CONTENT

CD1,TR38

A **Read and listen.**

Anthropology Journal

Lucia is an anthropology student. During a summer program she is studying the Quechua (Kech'wa) people and culture in the Andes Mountains. This is from her journal:

*This week, we are visiting a number of small villages and learning about the values, customs, and rituals of the people. Yesterday our group climbed very high, so we are in a beautiful environment today. I **see** the "Big Mountain" in the distance and I **hear** the wind and a waterfall. The waterfall **sounds** very powerful. The air up here **smells** fresh and the food **tastes** good. Right now, I **am looking at** the little village where the people are preparing dinner. I'**m tasting** a purple potato and it's delicious. Yesterday, I tasted quinoa for the first time, and it was also very good. I **am** also **listening to** the stories and songs of the Quechua people. Their values about community and family **seem** very strong. The value of "mutual help" is also strong. When we do something for them, they do something for us. This **feels** good to me.*

a community: a group of people that work, play, live together

mutual: sharing similar feelings, ideas, tastes

quinoa: a grain similar to rice

B **Lucia's journal is about present ongoing activity. However, some of the verbs are not in the progressive tense. Write those verbs on the lines. Then find the verbs that are similar in meaning to those verbs and write them on the other lines.**

Simple	Progressive
hear	*am listening to*
_____	_____
_____	_____

Verbs of Perception

Simple		Progressive	
see	I **see** the mountain in the distance.	look at/watch	I **am looking at** the view.
hear sound	She **heard** the waterfall. It **sounded** powerful.	listen to	She **was listening to** the waterfall.
taste	The food **tastes** delicious.	taste/try	I **am tasting** a purple potato.
smell	The garlic **smelled** strong.	smell	The horse **was smelling** my pack.
feel	Alpaca fur **feels** soft.	touch	I **was touching** the blanket.

Notes:

- Use a simple verb form (1) when the verb has a stative meaning, that is, it does not continue, for example, *She heard the waterfall.* or (2) when the subject is not the agent, for example, *The food tastes delicious.*

  Incorrect: ~~*Are you seeing that mountain in the distance? Yes, I am seeing it.*~~

  Correct: *Do you **see** that mountain? Yes, I **see** it.*

- Use a progressive verb form when there is ongoing action and the subject is the agent, for example, *I am looking at the view.* (I = subject = agent)

  Incorrect: ~~*Do you look at that mountain in the distance right now? Yes, I look at it. It's beautiful.*~~

  Correct: *Are you **looking at** that mountain? Yes, I'm **looking at** it.*

C **Fill in the blanks with progressive or simple verb forms.**

1. **A:** How do you like their cooking?

   B: It's good. You know, while I ___*was tasting*___ the soup yesterday, I ___*tasted*___ lemon. (taste/taste)

2. **A:** Did you see anything interesting?

   B: Yes, while I _____ the mountains, I _____ a mountain goat. (see/look at)

3. **A:** When did the thunder strike?

   B: At 3:00, I _____ a story about a Quechua ritual. Suddenly, I _____ the thunder. So it was a few minutes after 3:00. (hear/listen to)

4. **A:** Hey, Lila, what are you doing?

   B: I _____ this soup. It _____ too spicy. (taste/taste)

5. **A:** What is he doing?

   B: He _____ the ground to find out if it is wet. If it

   _____ too wet, he won't sit on it. (feel/touch)

6. **A:** (on the telephone) Do you like the Andes?

   B: I sure do. Every day I _____ something interesting. Right

   now, I _____ a purple potato. (see/look at)

CD1,TR39

D **Listen and** (circle) **the correct answer.**

Example: How is the soup?
   a. It's tasting good.
   (b. It tastes good.)

1. a. I am tasting the soup.
    b. The soup tastes good.

2. a. I saw a movie on TV about Quechua culture.
    b. I was watching a movie on TV about Quechua culture.

3. a. Yes, we heard an interesting lecture about Quechua beliefs.
    b. Yes, we were hearing an interesting lecture about Quechua beliefs.

4. a. She was smelling the chicken burning.
    b. She smelled the chicken burning.

5. a. Yes, it tasted very good.
    b. Yes, it was tasting very good.

6. a. I felt a hot stove.
    b. I touched a hot stove.

■ **COMMUNICATE**

E **GROUP WORK** **Find pictures in magazines of people doing/experiencing the verbs**
in the list. Create a brief description of one of the pictures. Present it to the class.

- look at/see
- listen to/hear
- touch/feel
- taste/taste

Here is a woman and she is listening to her iPod. She just downloaded a new song from her favorite singer. The woman hears the drums and starts to dance. The new song sounds great, and the woman is happy.

GRAMMAR IN CONTENT

CD1,TR40

A Read and listen.

Quechua Beliefs and Values

In Peruvian Quechua culture, the highest mountains **have** an important meaning. The people **believe** a mountain is alive, and they **think** a mountain has a mind and feelings. They **know** the mountain isn't a human, but they **respect** it like a human.

The Quechua people **don't own** televisions and **don't possess** many things. They have their houses, families, and animals. They have a very strong relationship with their animals, and they **love** and **appreciate** their animals as members of their nuclear and extended families.

The Quechua people also have a strong sense of "reciprocity." This **means** they respect and help each other. If someone **needs** help or **wants** some food, they will give it. If something **belongs** to them, they are happy to share it because the person who receives help will give it back in some way.

to appreciate: to be thankful about something

B Look at the reading. The stative verbs in bold show no action. They show a feeling (emotion), a thought (cognition), or something a person has (possession). Write each verb in the proper column below.

Emotion	Cognition	Possession
1. _____	1. _____	1. *have*
2. _____	2. _____	2. _____
3. _____	3. _____	3. _____
4. _____	4. _____	4. _____
5. _____		

Stative Verbs of Emotion/Cognition/Possession

Emotion (Feel)		Cognition (Think)		Possession (Have)	
love	need	believe	understand	have	possess
hate	want	think	know	belong	own
like	dislike	mean			
respect					

Notes:

- In general do not use these non-progressive verbs in a present progressive or past progressive tense when you write.

  Incorrect: ~~Are they loving their animals? Yes, they are loving their animals.~~

  Correct: *Do they love their animals? Yes, they **love** their animals.*

- Use progressive tense with *think about,* for example, *I am **thinking about** the question.*

- Use progressive tense with *have* in idioms where *have* means experience: *We're **having fun.** We're **having a party.** They're **having a good time.** She's **having problems.** She's **having difficulty** with her pronunciation.*

C **Fill in the blanks with the simple present or present progressive form of the verb.**

A: Hey, Anna, how is your anthropology class going?

B: Oh, I (enjoy) *'m enjoying* _____ it. I (like) _____ the professor's
(1)   (2)
lessons about other cultures.

A: What (learn) _____?
(3)

B: Oh, we (study) _____ beliefs and customs in different cultures.
(4)

Now, I (understand) _____ many other cultures around the
(5)

world. For example, this week, we (think) _____ about the value
(6)

of mutual help. I (believe) _____ it is important, but it is not a
(7)

strong value in my culture. I (think) _____ my culture (need)
(8)

_____ more of this value right now.
(9)

A: (do) _____ you (know) _____ anybody from a
(10)   (11)
culture where that value is strong?

B: No, but now, after the professor's examples, I (know) _____ what
(12)

it (mean) _____.
(13)

D Correct the errors in the anthropology journal. There are eight errors.

Today, we are staying in a small village with
about 30 people. The people here ~~are loving~~ song and
(love)
dance. Right now they have a dance festival. They
are teaching us about their culture through their
music. They are having many interesting ways to show
us their values and beliefs. They are understanding
the importance of family and community, and they
are also knowing a lot about nature. I am having
difficulty with the language, but our guide is helping
me. I want to speak with the people myself, but I am
needing a lot of practice. I am knowing a lot about
this culture, and I'm liking the way the people live.

■ **COMMUNICATE**

E **PAIR WORK** Tell your partner about your values, beliefs, and customs. Use the verbs below and other verbs to compare the past and present. Use the progressive form when you can.

| love | need | have | own | think | mean | understand | know | hate | want |

GRAMMAR AND VOCABULARY Write about yourself. Fill in the blank with the correct affirmative or negative form of the verb in parentheses.

1. I (have) _____ a strong relationship with my nuclear family.

2. In my culture, money (be) _____ an important value.

3. People (love) _____ nature more than their cars in my culture.

4. Right now, my extended family (live) _____ in a village.

5. At the present, most people in my culture (own) _____ two cars.

6. Right now, I (hear) _____ my classmates talking.

7. People in my culture (believe) _____ a mountain has a mind and feelings.

PROJECT Follow these steps to study the culture you are living in.

1. Choose a situation to observe in your everyday life, for example, your college campus, a party, a gym, a restaurant, a shopping mall, and so forth.

2. Put yourself into the situation. Observe and listen to the people and activities in the situation. Take notes on these questions:

   - What do you see and hear?
   - How do things feel, smell, taste?
   - What are you and/or other people listening to, looking at, tasting, smelling, touching?
   - What cultural values, beliefs, and customs do you understand from this situation?

3. Write a journal entry about your observations and ideas. Write in the present tense to bring your reader into the experience.

 INTERNET Search for information about one of these cultures: *Navaho, Maya, Lakota, Maori,* or *Inuit.* Read about their beliefs, values, and customs. Report something interesting you learned to the class.

Economics: Money and Trade

■ CONTENT VOCABULARY

Look at the pictures. Do you know the words?

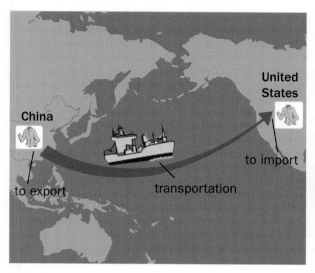

to trade

to exchange

labor

Write the new words in your vocabulary journal.

■ THINK ABOUT IT

In your writing journal, write for five minutes about any of these questions.

1. What food or clothing products does your native country export?
2. When you go shopping, what products do you buy that are exported?
3. What kinds of things do people buy on the Internet?

■ GRAMMAR IN CONTENT

A Read and listen.

CD1,TR41

The History of Money

Professor: Long ago, before there was money, **people** exchanged **objects** and **services**. This was called *bartering*. Can you imagine? This would mean you give me five **potatoes**, and I give you three **peaches**. For example, if a farmer had ten **cows**, he went to market and exchanged one cow for three **sheep**. You know, they say that Marco Polo traded his **owls** for a ship. Also, another example—in the fishing **communities** of northern Canada, people traded whale's **teeth** and **seashells** for **clothes** and **blankets**.

Student: So, when did people begin to use money?

Professor: Well, in 687 BCE the Lydians began to make **coins**. They lived in the area that is now western Turkey. The minting of coins as currency spread to Greece (from 600 to 570 BCE, then to Persia in 546 BCE), and then to the Romans, among others. China independently began minting coins (600 to 300 BCE). Today, trade is much more than an exchange of objects and services. Some **countries**, for instance, export **products** when they cannot use all of them in their own countries. It is a way to make a profit and earn foreign currency.

currency: bills and coins of a specific country

to mint: to manufacture money

B The words in bold are plural forms of nouns. What are the three *irregular* plural forms?

_____   _____   _____

Write the singular form for these nouns. Then write the rule for the plural.

countries: _____ Rule: _____

peaches: _____ Rule: _____

Count Nouns: Regular Singular and Plural Forms

Rule	Ending	Singular	Plural
After vowels After voiced consonants After voiceless consonants After vowel + -y After some nouns ending in o (*avocados, pianos, photos, autos*)	-s	one bee one pig a profit a toy a radio a mango	two bees two pigs some profits some toys some radios some mangos
After s, sh, ch, ss, x, z After some nouns ending in o (*heroes, mosquitoes*) Change the f to v and add -es (Except *roofs, beliefs, chiefs*)	-es	a box one potato one tomato a knife a leaf	a lot of boxes two potatoes two tomatoes a lot of knives some leaves
Change y to i and add -es	-ies	a country	some countries

Notes:

- A count noun has a plural form, for example, *cow* → *cows*. We can count it, for example, *one cow, two cows.*
- Use *a/an* with singular count nouns. Use **some** and **a lot of** with plural count nouns.

Count Nouns: Irregular Singular and Plural Forms

Type of Plural	Singular	Plural
Vowel or word change	one man/woman a tooth one foot a child one person one mouse	two men/women some teeth two feet some children two people two mice
Same word (no change)	one sheep one deer a fish	three sheep two deer some fish
Borrowed from other languages	a crisis one cactus	some crises two cacti (or two cactuses)

C Use the rules in the chart. Write the plural form of each noun.

1. Three (boy) _____*boys*_____ tried to trade their two pet (mouse) _____ for the hats of three (fireman) _____.

2. Two (bus) _____ stopped, and two (thief) _____ ran onto one of them. They tried to sell their stolen (toy) _____ and (radio) _____ to the (person) _____ on the bus.

3. Four (man) _____ and five (woman) _____ went to the market to trade (mango) _____, (papaya) _____, and (potato) _____.

4. The three (child) _____ went on the Internet and traded two (compass) _____ and three (box) _____ of magic cards.

D Write the plural form of the noun in bold.

1. **A:** Can we use this **box** to transport the bananas?

   B: No, use these _____*boxes*_____ here.

2. **A:** What happens if a country has a strong **economy?**

   B: Sometimes, other _____ may get stronger.

3. **A:** Do you want to trade?

   B: OK. I'll trade you one sweet **potato** for three plain _____.

4. **A:** A **child** is working at the factory.

   B: That kind of labor is not for _____.

5. **A:** Who should we talk to?

   B: There is a **person** in the office with good ideas, and there are two _____ in another company with some information.

6. **A:** I think Richard is going through a **crisis.**

   B: Well, don't worry. Some _____ teach us important lessons.

E Listen and complete the response with a plural noun. Then practice pronouncing each of the sentences with a partner.

1. No, thanks. I already have two _____glasses_____.

2. No, I never make _____.

3. Yes, she always gives me a lot of hugs and _____.

4. No, that company doesn't sell _____.

5. Yes, there are three _____ in my neighborhood.

6. No, thanks. I have some _____.

■ COMMUNICATE

F **PAIR WORK** Trade with your partner. Use singular and plural forms of the objects on your list. Then summarize your trading in writing.

I'll give you three ducks for six geese.

I don't think so. How about three ducks for one goose?

Student A	Student B
duck (3)	goose (6)
horse (4)	chicken (200)
cow (6)	sheep (10)
fish (10)	tomato (50)
banana (100)	watch (2)
video (20)	radio (2)

■ GRAMMAR IN CONTENT

A Read and listen.

CD1,TR43

International Trade

For many **years**, **people** traded face-to-face. In the early 1900s, when **methods** of **transportation** improved, **companies** began to trade **objects** such as **food**, **furniture**, **clothing**, and **jewelry** without meeting face-to-face. Now, **countries** all over the world trade through exports and imports. Brazil exports **coffee** and **sugar** to countries all over the world. Spain exports **olives** and **nuts** to other countries throughout Europe. The U.S. imports many **clothes** and other **products** from China. The U.S. also imports **fruit**, especially **bananas** and **mangos** from countries in Central and South America. The economic **health** and **well-being** of a country depends on this trade, since trade can affect the level of **poverty** or **wealth** in a country.

B The words in bold are nouns. Write the count and noncount nouns in the box.

Count	Noncount
years	

Noncount Nouns

Concrete

food/meat/cheese
coffee/tea/wine/milk/soda
rice/wheat/corn/sugar/salt
oil/water/air
cotton/wool/silk

Abstract

labor	energy	time
transportation	work	knowledge
information	poverty	
education	wealth	

Groups

| furniture | jewelry | money |
| cosmetics | homework | fruit |

Subjects

| history | biology | science |
| economics | mathematics | engineering |

Notes:

- A noncount noun usually has no plural form, for example, *informations*. We can't count it.

  Incorrect: ~~one information, two informations~~

  Correct: *some information; a lot of information*

- Use *some* and *a lot of* with noncount nouns.

- Some noncount nouns can be count nouns with a specific meaning:

  two coffees = two cups of coffee.

  fruits/foods = the individual kinds that make up the whole group, for example, *Brazil exports many tropical fruits such as papayas and mangos.*

C **Part 1: If the word is a count noun, write *a/an* and the singular form. Then write a number and the plural form. If the word is a noncount noun, write *some* and the noun. Write *x* if there is no form.**

	Singular	Plural	Noncount
1. chair	a chair	two chairs	x
2. furniture	x	x	some furniture
3. fruit			
4. energy			
5. labor			
6. soybean			
7. math			
8. clothes			
9. avocado			

Part 2: Use the nouns from Part 1 to make short conversations with your partner. Use the model.

Are you selling a chair?

Great! I need some furniture.

Yes. In fact, I'm selling two chairs.

D (Circle) the correct word.

International trade is increasing every day. (Car / (Cars)),
(1)
(computer / computers), (cloth / clothes), and (food / foods) (is / are) all
(2)   (3)   (4)   (5)
major (import / imports) and (export / exports) on the world market. However,
(6)   (7)
(crime / crimes) (is / are) often a big (problem / problems) with international
(8)   (9)   (10)
(trade / trades). Some small, unknown (company / companies) (is / are) putting
(11)   (12)   (13)
famous brand (name / names) such as "Nike" on their (product / products),
(14)   (15)
without permission. Then, those (company / companies) (use / uses) a lot of cheap
(16)   (17)
(labor / labors) and (sell / sells) their (shoe / shoes) at high (price / prices)
(18)   (19)   (20)   (21)
with the famous brand (name / names). Their (sale / sales) are high because of
(22)   (23)
the brand name, and they show strong (profit / profits) because their business
(24)
(cost / costs) are so low.
(25)

E Correct the errors in the e-mail. There are 14 errors.

To: Nancy@csb.net
From: snowlion

In my economic class, I am studying moneys and trade. It is an interesting class, but I have a lot

of homeworks. Sometimes, the idea are difficult to understand, but the professor gives us a lot of

informations. He finds creative way to teach us. For example, he brought some jewelrys to class—some

watch, ring, and bracelet. He also brought some fruit, like apple, orange, and banana. We discussed

many ideas about trade, and we practiced with those object.

F **PAIR WORK** Student A, look at this page. Student B, look at page 299. Take turns. Use the words to ask your partner about last year's exports. Fill in the chart.

Are eggs a major export for Italy?

Yes, Italy exported $69 million in eggs last year.

EXPORTS	INDIA	ITALY	CHINA	BRAZIL	U.S.	NIGERIA
	57 million	69 million	71 million	23 million		0
		350 million			1 billion	
	320 million		110 million	200 million		
		520 million		2 billion		0
	26 million		1 billion		265 million	
		870 million	2 billion	11 million		0

Amounts in U.S. dollars. (Estimates based on past years.)

GRAMMAR AND VOCABULARY

1. Write the correct form of the noun (singular, plural, or noncount) in each blank.
2. In the space after the item number, write *A* if you agree with the statement and *D* if you disagree with the statement. Write *DK* if you don't know.
3. Discuss with your class.

I think world trade levels affect the lives of many people.

I agree with that. If Japan is exporting a lot of cars, we can buy them more easily.

1. ___ World trade levels affect the ___*lives*___ of many _____.
   (life)   (person)

2. ___ Countries with a lot of _____ don't have a lot of _____.
   (export)   (poverty)

3. ___ My native country is not in an economic _____ right now.
   (crisis)

4. ___ A lot of _____ brings a lot of _____.
   (wealth)   (problem)

5. ___ The _____ in this city don't have a lot of _____ about world trade.
   (newspaper)   (information)

6. ___ A lot of cheap _____ helps a _____ make high _____.
   (labor)   (company)   (profit)

7. ___ Before you leave for another country, you should exchange your money for some foreign _____.
   (currency)

PROJECT Form a group with three to five students.

1. Each student in your group chooses a different type of store, for example, a grocery store, clothing store, shoe store, and so on.
2. Go to the store and read the product labels. Where are the products from?
3. Share the information with your group.

INTERNET Choose any country in the world. Type this phrase into your search engine: "(Name of country) exports." Write down three products the country exports. Report to your class.

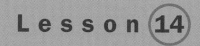

PART 1
Units of Measure

PART 2
Much/Many/A Lot Of

PART 3
A Few vs. *Few/A Little* vs. *Little/*
Very vs. *Too*

Nutrition:
Diet and Health

■ CONTENT VOCABULARY

Look at the pictures. Do you know the words?

grains

protein

fruit

fat

vegetables

dairy

Write the new words in your vocabulary journal.

■ THINK ABOUT IT

In your writing journal, write for five minutes about any of these questions.

1. Do you think you follow a healthy diet? Why or why not?
2. How much meat, fruit, fat, protein, and sugar do you eat?
3. How many vegetables do you eat?

PART ONE

■ GRAMMAR IN CONTENT

A Read and listen.

CD1,TR44

A Healthy Diet

The study of nutrition—the science of food—helps us to understand the relationship between diet and health. When you eat more calories than you need, you gain weight. If you eat **a bowl of** ice cream or **a piece of** cake from time to time, the sugar and fat won't hurt your body. However, **two bowls of** ice cream with lunch, **a slice of** pie after dinner, and **three pieces of** cake before you go to sleep is too much sugar and fat in one day. If you drink eight **glasses of** water every day, it's good for you, but it's not healthy to drink eight **cups of** coffee or eight **cans of** soda every day. The water is going to keep your body healthy, but drinking too much coffee or soda could cause health problems.

calories: a measure of the amount of energy produced by food

a diet: a person's regular eating habits

B Look at the reading. Each phrase in bold shows the quantity (how much) of the noun after it.

1. What word do you find in each of these phrases? _____
2. Which type of nouns do the quantity expressions describe?

___ count   ___ noncount   ___ both

Specific Quantity Expressions	
Servings	**Measurements**
a cup of coffee/tea/cocoa/soup	**a cup of** sugar/flour/milk/rice
a bowl of cereal/soup/ice cream/rice	**a teaspoon of** sugar/salt/honey
a slice of bread/toast/meat/cheese/pizza/pie	**a gallon of** milk/juice
a piece of cake/fruit/fish/chicken/candy	**a pound of** meat/vegetables/sugar/cheese
a glass of water/milk/juice	**a gram of** sugar/protein/carbohydrates

Specific Quantity Expressions

Containers	Others
a **bag/package of** chips/pretzels/nuts a **box of** cereal/pasta/crackers a **can of** soda/juice/soup a **carton of** milk/juice/ice cream/yogurt a **bottle of** water/soy sauce/ketchup a **jar of** peanut butter/jam/pickles	a **loaf of** bread a **stick of** butter/margarine a **head of** lettuce/cabbage a **bunch of** bananas/grapes/celery/carrots

Note:

All of the specific quantity expressions have plural forms because they are count nouns, for example, *two slices of bread, three teaspoons of honey.*

C Fill in the blanks with quantity expressions.

Ling used to drink four _____*cups of*_____ coffee every day with two
(1)

_____ sugar in each cup. Now, she has _____ juice in
(2) (3)

the morning, and _____ green tea in the afternoon. For lunch, she
(4)

sometimes has two or three _____ cheese with lettuce and tomato
(5)

on _____ bread. For dinner, she likes _____ soup with
(6) (7)

vegetables and rice. She used to eat _____ ice cream for dessert. Now
(8)

she has one or two _____ fruit instead.
(9)

D Work with a partner to complete the conversation with quantity expressions. Then listen to the dialogs and check to see if you both wrote a correct quantity expression.

CD1,TR45

Do you want _____*a bowl of*_____ cereal? No thanks, I just had
(1)

_____ toast. You know, _____ butter has 800 grams of
(2) (3)

fat. That means the butter on your toast comes to about 100 grams of fat. Really?

Next time I think I'll have _____ fruit instead. I want to have a
(4)

healthy diet too, so I'm going to drink _____ water and eat least three
(5)

_____ of fruit every day. Good idea.
(6)

■ COMMUNICATE

E **PAIR WORK** Take turns. Ask your partner about the food and drinks in his/her diet. Use the verbs and nouns from the lists.

Do you drink coffee?

Yes, I usually drink two cups of coffee a day.

Nouns					Verbs		
bread	juice	cheese	soup	chips	drink	like	make
sugar	water	meat	milk	soda	eat	use	have

PART TWO	*Much/Many/A Lot Of*

■ GRAMMAR IN CONTENT

A **Read and listen.**

CD1,TR46

protein: a nutrient the body needs for good health. It comes from meat, fish, dairy products, legumes (beans, lentils, etc.), or tofu.

The Food Pyramid

Instructor: OK everybody, today we're going to talk about the Food Pyramid. We can use the pyramid to eat the right amount of protein, grains, dairy, fruits, and vegetables.

Student 1: **How much** protein do we need every day?

Instructor: That's a good question. **Many** people think protein is the most important food, and they eat **a lot of** meat. But as you can see, you don't need **very much** protein to stay healthy.

Student 2: Whole grains are really important, aren't they? **How many** servings of grains do we need every day?

Instructor: We need **a lot of** servings of whole grains every day—four to eight servings. And, you know, most whole grains have a lot of vitamins and protein. **How much** protein do they have? You can find out when you read the food labels.

B In the reading, underline the nouns that follow *much, many,* and *a lot of.* Are they count or noncount? (Circle) the correct answers below.

1. **much**   Count   Noncount
2. **many**   Count   Noncount
3. **a lot of**   Count   Noncount

	Count: *Many/A Lot Of*	Noncount: *Much/A Lot Of*
Affirmative	**Many** people eat meat. **Too many** people have poor diets. There are **a lot of** calories in this meal.	**Too much** fat is not good. They eat **a lot of** meat.
Negative	There aren't **many** vegetables in your diet. There aren't **a lot of** vitamins in coffee.	We don't need **much** protein. There isn't **a lot of** fat in this meal.
Questions	**How many** servings of grains do we need? Are there **many** calories in your meal? Do you eat **a lot of** vegetables?	**How much** protein do we need? Is there **much** sugar in that cereal? Do you eat **a lot of** meat?

Notes:

- In general we don't usually use *very much* or *much* in affirmative statements; use *a lot of* or *too much*.
  Incorrect: ~~I eat *very much* fruit.~~   Correct: I eat *a lot of* fruit.
- Use *a lot of* with both count and noncount nouns.

C **Write a question using the words and phrases provided. Use *much/many/ a lot of*. Practice asking and answering the questions with a partner.**

How many calories does an apple have?

An apple doesn't have many calories – only about 58.

1. calories / apple (58)

   How many calories does an apple have?

2. fat / a piece of steak (18 grams)

   _____

3. sugar / a bowl of ice cream (28 grams)

   _____

4. vitamin C / a glass of orange juice (80 milligrams)

   _____

5. calcium / a cup of yogurt (49% of daily requirement)

   _____

D Circle the correct answer.

The college snack bar sells (much / many) unhealthy snacks. There aren't
                                                    (1)

(much / many) choices if you want to eat something nutritious. When I read
       (2)

(much / many) of the package labels, I can see that there isn't (much / many)
       (3)   **(4)**

protein and there aren't (much / a lot of) vitamins. Nevertheless, (a lot of / much)
                                   (5)   **(6)**

students eat this food for lunch because they don't have (much / many) time or
                                                                              (7)

money.

■ **COMMUNICATE**

E PAIR WORK Student A: Look at the nutrition chart at the bottom of the page. Your
partner will look at the chart on page 300. Take turns with your partner. Use the
words below. Ask your partner a question. Your partner will answer the question.

How many servings are
there in a box of pasta?

There aren't many servings
in one box; only three.

Student A Questions

1. fat/cheeseburger
2. calories/apple
3. protein/brown rice
4. calcium/cheese
5. vitamins/carrot juice

Student A Nutrition Chart		
Food	**Serving**	**Nutrition**
pasta	3 servings in a box	40 grams of carbohydrates per serving (1 cup)
ice cream	small bowl ($\frac{1}{2}$ cup)	$3\frac{1}{2}$ teaspoons of sugar
oatmeal	1 cup (small bowl)	150 calories
whole wheat toast	1 slice	1 gram of fat
peanut butter	2 tablespoons	16 grams of fat

■ GRAMMAR IN CONTENT

A **Read and listen.**

CD1,TR47

School Lunches

Paul: What did you find out about the elementary school lunch program for your report?

Nadia: Well, the children get very **few** fresh vegetables. They might get **a few** carrots or celery sticks. Also, the meals have **too many** calories, **too much** fat, and **too many** simple carbohydrates.

Paul: What about protein?

Nadia: Well, there is **a little** protein at each meal, but they often have protein with a lot of fat, like the cheese on pizza. You know, I think the children get **too little** healthy food in these lunches.

carbohydrates: nutrients found in grains, sugar, fruit, or starch that give the body energy

B **In the dialog above, underline the nouns that follow *few* and *little*. Write a rule about count and noncount nouns with *few* and *little*.**

_____

A Few/Few/A Little/Little		
	Positive Small Quantity (+)	**Negative Small Quantity (–)**
Count	a few They got **a few** pieces of fruit.	few The children get **(very) few** fresh vegetables.
Noncount	a little They get **a little** protein at each meal.	little I think the children eat **(too) little** fruit.
Very vs. Too		
Very	Use **very** before *much/many/few/little* to emphasize the quantity.	She eats **very little** sugar. She doesn't eat **very much** sugar.
Too	Use **too** before *much/many/few/little* for a negative meaning.	She eats **too little** protein. She eats **too much** sugar.

Note:

In general don't use **too** for positive meaning. Incorrect: ~~These grains have too much nutrition.~~

Correct: These grains have **a lot of** nutrition.

CD1, TR48

C Listen. Does the sentence express a positive (+) or a negative (−) quantity? (Circle) the correct answer.

1. (positive (+)) negative (−)   5. positive (+) negative (−)

2. positive (+) negative (−)   6. positive (+) negative (−)

3. positive (+) negative (−)   7. positive (+) negative (−)

4. positive (+) negative (−)

D Read about Lien's diet. (Circle) the closest meaning.

1. I am very careful about my diet, so I eat little fat and sugar.

   a. She doesn't eat a lot of fat and sugar.
   b. She eats a lot of fat and sugar.

2. I had three pieces of chocolate yesterday, so I won't have any chocolate today.

   a. She had a few pieces of chocolate yesterday.
   b. She had a little piece of chocolate yesterday.

3. I'm not a vegetarian, but I don't eat much meat.

   a. She eats a lot of meat.
   b. She doesn't eat a lot of meat.

4. I like to cook nutritious meals, but I have little time to do it.

   a. She doesn't have much time to cook.
   b. She has a lot of time to cook.

5. I usually take a few healthy snacks to school with me.

   a. She takes some snacks.
   b. She takes many snacks.

6. Sometimes, I don't use enough salt, and my food is tasteless.

   a. Sometimes she uses too little salt in her food.
   b. Sometimes she uses a little salt in her food.

7. Some of my friends think I follow too many rules in my diet.

   a. Her friends think she has a lot of rules and that's good.
   b. Her friends think she has a lot of rules and that's bad.

E PAIR WORK You will look at Brian's food diary on this page. Your partner will look at Jenny's food diary on page 301. Take turns. Ask and answer questions about the diets. Use these words: fruit, protein, vegetables, fat, sugar.

How much fruit did Brian eat?   He ate too little fruit—only a few servings in three days.

Brian	Breakfast	Snack	Lunch	Dinner	Snack
Monday	3 cups of coffee/ 2 donuts	soda/chips	hamburger/ french fries/ soda	pizza with meat/salad	2 bowls of ice cream
Tuesday	3 cups of coffee/bacon/ toast with butter	carrots/ nuts/ candy bar/ soda	beef sandwich/ chips/cookies/ soda	beef burrito with cheese and beans	soda/chips
Wednesday	orange juice/ 3 cups of coffee/coffee cake	soda/chips	2 peanut butter sandwiches/ apple/chocolate cake/glass of milk	roast beef/ poatoes/ salad	ham sandwich with butter and cheese

GRAMMAR AND VOCABULARY Keep a food diary for a week. Then write a summary of your nutrition. Use the grammar and vocabulary from the lesson.

My diet is good, but I could eat better. I eat too few fruits and vegetables. Last week, I only ate two servings of vegetables and a few pieces of fruit. I also eat too many calories at each meal and too much fat and sugar.

PROJECT Go to a local grocery store.

1. Choose two food items that have nutrition facts on a label. Take notes or bring the two items to class if possible.
2. Your group members will ask you questions about the food. Report to your group on the two items. Use the grammar and vocabulary from the lesson.
3. Write a paragraph about the food item. Describe the nutritional value.

 INTERNET Type one of these foods—apple, cheese, steak, hamburger, ice cream, broccoli, cookie, banana, rice—and "nutrition chart" into a search engine. Take notes on the nutrition information. Report to your class.

PART 1
Quantity: *Some/Any/No/None*

PART 2
General vs. Specific: Articles and
Quantity Expressions

PART 3
*Some/Others/One/Another/
Other/The Other/The Others*

Lesson ⑮

Linguistics:
Language Learning
Stages

■ CONTENT VOCABULARY

Look at the pictures. Do you know the words?

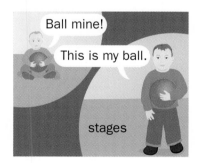

Write the new words in your vocabulary journal.

■ THINK ABOUT IT

In your writing journal, write for five minutes about this question: What stages do you think you went through learning English?

■ GRAMMAR IN CONTENT

A Read and listen.

CD1,TR49

acquisition: process of getting or learning something

First Stages

Professor: Today we will begin discussing the stages of child language acquisition. At zero to four months, crying is the language of infants. In these first few months, they make **some** sounds, but they produce **no** words. You may think there is **no** communication with such young infants, but that's not true. They can't say **any** words, and they don't have **any** language comprehension, but they can recognize the voices of their mother and father.

Student 1: How do we know this? Are there **any** studies with babies and their parents?

Professor: Yes, we'll look at **some** interesting research about this. For example, in one study, infants knew the location of the mother by her voice.

Student 2: Is there **any** information about that research in our book?

Professor: Well, there is **some** research in the book, but **none** about that specific study.

B Look at the above dialogue.

1. Which words are used with negative statements?   ___ some   ___ any

   ___ no   ___ none

2. Which words are used in affirmative statements?   ___ some   ___ any

   ___ no   ___ none

3. Which words have negative meaning?   ___ some   ___ any

   ___ no   ___ none

	With Count Nouns	With Noncount Nouns
Affirmative	Adj.: They use **some words**. Pronoun: They use **some**.	Adj.: They pick up **some intonation**. Pronoun: They pick up **some**.
Negative	Adj.: They use **no words**. Pronoun: They use **none**. Adj.: They can't say **any words**. Pronoun: They can't say **any**.	Adj.: There is **no communication**. Pronoun: There is **none**. Adj.: They don't have **any comprehension**. Pronoun: They don't have **any**.
Questions	Adj.: Are there **any studies**? Pronoun: Are there **any**?	Adj.: Is there **any information**? Pronoun: Is there **any**?

Notes:

- We use a pronoun form (**some, any, none**) if we've already mentioned the noun.
- Use **no** as an adjective; use **none** as a pronoun.
  Incorrect: ~~They use none words.~~   Correct: *They use **none**.*

C **Based on the reading, fill in the blanks with *some, any,* or *no.***

1. Students in this class will learn ___some___ facts about language learning.

2. Infants can't say _____ words when they are four months old.

3. Newborns have _____ spoken communication with their parents.

4. Infants can recognize _____ voices when they are born.

5. There are _____ studies about young infants' language.

D **Fill in the blanks with *any, some,* or *no.***

Keira was 21 months old, and she wasn't repeating ___any___ words when her mother spoke. Her mother was
(1)
worried, so she took Keira for _____ hearing tests. Keira
(2)
passed all the tests, so she clearly had _____ problems
(3)
with her hearing. The doctor asked her mother, "Does Keira have _____ brothers
(4)
or sisters?" When the doctor heard that Keira had a three-year-old brother, he gave

Keira's mother _____ advice. "Keira doesn't have _____ speech problems.
(5)   (6)
She is just listening to her brother. There is _____ reason to worry. Just wait
(7)
and have _____ patience. She will begin speaking soon."
(8)

E Listen and (circle) the correct choice.

CD1,TR50

1. a. Yes, they have some.
   b. Yes, they have any.

2. a. No, they use none gestures.
   b. No, they use none.

3. a. No, they don't say any words yet.
   b. No, they don't say no words yet.

4. a. No, they just make some sounds.
   b. No, they just make any sounds.

5. a. You're right. There is no any intonation.
   b. You're right. There isn't any.

6. a. That's right. There isn't any.
   b. That's right. There isn't no.

7. a. You're right. It has any in the back.
   b. You're right. It has none in the back.

■ COMMUNICATE

F PAIR WORK Discuss the language learners in your class. Take turns. Ask a question with *any*. Use *some/any/no/none* to answer.

Are there any Italian speakers in your class?

No, there aren't any, but there are some Spanish speakers.

1. Italian speakers/in your class?
2. classmates/speak/Finnish?
3. you/have/comprehension/when/listen/to the radio/in English?
4. Thai speakers/in your class?
5. you/have/friends/from Taiwan?
6. instructor/speak/Slavic languages?
7. you/take/English classes/last year?
8. English tutoring/at your school?
9. words/in your language/with *ion*/at the end/of the word?

■ GRAMMAR IN CONTENT

A Read and listen.

CD1,TR51

Studying for the Exam

Student 1: OK, what is babbling?

Student 2: Umm, at four to six months, **a** baby starts to practice **the** sounds, intonation, and rhythm of **the** language. They imitate **the** language they hear, and their parents reinforce **the** language they produce.

Student 1: Right. What does it mean when we say **children** learn language in stages?

Student 2: Well, for example, **all children** make vowel sounds first. Next, they add consonant sounds. At this stage, **some children** will use gestures when they want something. And **most of them** can understand intonation. But **each child** goes through **the** stages. OK, my turn. Explain **the** pre-birth heart rate test.

Student 1: Umm, **the** heart rates of **the** unborn babies decreased at **the** sound of **the** mothers' voice. **Each of the** babies in the study recognized **the** mother's voice. **Many of them** recognized their fathers' voices. **None of the babies** had an increased heart rate when he or she heard its parents' voices.

B Look at the dialog above. What is the difference between *a* and *the?* What is the difference between *none, some,* and *most?* Write two or three rules about these terms.

_____

_____

General vs. Specific

A/An/Ø Article vs. *The*

General	Specific
An infant practices sounds.	**The child** is imitating his mother.
A child imitates his/her mother.	I heard **a child** imitating his mother.
Children learn language in stages.	**The children** also learned Spanish.

General vs. Specific

Quantity Expressions

General	Specific
All children develop errors.	**All of the children** used past tense.
Every child has some vocabulary.	**Every one of the children** has a book.
Each child learns in stages.	**Each (one) of the children** spoke Spanish.
Most vocabulary comes later.	**Most of the vocabulary** was correct.
Many children create nonsense words.	**Many of the children** understand English.
Some children speak two languages.	**Some of the children** speak Spanish.
No child was left alone.	**None of the children** was left alone.

Notes:

- In some cases, use *the* for generalization, for example, *The computer is a necessary tool.*
- Don't use an article (Ø) with plural count nouns and noncount nouns to make a generalization, for example, *Babies can understand intonation.* (= all babies)
- Don't forget *the* after *of* in definite contexts: Incorrect: ~~*All of children*~~ Correct: ***All of the children***
- Use count nouns after *each, every,* and *many.*
- Use singular nouns/pronouns and verbs after *each* and *every.*
  Incorrect: ~~*Each children have some vocabulary.*~~
  Correct: ***Each child*** OR ***Each of the children*** *has* some vocabulary.

C Fill in the blank with an article (*a, an, the, Ø*) or quantity expression to make a true statement.

1. _____*A*_____ sentence has a subject and a verb.

2. _____ plural count nouns end in *-s.*

3. _____ students in my class are learning English.

4. _____ language student goes through stages.

5. _____ English grammar is difficult.

■ COMMUNICATE

D PAIR WORK Work with a partner. Discuss your language learning experience. Use the words and quantity expressions listed such as *every language learner, most children, some instructors,* and so on.

> I think every language learner imitates the language they hear.

> Yes, but not all language learners have a good ear for pronunciation.

■ GRAMMAR IN CONTENT

A Read and listen.

CD1,TR52

Observation Report

Today I visited the Child Development Center for my linguistics class. **Some children** were babbling. **Others** were speaking. **One child** was at a very early stage of speaking. He was saying a single word at a time, for example, "ball" or "book." **Another child** was speaking in two-word sentences. **Another one** was using very strong intonation: "ME ball NOW!"

I also observed some older children playing together. **One** was speaking in four-word sentences. **The other** said nothing. While these two were playing together, **the others** were singing.

B Based on the reading, write *T* if the statement is true. Write *F* if it is false.

1. _F_ Only two children were speaking.

2. ___ One child couldn't say any words yet.

3. ___ One child was using strong intonation.

4. ___ Two of the children were speaking about a puzzle.

5. ___ Two older children were playing together.

Some/Others/One/Another/Other/The Other/The Others	
Singular	**Plural**
Adj.: **One child** said, "ball."	Adj.: **Some children** were babbling.
Pronoun: **One** said, "ball."	Pronoun: **Some** were babbling.
Adj.: **Another child** said, "ball mine."	Adj.: **Other children** were speaking.
Pronoun: **Another** said, "ball mine."	Pronoun: **Others** were speaking.
Adj.: **The other child** said nothing.	Adj.: **The other children** were singing.
Pronoun: **The other** said nothing.	Pronoun: **The others** were singing.

Notes:

- Use *the other* or *the others* when it's the last one(s) mentioned.
- Use a number before *others* when necessary, for example, *Two others were playing*.
- You can use *one/ones* after *another/the other* to replace a noun, for example, *Another one said "ball mine." The other ones were singing.*

C Look at the picture of the Language Learning Lab. (Circle) the correct answers.

The Language Learning Lab is very busy today. (One / Some) of the
(1)
students are working with tutors. (The others / Others) are using the
(2)
computers and the DVD player. (The others / Others) are participating
(3)
in a conversation group. (One / Some) tutor is helping a student with a
(4)
paper. (Another one / The other one) is helping a student with a reading.
(5)
(Two of the / The other two) students are working on the computers.
(6)
(One of them / Some of them) is typing an assignment. (The other / Another) is
(7)   (8)
taking notes about the grammar.

D Complete new sentences about the picture in exercise C. (Answers may vary.)

1. Some of the students _____.

   Others _____.

2. One of the tutors _____.

   The other _____.

3. Some of the students _____.

   The others _____.

4. Two of the students _____.

   Two other ones _____.

■ C O M M U N I C A T E

E **WRITE** Observe a group of people, for example, your class, students at your school, a group of children. Write a paragraph about one specific characteristic of the group, for example, their country, their clothes, their language, their activity. Use *some . . . others/one . . . another/other/the other/the others.*

> There are 18 students in my class. Some live here permanently, and others are here on a student visa. One of the students is from Uzbekistan. Another one is from Poland, and another is from Lebanon. Two others are from Latin America. One of them is from Brazil, and the other is from Argentina. Three other students are from Mexico, and two others are from Armenia. The others are from Asia. One is from Korea. Another one is from Vietnam, and the others are from China.

GRAMMAR AND VOCABULARY Fill in the blank with the correct word and put it in the correct form.

consonant	recognize	stage	gesture	imitate
intonation	babble	vowel	comprehension	

1. In some English questions, the _____ rises at the end.

2. Most newborn babies can _____ the voices of their parents.

3. Second language learners don't _____ before they speak.

4. Many successful second language learners _____ native speakers.

5. Some letters are _____, and others are _____.

6. Each language learner goes through _____.

7. A language teacher uses _____ to help students with _____ of words.

PROJECT Form groups and conduct a survey about language learning.

1. In a small group, write one question about language learning to ask your classmates, for example, "What is the hardest thing about learning English?" Each group should choose a notetaker.
2. Each notetaker moves to a new group and asks the question. Those group members give their answers. The notetaker takes notes on their answers. Each notetaker then moves to a new group. Repeat this until each notetaker has visited each group.
3. The notetakers return to their original groups and summarize the responses. The group members choose a few of the most interesting answers.
4. The groups take turns reporting their survey. First, the notetaker repeats the question. Then each member of the group reports one key finding.

 INTERNET Enter "language development and children" in a search engine. Take notes on one interesting fact. Tell your class what you learned.

A Read the student presentation for a nutrition class. Write the correct tense/form of the verb in parentheses OR choose from the words in parentheses. If there is no choice, add a word(s) or write Ø if no word is necessary.

Rob: In our presentation today, we (discuss) <u>'ll discuss</u> the relationship
(1)

between cultural values and nutrition. Before we (begin) _____, we
(2)

(explain) _____ our interest in this subject. Then, we (give) _____ you
(3)   (4)

(a few/a little) _____ (information/informations) _____ about (a few/a
(5)   (6)

little) _____ cultures that have interesting (idea/ideas) _____ about
(7)   (8)

nutrition. We (listen) _____ to some tapes of (a few/few) _____ people
(9)   (10)

discussing their (believes/beliefs) _____. After we (give) _____ you
(11)   (12)

some background information on (a little/a few) _____ cultural groups,
(13)

you (see) _____ the results of our work. When we (finish) _____, you
(14)   (15)

(have) _____ a chance to ask questions.
(16)

Molly: OK. First, we (give) _____ you (a few/some) _____ background
(17)   (18)

in this topic. (Much/Many) _____ cultures have (very/too) _____
(19)   (20)

strong ideas about food and nutrition. In some cultures, people (are believing/

believe) _____ all food (has/is having) _____ an effect on our thoughts
(21)   (22)

and feelings, (wishs/wishes) _____, and (dreames/dreams) _____. In
(23)   (24)

(other/the other) _____ cultures, people (think/are thinking) _____
(25)   (26)

more about the effect of each kind of food on our (bodys/bodies) _____.
(27)

For (other/others) _____ cultures, there is (too little/too few) _____
(28)   (29)

(information/informations) _____ about the meaning of food for us to
(30)

draw conclusions.

B Read the conversation between two students. Write the correct tense/form of the verb in parentheses OR choose from the words in parentheses. Write Ø if no word is necessary.

A: (see) _____ (1) you _____ (2) weather report?

B: No, but I (hear) _____ (3) it this morning on the radio. If the temperature (continue) _____ (4) to decrease, (much/many) _____ (5) of _____ (6) cities on the East Coast (have) _____ (7) freezing temperatures by (very/the) _____ (8) weekend. Also, by Saturday, (most of/most of the) _____ (9) people in the Midwest (fight) _____ (10) floods caused by a series of rainstorms. There (be) _____ (11) also serious predictions for (the/a) _____ (12) western area of (the/a) _____ (13) country.

A: _____ (14) you ever (think) _____ (15) about the cause of such severe weather conditions? I mean, _____ (16) you (believe) _____ (17) global warming (be) _____ (18) the cause?

B: (a lot of/much) _____ (19) scientists now (believe) _____ (20) these serious weather conditions are due to (a/an) _____ (21) increase in (a/the) _____ (22) temperature of (the/an) _____ (23) ocean. They (will think/think) _____ (24) Earth (experience) _____ (25) (other/another) _____ (26) Ice Age in 100 years.

LEARNER LOG Check (✔) *Yes* or *I Need More Practice.*

Lesson	I Can Use . . .	Yes	I Need More Practice
11	Future Time Clauses: *After/Before/When/As Soon As,* Future Conditional with *If* Clauses, Future Progressive		
12	Verbs of Perception: Non-Progressive vs. Progressive, Verbs of Emotion/Cognition/Possession: Non-Progressive		
13	Count Nouns, Count vs. Noncount Nouns		
14	Units of Measure, *Much/Many/A Lot of, A Few vs. Few/A Little vs. Little/Very vs. Too*		
15	*Some/Any/No/None,* Articles and Quantity Expressions, *Some/Others/One/Another/Other/The Other/The Others*		

PART 1
Adjectives and Adverbs

PART 2
Participial Adjectives

PART 3
Nouns as Adjectives

Lesson 16

Career Development I: Personality Profile

■ CONTENT VOCABULARY

Look at the pictures. Do you know the words?

a customer service representative

a computer technician

an engineer

Write the new words in your vocabulary journal.

■ THINK ABOUT IT

In your writing journal, write for five minutes about this question: What career do you think matches your personality? Why?

■ **GRAMMAR IN CONTENT**

CD2,TR1

A **Read and listen.**

Personality Profile

    Think about your **personal** characteristics. Are you **rational** or **emotional**, **lazy** or **hard-working**, **calm** or **nervous**? Are you **polite** or **impolite** with others? Do you work **quickly** and **efficiently**? Do you think **fast** and work **hard**? Or do you think and work more **slowly** and **carefully**? Do you like to work **independently** or are you **dependent** on other people?

    Your answers to these questions will help you to make the **right** choice in a career. For example, the best teachers and nurses are **very patient, caring** people. A teacher works **patiently** with students, and a nurse has **a caring** attitude toward sick people. Business careers attract **hard-working** people— people who work **hard** to get ahead.

a personality profile: a summary of your personality

B **Go through the reading and underline the nouns and pronouns once. Underline the verbs twice. The adjectives and adverbs are in bold.**

1. Find one adjective that describes a noun. Write both words:

   adjective: _____ noun: _____

2. Find one adjective that describes a pronoun. Write both words:

   adjective: _____ pronoun: _____

3. Find one adverb that describes a verb. Write both words:

   adverb: _____ verb: _____

4. Find one adverb that describes an adjective. Write both words:

   adverb: _____ adjective: _____

Adjectives	
An adjective describes a noun (person, place, thing). Adjectives come directly before a noun or after a linking verb such as **be**.	adjective noun Teachers are **patient** people. noun adjective Salespeople are **ambitious**.

Adverbs

Regular

An adverb describes a verb/action (how you do something). To form a regular adverb, add the *-ly* ending to an adjective.	verb adverb Teachers listen **patiently**. verb adverb Salespeople work **ambitiously**.

Irregular	**Adjective**	**Adverb**
The adverb form does not add the *-ly* ending.	He is a **good** teacher. She is a **fast** worker.	He teaches **well**. She works **fast**.

Notes:

*He works **hard**.* = He is a hard worker. (Incorrect: ~~He works *hardly*.~~)

He ***hardly*** works. = He doesn't work very much.

They work ***late*.** = They work late hours. (Incorrect: ~~They work *lately*.~~)

They have worked hard ***lately*.** *(lately = recently)*

C Check (✔) the characteristic that describes you. Then write *Adjective* or *Adverb* next to the sentences.

1. a. ___ I am slow and calm. _____*Adjective*_____

   b. **✔** I move and talk quickly. _____*Adverb*_____

2. a. ___ I am not a hard worker. _____

   b. ___ I work hard at any job. _____

3. a. ___ I work fast, especially when I have a deadline. _____

   b. ___ I am not a fast worker, even when I have a

   deadline. _____

4. a. ___ I react emotionally to most situations. _____

   b. ___ I am a rational and thoughtful person. _____

5. a. ___ I feel better when I am dependent on others. _____

   b. ___ I work best when I am working independently. _____

D Read the personality profile below. (Circle) the correct word.

Yu-Chung is a ((calm) / calmly) and (rational / rationally) person. She
₍₁₎   (2)

works (good / well) when she is (independent / independently). She has a
₍₃₎   (4)

(quick / quickly) mind and a(n) (special / especially) good mind for mathematics.
₍₅₎   (6)

When she works with numbers, she is (careful / carefully) and (correct / correctly).
                     (7)   (8)

She likes people, but she doesn't meet new people (easy / easily), and she feels
                     (9)

(shy / shyly) at first. Her counselor gave her some (good / well) advice and told her
₍₁₀₎   (11)

to think about a career in accounting.

E Listen to the question. (Circle) the correct answer.

CD2,TR2

1. a. Maybe. Are you also punctual?
    b. Maybe. Are you also punctually?

2. a. Let's see, in a lot of sales jobs, you work very independently.
    b. Let's see, a lot of salespeople are very independently.

3. a. No, I don't very cooperative.
    b. No, I'm not very cooperative.

4. a. You're right. Good managers can't be too emotional.
    b. You're right. Good managers are not too emotional being.

5. a. No, I'm thinking about it careful.
    b. No, I'm carefully thinking about it.

6. a. No, I can work hard, but not at night.
    b. No, it's hardly for me to work at night.

7. a. Yes, I can communicate good with people.
    b. Yes, I'm a good communicator.

■ **COMMUNICATE**

F **PAIR WORK** Take turns with your partner. Ask your partner about a possible future
career for him/her. Your partner will answer with an adjective and/or adverb. Use
the list in Appendix 3 for more adjectives and adverbs. Follow the model.

Do you think you could
be a good nurse?

No, I don't think so. A nurse must give
patients their medicine carefully. I'm too
nervous and I'm not careful enough.

■ GRAMMAR IN CONTENT

CD2,TR3

A **Read and listen.**

> ### Career Profile
>
> **Professor:** Now that you have an idea about your personality profile, what careers do **you** think match your characteristics?
>
> **Student 1:** Well, I'm **interested** in books, and I feel **relaxed** when I'm in the library.
>
> **Professor:** Yes, it sounds like you could become a librarian. For you it would be a **relaxing** and **interesting** job.
>
> **Student 2:** Not me. I want an **exciting** career with a lot of possibilities. I'd like to be a lawyer.
>
> **Teacher:** I see. Well, maybe you're **fascinated** by travel and contact with different cultures. And it may be **surprising** to you, but a librarian finds the system of a library **fascinating**. But that's why it's important to find a match between your personality and a career.

B **Look at the dialog. Each adjective in bold has both an *-ing* and an *-ed* form. Which form describes how the modified noun feels (feeling)? Which form describes what the modified noun is like (characteristic)?**

Participial Adjectives

-ed	*-ing*
I feel **relaxed** when I'm in the library.	It is a **relaxing** job.
I'm **interested** in books.	Books are **interesting**.
He's **fascinated** by travel.	He finds travel **fascinating**.

Notes:

- Participial adjectives come from verbs, for example, *The library **relaxes** me. I feel **relaxed**.*
- Use the *-ed* ending to describe a person's *feeling*. Use the *-ing* ending to describe the *characteristic* of a person, place, or thing.
- Don't use the *-ing* ending to describe your feelings about an experience.

  Incorrect: *Do you feel comfortable in the library? ~~Yes, I feel relaxing.~~*

  Correct: *Yes, I feel **relaxed**.*

C The base form of the verb is provided. Write the correct *-ing* or *-ed* adjective form of the word.

Nathan is (interest) _____interested_____ in an acting career, and
(1)

his parents are very (surprise) _____ about this. For
(2)

him, this career is (fascinate) _____. He is (amaze)
(3)

_____ every time he sees a good actor perform on
(4)

stage. A good actor remembers so many lines and doesn't seem (embarrass)

_____. Nathan knows his parents feel (annoy)
(5)

_____ and (disappoint) _____ with him,
(6)   (7)

but he can't help it.

D Listen to the conversation. Write the participle when you hear it.

CD2,TR4

A: How do you like the career class?

B: I'm not very _____interested_____ in the careers we're talking about.
(1)

A: Really? Why aren't they _____ to you?
(2)

B: Accounting, for example, isn't very _____. I need a more
(3)

_____ job, so I can enjoy the hard work.
(4)

A: It sounds like you won't be _____ with a desk job.
(5)

B: No, for me, a desk job would be too _____.
(6)

■ COMMUNICATE

E **PAIR WORK** Talk about different careers. Practice the *-ing* and *-ed* forms of the participial adjectives.

Do you think a lawyer is ever surprised by the details of a case?

Yeah, and a lawyer's client can be surprised when they receive the bill!

Yes, I think lawyers often get surprising information when they work on a case.

■ GRAMMAR IN CONTENT

CD2,TR5

A Read and listen.

Career Decisions

In an **evening** class at **City** College, Amiya and her classmates are looking at **career** profiles. Amiya is a **22-year-old** student majoring in art. She also works a **Saturday** shift at an **art** store near the college. She is interested in art, so she is thinking about possible careers in this field. Because she is not a "**people** person," she could be satisfied as a **studio** artist.

a people person: someone who likes being with others

B In the reading, each of the nouns in bold describes another noun, so it becomes an adjective. Find the noun or the noun phrase that each noun in bold describes. Then write the *adjective + noun* phrase here.

1. _____Career Decisions_____   5. _____

2. _____   6. _____

3. _____   7. _____

4. _____   8. _____

Nouns as Adjectives	
Noun	**Noun as Adjective**
(noun) Karinka teaches **art**.	(adjective) Karinka is an **art** teacher.
(noun) Stefan already chose a **career**.	(adjective) Stefan read his **career** profile.
(noun) (noun) Lien is 22 **years** old and attends **college**.	(adjective) (adjective) Lien is a **22-year-old college** student.

Note:

• When a plural noun becomes an adjective, drop the **-s** ending.

Incorrect: ~~She is a 22 years old student.~~

Correct: *She is a 22-year-old student.*

C Fill in the blanks with a noun phrase: (noun as adjective) + noun.

In the Counseling 17 class yesterday, the students thought about

the reasons for their interests in a career and then reported on their

_____*career interests*_____. Sam wants to be a
(1)

_____ because he knows a mechanic who
(2)

works on cars, and this friend enjoys his job. Carol would like a job in an office

because in an _____ she can use her
(3)

computer skills. Lien will become a geologist because geologists do interesting

work in the field, and the geological _____
(4)

is fascinating to her. James is interested in becoming a professor at

a college. As a _____ he would
(5)

teach his students important ideas about literature. Tina wants to be a

_____ because as a nurse in a school, she
(6)

can work with children. Stephanie is studying biology so she can work as an

assistant in a lab. As a _____ she will work on
(7)

important projects. Leo will be a technician who works on computers. He knows that

_____ solve problems.
(8)

D Oral Practice: Combine any noun from List 1 and any noun from List 2 to make a
sentence. Work with a partner to make as many combinations and sentences as
you can.

 I am completing my *personality profile* to help me think about the future.

<table>
<tr><td colspan="2">**List 1**</td><td colspan="2">**List 2**</td></tr>
<tr><td>personality</td><td>25 years old</td><td>nurse</td><td>choice</td></tr>
<tr><td>school</td><td>career</td><td>job</td><td>clerk</td></tr>
<tr><td>college</td><td>hospital</td><td>profile</td><td>teacher</td></tr>
</table>

■ COMMUNICATE

E **PAIR WORK** Take turns with your partner. Ask and answer the questions, using full sentences and additional information when possible. Use one of the nouns in bold as an adjective in your answer.

> Are you a student of **English?**

> Yes, I'm an English student at City College.

1. Are you a **student** of **English?**
2. Do you have a **dream** to follow a certain **career?**
3. Do you have any **skills** that are useful for a **job?**
4. Do you have a **plan** for the next **five years?**
5. Can you give me a **profile** of your **personality?**
6. Would you like to have a **job** working at a **desk** most of the time?
7. Does the **education** you receive in **college** prepare you for the **career** you will have in the **future?**
8. How can students get help with their **decisions** about **careers?**
9. Does a teacher need **skills** that help with good **communication?**

GRAMMAR AND VOCABULARY Write a paragraph about your personality profile. Describe a career that matches it. Use the grammar and vocabulary from this lesson.

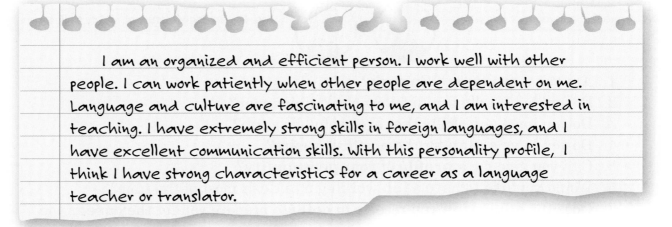

> I am an organized and efficient person. I work well with other people. I can work patiently when other people are dependent on me. Language and culture are fascinating to me, and I am interested in teaching. I have extremely strong skills in foreign languages, and I have excellent communication skills. With this personality profile, I think I have strong characteristics for a career as a language teacher or translator.

PROJECT Take a survey.

1. Work in groups of three and choose a career, for example, nursing, teaching, sales, etc.
2. Each student in your group will interview two people at your school or in your community about the career your group chose. Each of you should ask these questions:
   - Could you describe the personality profile of a (nurse)?
   - Do you think (nurses) have an (interesting/exciting/dangerous, and so forth) career? Why?
3. In your group, combine and summarize the results of your survey.
4. Report to the class.

 INTERNET Enter "lists of careers" into a search engine. Find one career that you didn't know about. Take notes. Describe the career to your classmates.

PART 1
Gerunds and Gerund Phrases

PART 2
Verbs + Infinitives; Verbs +
Infinitives or Gerunds

PART 3
Prepositions Followed by Gerunds

Lesson 17

Career Development II:
Goals and Values

■ CONTENT VOCABULARY

Look at the pictures. Do you know the words?

to imagine

I could become
a surgeon.

Or perhaps I should
become a social worker.

to consider

This is the best computer.
You should buy it.

OK. I'll buy it.

to persuade

Write the new words in your vocabulary journal.

■ THINK ABOUT IT

In your writing journal, write for five minutes about one of these questions.

1. What are your career goals?
2. What is important to you in a career?

■ GRAMMAR IN CONTENT

CD2,TR6

A Read and listen.

Choosing a Career

Professor: **Choosing** a successful career requires a lot of thought and effort. During the semester, you'll learn about many different jobs, and you'll imagine **working** at certain jobs. You'll also keep **thinking** about your views of success.

Student 1: How can we know *now* if we're going to like a career we choose?

Professor: **Deciding** on a career is not a simple process, but we'll do some exercises that will help you. First, list your values and goals. **Knowing** your values and goals helps you to choose a career. This includes **defining** your idea of success.

Student 2: For me, success is **becoming** the owner of a big company.

Professor: I see. Well, you know, many young people share your idea about success. However, many people don't know about the work involved in owning a business. You may regret not **considering** other types of satisfying jobs.

B Look at the dialog. The words in bold are gerunds. Check *Subj* if the gerund is the subject. Check *Obj* if the gerund is an object.

	Subj	Obj			Subj	Obj
choosing	✔	_____		knowing	_____	_____
working	_____	_____		defining	_____	_____
thinking	_____	_____		becoming	_____	_____
deciding	_____	_____		considering	_____	_____

Gerunds and Gerund Phrases

A gerund is the base form of a verb + *ing* that is used as a noun.	**Teaching** can be an interesting career.
A gerund or gerund phrase can be the *subject* or *complement* of a sentence. Use the third person singular form of the verb after a gerund subject.	(subject) **Deciding on a career** is not simple. (complement) My dream job is **teaching children.**
A gerund or gerund phrase can be the *direct object* of a verb.	(direct object) You'll imagine **working at certain jobs.**

Verbs + Gerunds

Certain verbs must be followed by a gerund:

enjoy	imagine	risk	include
suggest	avoid	go	consider
delay	discuss	regret	involve
miss	keep	quit	appreciate

Don't use an infinitive after these verbs.

You'll **consider entering** a career.

They **involve listing** your values.
This **includes defining** your idea of success.

Incorrect: ~~I enjoy to work at home.~~
Correct: I **enjoy** *working* at home.

Note:

There are many gerunds that can follow *go* to describe activities, for example, *go shopping, go swimming, go running,* and so on.

C **Fill in the blanks. Use the correct form of the verbs in parentheses.**

Cecile is a college counselor. She (enjoy/help) _____ (1) students with their career plans. When a student asks her for advice, she usually (suggest/write) _____ (2) a list of career goals. Then they (discuss/achieve) _____ (3) each of the goals. The first session always (include/find out) _____ (4) which goals are possible to achieve. When they (finish/talk) _____ (5) about goals, they draw up a plan of action.

D **GROUP WORK** Complete the statements about careers. Use gerunds and gerund phrases.

> For me, a successful career is working at a good job and enjoying life at the same time. How about you?

> I think a successful career is developing many different skills as you move through your career.

1. For me, a successful career is _____.

2. _____ is the most important goal for me in a career.

3. I can't imagine _____.

4. My dream job is _____.

PART TWO	Verbs + Infinitives; Verbs + Infinitives or Gerunds

■ GRAMMAR IN CONTENT

CD2,TR7

A Read and listen.

Chapter Introduction

In this chapter, you will **attempt to identify** your career goals and think about a career that satisfies those goals. Let's begin with a case study. Sean, a first year college student, **hopes to work** in a friendly environment, and he **intends to help** others through his career. He **likes to work** both indoors and outdoors and he **prefers to be** self-employed. His father **wants him to become** a doctor, but he doesn't **want to be** a doctor. He **likes working** with animals, so his career counselor **advised him to read** about veterinarians. He never **considered becoming** a veterinarian, but now it **seems to be** the right career for him. He **intends to have** his own practice, so he can be self-employed. You can see how Sean's counselor **helped him to choose** a career that matches his goals.

a veterinarian: a doctor for animals

a case study: an in-depth examination of one person or situation

B Which verb in the reading is followed by both an infinitive and a gerund?

_____ Which three verbs are followed by a pronoun before the

infinitive? _____ _____ _____

Verbs + Infinitives

Without Object

Certain verbs are usually followed directly by an infinitive form of a verb. There is no object between the verb and the infinitive: aim decide hope refuse intend seem	I **hope to work** in a friendly environment. She **intends to help** people in her career. Incorrect: ~~I hope me to earn a good salary.~~ Correct: I **hope to earn** a good salary.

With Object

Some verbs require an object (noun or pronoun) before the infinitive: teach advise remind require hire persuade	She **reminded** *them* **to complete** the forms. The college **requires** *you* **to see** a counselor. She **taught** *her students* **to revise**.

With or Without Object

If an object comes between these verbs and the infinitive, the meaning changes: need choose want help(s) prepare expect	Sean's father **wants to become** a doctor. (Result: Sean's father wants to be a doctor **himself**.) Sean's father **wants** *him* **to become** a doctor. (Result: Sean's father wants **Sean** to become a doctor.)

Verbs + Infinitives or Gerunds

Some verbs can be followed by an infinitive *or* a gerund: like begin love hate attempt stop prefer start try can't stand	I **like** *to work* outside. I **like** *working* outside. Some people **prefer** *to be* self-employed. Some people **prefer** *being* self-employed.
There is a clear difference in meaning with these verbs: stop remember forget	We **stopped** *to talk*. (to = in order to) (First, we stopped. Then, we talked.) We **stopped** *talking*. (First, we were talking. Then, we stopped.) **Remember** *to fill* out the form. (First, remember. Second, fill out the form.) I **remember** *filling* out the form. (First, I filled out the form. Second, I remember.)

Note:

Verbs that are followed by infinitives can be followed also by an adverb before the infinitive. Example:

I **hope** *someday* **to work** as a doctor.

C **Fill in the blanks with the correct form of the verbs in parentheses. Add a pronoun if necessary. Use the affirmative or negative form of the first verb as needed.**

Grace's father (want/become) ___*wants her to become*___ a nurse, but

Grace (intend/study) _____ architecture. She (refuse/choose)

$\underset{(1)}{\rule{0pt}{0pt}}$

_____ a nursing career just because her father (expect/do)

$\underset{(2)}{\rule{0pt}{0pt}}$

_____ that. Grace (love/design) _____

$\underset{(3)}{\rule{0pt}{0pt}}$ $\underset{(4)}{\rule{0pt}{0pt}}$

buildings, and she (hope/work) _____ for a big company in

$\underset{(5)}{\rule{0pt}{0pt}}$

Shanghai. Grace usually (love/talk) _____ to her father, but

$\underset{(6)}{\rule{0pt}{0pt}}$

she cannot (persuade/listen) _____ to her point of view right

$\underset{(7)}{\rule{0pt}{0pt}}$

now. She (need/be) _____ patient, and perhaps her father (will

$\underset{(8)}{\rule{0pt}{0pt}}$

start/understand) _____ her when she is successful.

$\underset{(9)}{\rule{0pt}{0pt}}$

D **Fill in the blanks with a gerund or infinitive form of the verb in parentheses.**

1. **A:** Why are you so late for class?

   B: I stopped (see) ___*to see*___ a career counselor.

   A: Why can't you go after class?

   B: The counselors stop (see) _____ students at 4:00.

2. **A:** What time did you go to bed last night?

   B: I stopped (study) _____ at 11:00. Then, I remembered

   (send) _____ an e-mail to my study buddy. She needed the

   assignment. So, I remember (get) _____ to bed by 11:30.

3. **A:** Are you sure this information is correct?

   B: Yes, I remember (see) _____ it on a Web site. A: Well, don't

   forget (add) _____ the Web site information to your paper.

4. **A:** I'll never forget (read) _____ my first Shakespeare play.
   That's when I decided on an English teaching career.

   B: Yes, I remember (decide) _____ on a nursing career after my
   first stay in a hospital.

E **Correct the errors in the case study report. There are eight errors.**

    In the case study, Sean's father advises ~~him~~ to become a doctor, but Sean doesn't want go to medical school. He likes to helping others, but he can't stand work in a big hospital. When his career counselor reminds to think about his goals and values, he decides becoming a veterinarian. Now, he is starting getting excited about this career. He is happy because he chose a career that he will enjoy. His counselor taught to think about important values.

■ **C O M M U N I C A T E**

F **GROUP WORK** Below is a bar graph of responses to a questionnaire. College students answered this question: *What do you want most from a career?*

Part 1. Discuss the results in a group of students. Use verbs that are followed by infinitives (*want, need, plan, intend, prefer, expect, refuse, hope, aim*). Use both negative and positive statements.

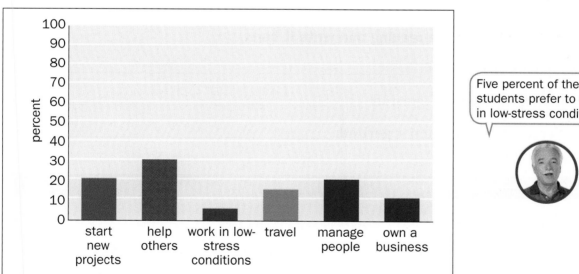

> Five percent of the students prefer to work in low-stress conditions.

Part 2. Now, in your group ask and answer the same questions about yourselves. Write the percentages, for example, 0%, 25%, 50%, etc. Then make your own bar graph.

■ GRAMMAR IN CONTENT

CD2,TR8

A **Read and listen.**

Passion

Professor: Many people decide on a career **by thinking** about money or status alone. This is a big mistake. A surgeon might make a good income, but good surgeons **care about healing** people. If a social worker doesn't **believe in improving** people's lives, she won't be **good at helping** others. You have to find your passion.

Student: What do you mean by passion?

Professor: **Before thinking** about money or status, think about this: What career do you **look forward to working** at for a long time? What job are you **enthusiastic about doing** for many years? If the passion is there, the money will follow.

enthusiastic: excited and interested in something

B **Find the following in the reading and write it here.**

1. preposition + gerund: _____

2. verb + preposition + gerund: _____

3. adjective + preposition + gerund: _____

Prepositions Followed by Gerunds	
Prepositions + Gerunds	
by before after without in for with to	Many people decide on a career **by thinking** about money or status.
Verb + Preposition + Gerund	
look forward to believe in care about help someone with	Good doctors **care about healing** people. He **believes in working** hard.

Prepositions Followed by Gerunds

Be + Adjective + Preposition + Gerund

be good at	be afraid of	She won't **be good at helping** others.
be interested in	be familiar with	They **are afraid of failing**.

Noun + Preposition + Gerund

have **an interest in**	have **a talent for**	I have **an interest in writing**.
have **a passion for**	have/get **a chance at**	He has **a passion for acting**.

C Use the phrases to make complete sentences. Follow the example.

1. sales manager / believe in / help other people

   A sales manager believes in helping other people.

2. scientist / good at / ask questions

   _____

3. math teacher / help students with / solve problems

   _____

4. police officer / care about / protect all people

   _____

5. surgeon / afraid of / make mistakes

   _____

6. engineers / interested in / design and build / new and exciting objects

   _____

■ COMMUNICATE

D **PAIR WORK** Take turns asking and answering questions about careers. Use prepositions followed by gerunds.

> Does a nurse care about helping other people?

> Yes, a nurse must care about helping people when they're sick.

GRAMMAR AND VOCABULARY Write a paragraph about your career values and goals. Use the grammar and vocabulary from this lesson.

> For me, a successful career means doing something I'm good at and enjoying my work. My passion is designing Web pages, and I want to help others, but I don't intend to become a social worker or a nurse. However, I imagine having a career in health. After taking one nutrition class, I became interested in learning more about this subject. It seems to be a possible career for me. I can imagine designing Web-based nutrition programs.

PROJECT Conduct a survey on career values and goals.

1. In your group of three or four students, write one question about career values or goals.
   Examples: For you, what is the most important value in a career (for example, money, enjoying the work, and so forth)? OR What kind of career do you hope to have (for example, sales, education, health, and so forth)?
2. Each person in your group should ask ten college students the question and write down the answers.
3. Share the results with your group.
4. Report your group's findings to your class.

INTERNET Go to a college website. Search "Career Development." List the resources that the college has to help students make decisions about careers. Report to your classmates on what you found.

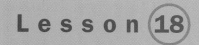
PART 1
Adjectives + Infinitive

PART 2
Too/Enough + Infinitive

PART 3
Adverbial Infinitives of Purpose:
To/In Order To

Astronomy: The Solar System

■ **CONTENT VOCABULARY**

Look at the pictures. Do you know the words?

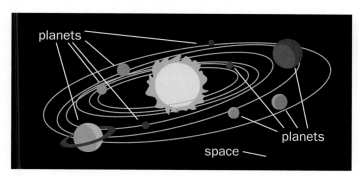

planets

planets

space

the Solar System

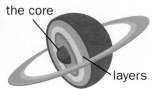

a crater

the core

layers

gravity

We found a new planet!

a telescope

to discover

What is my heart rate up here in space?

an experiment

Write the new words in your vocabulary journal.

■ **THINK ABOUT IT**

In your writing journal, write for five minutes about this question: Why do people want to know about life on other planets?

■ GRAMMAR IN CONTENT

A Read and listen.

CD2,TR9

The "New Earth"

Professor: In 2005, scientists were very **excited to discover** a new dwarf planet. At first, they called the dwarf planet the "New Earth" because it shared some characteristics with our planet. As soon as they saw this, they were **eager to find out** if it could support life.

Student: But then they were **surprised to find out** about its sun, weren't they? It was very close to the dwarf planet, right?

Professor: Yes, that's right, so the planet is very hot. They were also very **disappointed to learn** that one of its sides was frozen because the back side never faced the sun. It seems **impossible** for humans **to live** there.

dwarf: extremely small

B In bold you see adjectives followed by infinitives. Circle the adjectives and underline the verbs in the passage.

Adjectives + Infinitive

Animate Subjects

These adjectives usually have an animate subject. When used with an infinitive, the infinitive comes after the adjective.	<u>Scientists</u> were **excited to discover** a new planet. <u>They</u> were very **eager to find out** about it.

excited	surprised	disappointed	hesitant
careful	sad	happy	eager

Inanimate Subjects

These adjectives are often used with an inanimate subject (Noun or *It*). The infinitive comes after the adjective.

exciting	surprising	disappointing
possible	difficult	easy

Use *for* + **noun/pronoun** between the adjective and infinitive when necessary.

You can use the infinitive as the subject OR a gerund can replace the infinitive as the subject.

<u>It</u> is **exciting to discover** a new planet.
<u>The planets</u> are **difficult to see**.

<u>It</u> is **impossible (for humans) to live** there.

<u>**To discover**</u> a new planet is exciting.
<u>**Discovering**</u> a new planet is exciting.

C Read the conversation. Fill in the blanks with the correct form of the adjective in parentheses plus a verb from the list. Use *for* + pronoun if necessary.

spend	revise	~~get~~	hear	receive	see

A: Hey, Alisa, how is your astronomy class going?

B: Well, it was (excite) _____*exciting to get*_____ my mid-term test back. I did
(1)

quite well, but I was (disappoint) _____ only a C on my
(2)

term paper.

A: I'm (surprise) _____ that. You knew the subject so well,
(3)

and you're such a good writer.

B: Yeah, it was (surprise) _____ the grade too. Maybe I
(4)

just didn't develop my ideas completely.

A: Can you revise the paper?

B: It's (possible) _____ the paper for a higher grade, but
(5)

I'm (hesitant) _____ a lot of time on it. We already have
(6)

the assignment for the next paper.

D Correct the errors in Lionel's Astronomy Lab Journal. There are seven more errors.

$\overset{It}{\cancel{I}}$ was fascinating to do the lab activity this week. At first, it was difficult to

finding the stars given in the assignment, but I was exciting to see a few stars after

I focused the telescope. My partner and I were also able to do the math, so it was

excited for to answer the question by using the correct numbers. Next time I will be

careful taking better notes in class. If I have good notes and study before the lab, it

will be possible understand everything during the lab. Then, I will be easy to do the

lab assignment.

■ COMMUNICATE

E PAIR WORK Take turns. Ask your partner about the change from high school to college. Use an adjective and an infinitive.

> Were you afraid to fail when you started taking college classes?

> No, but I was afraid to take difficult classes.

PART TWO	*Too/Enough* + **Infinitive**

■ GRAMMAR IN CONTENT

CD2, TR10

A Read and listen.

to survive: to continue to live or exist

the atmosphere: the air space above Earth

Astronomy Quiz

Question: There is **enough oxygen and water** for us **to survive** on Earth. The soil is **healthy enough to grow** plants. Scientists are now trying to find ways for us to live on the moon and Mars. Why is this difficult? Is there **enough oxygen and water** for us **to survive** there?

Tanja's answer: Scientists think it is impossible to live on the moon because there is **not enough oxygen** for us **to live** there. Also, there is **not enough gravity to keep** us firmly on the ground. Finally, there is **not enough good soil to grow** plants.

Scientists are trying to find a way for us to live on Mars. There is some water on Mars, but **not enough**. Also, the atmosphere on Mars is **too thin to support** life.

B Look at the reading. Use one of the phrases in bold to answer each question.

1. Why can't we stay alive on the moon? _____ *There is not enough oxygen.*

2. Why can't we stay firmly on the ground on the moon?

_____

3. Why can't we grow plants on the moon?

_____

4. Why can't the atmosphere on Mars support life?

_____

Too/Enough + Infinitive

too + adjective + infinitive *not too* + adjective + infinitive	It is **too cold to have** a comfortable life. It is **not too hot** (for us) **to survive**.
adjective + *enough* + infinitive *not* + adjective + *enough* + infinitive	It is **warm enough to live** on Earth. It is **not warm enough to live** on Mars.
enough + noun + infinitive *not enough* + noun + infinitive *too much/many/few/little* + noun + infinitive	There is **enough oxygen** to survive. There is **not enough water** (for us) **to drink**. There is **too much wind to use** machines.

Note:

• Sometimes we use *for* + **noun/pronoun** before the infinitive to be clear about the subject of the infinitive, for example, *There is not enough water for us to live there.*

C **Write *T* if the statement is true and *F* if it is false. Then discuss your responses with your class.**

1. ___ Some stars are too far away for us to see.

2. ___ There is enough gravity on the moon to play tennis.

3. ___ There is too much gravity on Earth to play tennis.

4. ___ The moon is close enough for us to see without a telescope.

5. ___ There is not enough water for us to survive on Earth.

D **Complete the statements about yourself with an infinitive.**

1. I am too old _____ *to ask my parents to support me* _____.

2. I am too young _____.

3. I don't have enough money _____.

4. I have too little time _____.

5. My English is not fluent enough _____.

6. I study enough _____.

7. I know too little about astronomy _____.

E Student A, look at the chart on this page. Student B, look at the chart on page 301. Ask your partner questions about living on the planets. Take notes. Fill in the chart. Use *too/enough* + infinitive. Follow the model. Then write a paragraph using your notes and the information in the charts.

Is it warm enough to live on Mars?   No, it isn't. It's –55 degrees. That's too cold for us to live there.

Student A Questions:

1. warm/Uranus?
2. oxygen/Jupiter?
3. gravity/Jupiter?
4. land/Uranus?
5. warm/Pluto?

Student A information

	Average Temperature	Oxygen/ Atmosphere	Gravity	Other
Mars	–55°C (↓)	no oxygen (↓) 95% CO_2	38% of Earth (↓) (could cause health problems)	
Venus	+477°C (↑)	pressure 95 times greater than Earth (↑)	95% of Earth (*)	
Earth	+15°C (*)	• protects from the sun • has oxygen (*)	can walk freely (*)	water (*)
Uranus				
Jupiter				

Key: (↑) = too much   (↓) = too little/not enough   (*) = OK/enough

■ GRAMMAR IN CONTENT

A Read and listen.

CD2,TR11

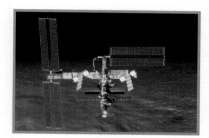

Astronomy Class

Professor:	In this astronomy class, we study the planet Earth and its relationship to the solar system—the sun, moon, stars, and other planets.
Student 1:	Why is this important?
Professor:	Well, **for understanding**. We learn about Earth **in order to understand** ourselves. Galileo used a telescope **to prove** Earth moves around the sun. Before that, some people still claimed Earth was the center of the universe. We study the planets **to compare** them and **to find out** if life is possible there.
Student 2:	Scientists do a lot of experiments out in space too, don't they?
Professor:	Yes, they do. **In order to do** experiments in space, there is a space station. But some very important discoveries were made before there was a space station. In the late 1960s, we learned a lot about gravity because of the moon missions. We used moon rocks **to learn** about the layers of the moon, and we measured "moonquakes" **to learn** about the core of the moon.

B Look at the dialog. The adverb phrases in bold are infinitives of purpose. They answer the questions "Why?" or "For what purpose?" Write the question for each phrase.

1. **Q:** _____ Why do we study Earth? _____

   A: In order to understand ourselves.

2. **Q:** _____

   A: To prove that Earth moves around the sun.

3. **Q:** _____

   A: To find out if life is possible there.

4. **Q:** _____

   A: To learn about the layers of the moon.

To

Use an infinitive of purpose to answer the questions *Why?* or *For what purpose?* You can place the adverbial infinitive phrase of purpose at the beginning of the sentence.	Galileo used a telescope **to prove** that Earth moves around the sun. Why did he use a telescope? **To prove** that Earth moves around the sun. **To prove** that Earth moves around the sun, Galileo used a telescope.

In Order To

Use *in order to* + base form of the verb to express purpose.	We have a space station **in order to do** experiments in space. Why do we have space stations? **In order to do** experiments in space. **In order to do** experiments in space, we have a space station.

Notes:

- An infinitive of purpose is an adverb phrase.
- Sometimes we use *for* + **gerund** to express purpose, for example, *Why is this important?* **For understanding.**
- An infinitive of purpose can help you to combine sentences:
  I took an astronomy class. I learned about the planets.
  I took an astronomy class **to learn** *about the planets.*

C **Complete the sentences by explaining the purpose. Use** *to/in order to/for.*

1. People drive cars _____to get from one place to another in very little time_____.

2. Scientists do experiments _____.

3. Astronomers study the planets _____.

4. Astronauts landed on the moon _____.

5. Galileo used a telescope _____.

6. Teachers give tests _____.

7. Students work part-time _____.

8. Babies cry loudly _____.

CD2,TR12

D Listen to the short dialogs and (circle) the correct answer.

1. Gina is taking astronomy
   a. to complete a General Education requirement.
   b. to learn about the planets.

2. Mika is going to the lab
   a. to do an experiment.
   b. to watch a video.

3. She learned about the layers of the moon
   a. to understand the effect of the layers on water.
   b. to get some water.

4. Mika will take another astronomy class
   a. to learn more.
   b. to complete a requirement.

■ **C O M M U N I C A T E**

E **PAIR WORK** Take turns with your partner. Ask and answer questions. Use *to/in order to/for* to express purpose. Use different tenses, for example, present/past.

Why are you studying English?

I'm studying English to get a college degree.

1. you/study/English?
2. astronomers/study/the planets?
3. scientists/build/a space station?
4. Galileo/use/a telescope?
5. we/study/grammar?
6. you/use/a dictionary?
7. you/carry/a cell phone?
8. you/use/e-mail?
9. you/take notes/in class?
10. you/study/pronunciation?

GRAMMAR AND VOCABULARY (Circle) the letter of the correct answer.

1. Galileo used a telescope
   a. for find sunspots on the sun.
   (b.) to find sunspots on the sun.

2. Earth is one of the
   a. space.
   b. planets.

3. It is exciting
   a. for to discover a new planet.
   b. for us to discover a new planet.

4. Earth has a hot _____ with many _____ around it.
   a. core..........layers
   b. layer..........cores

5. If you have a good _____, you can see the _____ on the moon.
   a. experiment.......core
   b. telescope.....craters

6. Scientists are _____ more about the solar system.
   a. eager for learning
   b. eager to learn

PROJECT **Form a group of four people to report on a planet.**

1. Choose a planet. Assign each group member one topic: gravity, atmosphere, temperature, or other information.
2. Read about the planet on the Internet or in the library, and take notes. Bring your information to class.
3. Prepare a report for the class. Explain why it would be difficult for people to live on that planet.

INTERNET **Enter "International Space Station" into a search engine. Read about the effects on the human body of living on the space station. Share the information with your classmates. Use the grammar from the lesson, for example, *They have enough* _____ *to* _____. *It is too* _____ *to* _____.**

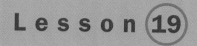

Business: Advertising

■ CONTENT VOCABULARY

Look at the pictures. Do you know the words?

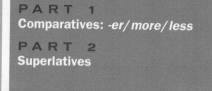

slogan

Be healthier than the rest. Drink Sun Orange Juice.

Step 1: Discuss nutrition.
Step 2: Compare to other juices.

a marketing strategy   advertising/an advertisement

products

a service

Write the new words in your vocabulary journal.

■ THINK ABOUT IT

In your writing journal, write for five minutes about any of these questions.

1. Do you know any advertising slogans? What are they?
2. What effect do those ads have on you? Do they persuade you to buy something?

■ GRAMMAR IN CONTENT

A Read and listen.

CD2,TR13

Comparative Advertising

Comparative advertising focuses on showing the difference between two products or services. A company uses this strategy to persuade the customer to buy a product or service. For example, a car company will say something like this: "Their car may look safe and comfortable, but our car is **safer** and **more comfortable** than theirs. And it uses less gas." An orange juice company will use a slogan: "Be **healthier** than the rest. Drink Sun OJ." A phone company will create ads about their service: "We have **more service people** than they do. Our people work **harder** and **more quickly** than theirs. They listen **more carefully** to your problems and solve them **more efficiently**." Such ads and slogans can persuade consumers to make a decision when they are ready to buy something.

B The words in bold are comparisons.

1. Find two adjectives ending with *-er:* _____ _____

2. Find two adjectives with *more:* _____ _____

3. Write a rule about the use of *more:* _____

    _____

Comparatives: *-er/more/less*	
Add *-er + than*	
1. One-syllable adjective/adverb	safe–**safer than** fast–**faster than**
2. Two-syllable adjectives with final unstressed *y*-ending (Change the *y* to *i* and add *-er.*)	happy–**happier** early–**earlier than**
Add *more/less* + adjective/adverb + *than*	
1. Adjectives/adverbs with three or more syllables	beautiful–**more beautiful than** skillfully–**less skillfully than**
2. Two-syllable adverbs ending in *-ly* if the corresponding adjective does not end in *ly* (slow–slowly)	slowly–**more slowly than** sharply–**more sharply than**

Comparatives: -er/more/less

Add -er OR more/less

1. Two-syllable adjectives with a stressed first syllable and an unstressed second syllable ending in -ly, -ow, or -le 2. Other two-syllable adjectives: *tender, stupid, quiet, etc.*	narrower–more narrow simpler–more simple quieter–more quiet than stupider–more stupid than

Add irregular comparative form + *than*

Irregular adjective and adverb comparative forms	good/well–**better than** bad/badly–**worse than** far–**farther than**

Add comparative form + noun + *than*

1. *more/less* + noncount noun + *than* 2. *more/fewer* + count noun + *than*	gas–**more gas than** noise–**less noise than** people–**fewer people than**

Note:

Omit the second part of the comparison if it is unnecessary, for example, *I like both cakes, but that one is better.*

C **Complete the advertising claims. Use correct comparative forms. You may choose to omit the *than* phrase in the comparison.**

1. Their sport shoe is comfortable and attractive, but _our sport shoe is more comfortable and more attractive than theirs_.

2. Their salespeople are friendly and helpful, but _____.

3. Their prices are low and they treat customers fairly, but _____.

4. Their service is quick and good, but _____.

5. Their restaurant is clean and their waiters work efficiently, but _____.

6. Their cooks prepare the food carefully and the food is delicious, but _____.

D Fill in the blanks with *less* or *fewer.*

Professor: We're going to look at these two magazine advertisements and compare them. Which one has ___fewer___ pictures?
(1)

Student 1: Ad #1 does. It is _____ crowded than Ad #2. It also has _____
(2)   (3)

people and _____ words.
(4)

Professor: Which one has the stronger idea?

Student 2: The negative idea in Ad #1 is very strong: "Their salespeople are

_____ helpful and they work _____ efficiently. There are
(5)   (6)

_____ salespeople, so they have _____ time to help the
(7)   (8)

customers. Customers get _____ help."
(9)

E Use the words to write a comparative advertising claim with the correct comparative form.

1. new bicycle/be/light

___Our new bicycle is lighter than theirs.___

2. TV show/be/funny

_____

3. have/a lot of/online support service

_____

4. shoes/be/beautiful

_____

5. drivers/arrive/punctually

_____

6. store hours/be/convenient

_____

7. gardeners/work/carefully

_____

8. professors/explain/clearly

_____

■ COMMUNICATE

F **PAIR WORK** Work with a partner. Create a comparative advertisement for each product or service. Use some of the details or create your own.

Our cars are better than theirs. Ours have more powerful engines and more comfortable seats.

Our cars are also safer and more reliable.

1. A car company trying to sell their new car: powerful engine/good service program/safe and reliable car
2. A cell phone company discussing their service: quick service/friendly people/ think creatively
3. A college or university advertising for more students: effective professors/ high student success rates/low fees/good job placement services
4. Computer: big screen/clear picture/cheap/easy to use/easy to add programs
5. Movie theaters: interesting movies/good popcorn/a lot of seats/comfortable seats

PART TWO	Superlatives

■ GRAMMAR IN CONTENT

CD2,TR14

A **Read and listen.**

A Radio Advertisement

Victor: Hey, Saleh, did you finish your advertisement for the Intro to Advertising class?

Saleh: Yeah, I just finished it. I created a radio ad for Golden University. Do you want to hear it?

Victor: Sure.

Saleh: OK, I'll read it like I'm on the radio. "Do you want **the best** education possible? Come to Golden University. Golden has **the highest** number of successful students of any college in the country, with the highest transfer rate and the lowest dropout rate. Golden's professors are **the brightest, most creative,** and **most interesting** you can find. 80% of Golden's professors have PhDs and many of them have studied and taught abroad. Other schools might have good programs and teachers, but Golden's programs are **better than** any other. Golden is **the best** school for a college student today. Don't make **the worst** mistake of your life by going to another college. Come to Golden!"

Victor: That's pretty good, Saleh. You persuaded me!

B Read the ad again. The superlative forms are in bold. Which word is the superlative of *good?* _____ Which word is the superlative of *bad?* _____

Superlatives		
-est	*the most/the least*	**Irregular Forms**
high–higher–the highest fast–faster–the fastest few–fewer–the fewest	the most creative the most interesting the least effectively the least noise	good–better–the best bad–worse–the worst far–farther–the farthest

Notes:

- Use *the* with superlatives.
- We often use a phrase after the superlative, for example, *It is the best college **in the country.***
- You can use a comparative with **"than any other"** or **"than any (of the) others"** to express the same idea as a superlative, for example, *This car is more economical than any other car.*

C Write the superlative form of the word in parentheses.

What is (smart) _____the smartest_____ strategy for an advertisement? First,
(1)

choose (important) _____ ideas about a product or service, and
(2)

think about (effective) _____ way to express those ideas. Sometimes
(3)

(simple) _____ ads are (good) _____. Sometimes,
(4) (5)

(bad) _____ ads have too much information and too many ideas.
(6)

Next, think about (funny) _____, (sad)_____, or
(7) (8)

(surprising) _____ way to present the ideas. How can you reach
(9)

(more) _____ people through your ad? How can you persuade (large)
(10)

_____ number of people? (Successful) _____ ads help the
(11) (12)

consumer to make the (wise) _____ decision.
(13)

CD2,TR15

D Listen to the advertisements and write the information about the colleges. Use a superlative form.

Pacific College	Atlantic College	Western College	Bright College	Simon College
most successful students				

E Correct the errors in Akira's essay about two bottled water ads. There are seven errors.

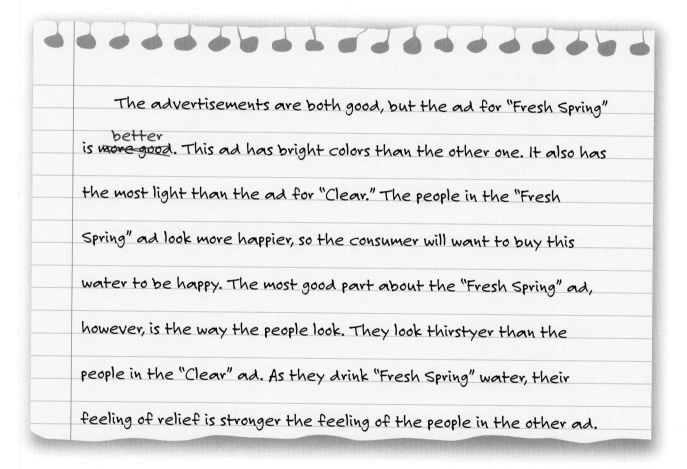

The advertisements are both good, but the ad for "Fresh Spring"

is ~~more good~~ *better*. This ad has bright colors than the other one. It also has

the most light than the ad for "Clear." The people in the "Fresh

Spring" ad look more happier, so the consumer will want to buy this

water to be happy. The most good part about the "Fresh Spring" ad,

however, is the way the people look. They look thirstyer than the

people in the "Clear" ad. As they drink "Fresh Spring" water, their

feeling of relief is stronger the feeling of the people in the other ad.

▪ COMMUNICATE

F **WRITE** Write an advertisement about your school, your neighborhood, or your city. Choose the most positive ideas. Use superlative forms. Use at least one fact or statistic.

GRAMMAR AND VOCABULARY Fill in the blanks with a word from the list. Write a comparative or superlative form for the words in parentheses.

product	advertising	decision	slogan	strategy	service

1. "Sport Drink: Fresher and Better" is an advertising _____.

2. When a company has a new _____, they have to sell it through the help of advertising. An advertisement shows the product is (good) _____ the others.

3. Sometimes companies use _____ to compare their product with others. The ads usually result in (high sales) _____.

4. Juan made his final _____ to attend White College when he read their Internet ad.

5. Right now, McFinn's Hamburger Company is using a smart advertising _____. They are putting ads on some of the city buses.

6. Phone companies and Internet companies need to advertise (good) _____ customer _____. If they don't, they will make (few) _____ sales.

PROJECT Write an advertising slogan.

1. Work with a group. Choose a product or service. Make a list of four to five good points about the product or service.
2. Write slogans and sentences to compare your product to similar products.
3. Create a poster with your advertisement. Add pictures and graphics. Present your poster to the class.

 INTERNET Look for a comparative advertisement on the Internet. Choose a favorite product or service and enter "advertisement and (name of product or service)" into a search engine. Bring the advertisement to class and share the comparisons with your classmates.

Literature: The Language of Poetry

■ CONTENT VOCABULARY

Look at the pictures. Do you know the words?

The feeling of loss is as deep as the ocean.

simile

The loss is an ocean.

metaphor

William Shakespeare, poet

similar

Christopher Marlowe, poet

Write the new words in your vocabulary journal.

■ THINK ABOUT IT

Read these two sentences. 1. *Life is long and difficult.* 2. *Life is like a long, rough road.* Which do you like better? Why do you think it's better? Why do poets and writers use similes and metaphors? In your writing journal, write for five minutes about these questions.

■ GRAMMAR IN CONTENT

A Read and listen.

CD2,TR16

a **margin:** edge

a **vale:** valley

continuous: not stopping

a **glance:** a quick look

Poetry Lesson

Professor: Today, we're going to read "I Wandered Lonely as a Cloud," a poem by the poet William Wordsworth. Let's start with the first two stanzas:

I wandered lonely as a cloud
That floats on high o'er vales and hills,
When all at once I saw a crowd,
A host, of golden daffodils;
Beside the lake, beneath the trees,
Fluttering and dancing in the breeze.

Continuous as the stars that shine
And twinkle on the milky way,
They stretched in never-ending line
Along the margin of a bay:
Ten thousand saw I at a glance,
Tossing their heads in sprightly dance . . .

Wordsworth uses similes in this poem. In the first line, he is saying: "While I was wandering, I felt **as lonely as** a cloud." In the second stanza, he is saying: "The daffodils were **as continuous as** the stars in the milky way." The similes help him to describe his feeling and his experience.

B Look at the poem in exercise A. Write *T* if the statement about the poem is true. Write *F* if it is false.

a.   ____ He felt as lonely as a cloud.

b.   ____ The daffodils were not as lively as dancers.

c.   ____ The daffodils were as bright as the stars.

d.   ____ The line of daffodils was not as long as the bay.

As . . . as for Comparisons

Adjectives

Affirmative	Negative
He felt **as lonely as** a cloud.	I am **not as lonely as** my sister.
The daffodils were **as yellow as** butter.	Her eyes are **not as dark as** mine.

Adverbs

Affirmative	Negative
She walks **as slowly as** a turtle.	She **doesn't walk as slowly as** her brother.
He moves **as fast as** a lion.	He **couldn't write as well as** the others.

Nouns

Count	Noncount
This poem has **as many stanzas as** that one.	Marlowe didn't write **as much poetry as** Shakespeare did.

Notes:

- Use *as . . . as* to show two equal things.
- You can omit the first *as,* for example, I wandered **lonely as** a cloud.
- You can omit the second part of the comparison if it is clear, for example, *My sister is very lonely. I am not as lonely.*

C **Fill in the blanks with a comparative structure. Use the words in parentheses.**

A: Hey, Steve, did you read the poetry homework?

B: Yeah, I did. This poem wasn't (difficult) ___as difficult as___ the first poem we
(1)
read. I didn't have (trouble) _____ understanding it.
(2)

A: Really? I didn't understand this poem (well) _____ you did.
(3)
For me, the language wasn't (clear) _____ the language in the
(4)
first one. However, I agree with the professor's comment about the poet. "His
words have (strength) _____ as the wind."
(5)

B: Well, in my view, his words weren't (strong) _____ the other
(6)
poet's words. For example: "Her sadness was (long) _____ the
(7)
night."

D **Listen and fill in the blanks.**

A: How is your new literature class?

B: Well, it's OK, but I don't like American Literature ___as much as___ British
(1)
Literature.

A: Really? But you had to read poems and plays by Shakespeare in British
Literature, didn't you?

B: Yes, but it _____ the poetry in this class. These poets use
(2)
_____ difficult words _____ Shakespeare. And
(3)   (4)
the ideas are more difficult. I'm reading this poetry just _____
(5)
because of the vocabulary and ideas.

A: Is the instructor good at explaining the texts?

B: He _____ Professor Patina. She helped me to understand
(6)
Shakespeare. I don't think my grade this semester will be _____
(7)
my grade last semester.

■ **COMMUNICATE**

E **GROUP WORK** **The similes below are common idioms. Discuss the meaning of
each simile. Then write a new one by changing the comparison. Share your similes
with the class.**

1. I feel as fresh as a daisy. ____*I feel as fresh as newly fallen snow.*____

2. His skin is tough as leather. _____

3. My son is as tall as a tree. _____

4. She has as many friends as people in this town. _____

5. Her heart is as cold as ice. _____

6. I am as hungry as a bear. _____

7. She is pretty as a picture. _____

8. I trust you as far as I can see. _____

F PAIR WORK Work with your partner. Write similes using the words below. Make a comparison to something in nature. Then share your similes with the class.

> Her eyes are as dark as the sky at midnight.

1. eyes/dark
2. hair/yellow
3. love/deep
4. hope/high
5. stomach/empty
6. heart/warm
7. anger/hot
8. have/rhythm

PART TWO	Comparative Expressions: *The Same as/Similar to/Different from/Like/Alike/Unlike*

■ GRAMMAR IN CONTENT

CD2,TR18

A Read and listen.

Lecture on Language

Professor: Similes and metaphors are **alike** in one important way. **Like** a metaphor, a simile compares two things. However, a simile uses the words *like* or *as*. For example: "Her eyes were **like** the sea." The writer uses a simile to say "A **is similar to** B."

Student 1: What is **the difference between** a simile and a metaphor?

Professor: A metaphor **is different from** a simile in an important way. In a metaphor, the writer is saying "A is **the same as** B." The writer tries to make the two things one. For example: "Love is a rose." **Unlike** a simile, a metaphor does not use the words *like* or *as* to compare.

B Look at the "Lecture on Language" reading. Which words and phrases in bold mean "similar" or "the same"?

_____   _____   _____

Which words and phrases in bold mean "different"?

_____   _____   _____

Comparative Expressions: *The Same as / Similar to / Different from / Like / Alike / Unlike*

Similar / The Same	Different
Poetry is **similar to** music. Poetry and music **are similar.** Hers is **the same as** mine.	A simile is **different from** a metaphor. Similes and metaphors **are different.** There's **a difference between** a simile and a metaphor.
Poetry is **like** music. Poetry and music **are alike.** **Like** music, poetry has rhythm.	Poetry is **unlike** music. **Unlike** a metaphor, a simile can have the word "like."

Notes:
- Use *like* and *unlike* as prepositions before nouns.
- Use *similar* and *different* as adjectives after *be* and linking verbs.
- Don't forget to use a noun after the prepositions.
  Incorrect: ~~Poetry and music are similar to.~~   Correct: *Poetry is **similar to** music.*
- Use "**different from**" for formal usage. Use "**different than**" in informal speech.
  Examples: *A metaphor is different from a simile. Your T-shirt is different than mine.*

C **Fill in the blanks with a comparative expression.**

1. **A:** Is there ___*a difference between*___ a breeze and a wind?

 (1)

   B: Yes. A wind is _____ a breeze because it's stronger.

 (2)

2. **A:** How is a poem _____ a song?

 (3)

   B: Well, a poem is _____ a song because they both have rhythm.

 (4)

   However, _____ a song, a poem isn't a piece of music.

 (5)

3. **A:** Professor Hurtz's reading of the poem was very emotional. There was so

   much feeling. Was Professor Ling's reading _____ his?

 (6)

   B: Yes, _____ his reading, her reading was very emotional.

 (7)

D Read the professor's notes about Jamal and Raquel. Complete the sentences. Then write a paragraph in your notebook about Jamal and Raquel based on the notes and the comparative sentences.

Jamal	Raquel
Class: English 46	Class: English 46
Topic: use of rhythm in poetry	Topic: use of rhyme in poetry
Problem: ideas	Problem: ideas
Strength: vocabulary	Strength: word choice
My suggestion: Develop the ideas	My suggestion: Develop the ideas

1. _____Like_____ Jamal, Raquel took English 46.

2. Jamal's topic _____ Raquel's topic.

3. Raquel's problem _____ Jamal's problem.

4. Jamal's strength _____ Raquel's strength.

5. The professor's suggestions _____.

E Listen to the comparison of William Shakespeare and Christopher Marlowe, famous English poets from the 1500s. Circle + if they are the same or similar. Circle – if they are different.

CD2,TR19

1. fame   +   (–)   4. education   +   –
2. age   +   –   5. writing style   +   –
3. social class   +   –   6. topics   +   –

F Correct the errors in Maya's comparison of two poems, "The Raven" by Edgar Allan Poe and "The Oven Bird" by Robert Frost. There are six errors.

The poem "The Raven" is similar ~~with~~ to "The Oven Bird" in some ways, but there are some differences the two poems. They are like because each poet uses a bird as a symbol. However, the feeling of "The Raven" is very difference from the feeling of "The Oven Bird." Is unlike "The Oven Bird," "The Raven" has a very dark feeling. In addition, the rhythm is different from. The rhythm of "The Oven Bird" is not as strong the rhythm of "The Raven."

G GROUP WORK Are they similar or different or both? Discuss with your group.

> What's the difference between high school and college?

> How is high school similar to college?

> Well, unlike high school, college offers a lot of choices.

> They're alike in a few ways. There is a lot of reading and speaking in both. Also, you have to work a lot by yourself.

1. high school/college
2. my language/English
3. reading a story/reading a poem
4. speaking English/writing English
5. writing a letter by hand/writing an e-mail message
6. the text of a poem/the words of a song
7. a poem with rhythm/a poem with rhyme

Connection | Putting It Together

GRAMMAR AND VOCABULARY Work with a partner. Find two poems. (Use the library or visit a poetry Web site such as www.poemhunter.com.) They can be two poems by the same poet or two poems by two different poets. Prepare a presentation on the similarities and differences between the two poems. Use the grammar and vocabulary from the lesson. Share your presentation with your classmates.

> Unlike the Frost poem, the poem by Dickinson is about beauty.

PROJECT Present a report about a poet.

1. Work with a partner. Choose a poet from your first language.
2. Do some research on the poet.
3. Make a presentation to the class about the poet.

 INTERNET Go to www.poemhunter.com or another poetry website. Find a poem with a metaphor or simile and share it with your class.

A Ms. Wu, an astronomer from JPL, is visiting a college astronomy class. Read her answer to a student's question. Write the infinitive or gerund form of the verb in parentheses OR choose from the words in parentheses. Add pronouns when necessary. If there is no choice, add the necessary word(s).

Nick: How did you become (interesting/interested) _____ in astronomy?
(1)

Ms. Wu: Well, when I was a (five-years-old/five-year-old) _____ girl, my
(2)

father was a (famous/famously) _____ astronomer, and he was
(3)

working (hard/hardly) _____ (discover) _____ a new crater
(4)   (5)

on the moon. I liked (spend) _____ time with him, and his work
(6)

was (fascinated/fascinating) _____ to me. I wanted him (teach)
(7)

_____ me about the solar system, the craters on the moon, and
(8)

space. However, during that period, he was (too busy/busy enough)

_____ (give) _____ me any extra time. One evening, he went
(9)   (10)

to the university, and my mother was on the telephone. There I was. It

was (frustrated/frustrating) _____ (look) _____ at my father's
(11)   (12)

telescope because it was impossible (use) _____ it. I wasn't (too
(13)

tall/tall enough) _____ (reach) _____ the telescope. I (quick/
(14)   (15)

quickly) _____ moved a small table in order (stand) _____
(16)   (17)

on it, but when I looked through the telescope, I was (surprised/

surprising) _____ (see) _____ (complete/completely) _____
(18)   (19)   (20)

darkness—no moon, no craters. At the moment of this (disappointing/

disappointed) _____ experience, I heard two voices behind me
(21)

saying, "*What* are you doing?" I (slow/slowly) _____ turned around
(22)

and both of my parents were staring at me without (smile/smiling)

_____. After (take) _____ the cover off of the telescope and
(23)   (24)

(tell) _____ me the new rules, my father agreed (give) _____ me
(25)   (26)

more (frequent/frequently) _____ lessons about the telescope and
(27)

the planets.

B The students in the poetry club are planning their annual student poetry conference. Write the infinitive or gerund form of the verb in parentheses OR choose from the words in parentheses. Add pronouns when necessary. If there is no choice, add the necessary word(s).

S1: OK. First, we need (decide) _____ on the lead poet for our event. We
(1)
have two possibilities: Chris Mead and Sonja Williams. Mead is (less/
fewer) _____ expensive _____ Williams, but she is not very good at
(2)   (3)
(read) _____ her poetry to large groups. She isn't _____ emotional
(4)   (5)
_____ Williams. However, like I said, Williams costs _____
(6)   (7)
_____ Mead. On the other hand, Williams isn't _____ eager
(8)   (9)
(participate) _____. That's why she's willing to (receive) _____
(10)   (11)
_____ money.
(12)

S2: Yeah, but also, Mead's poetry isn't the (same/same as) _____ Williams's
(13)
poetry. Their themes are (similar to/similar) _____, but their use of
(14)
metaphor and rhyme is very (different/different from) _____. To tell
(15)
you the truth, I think Williams is (simple/simply) _____ a (better/best)
(16)
_____ poet.
(17)

S2: Do we have _____ money (pay) _____ Williams?
(18)   (19)

S3: If we plan our advertising (wise/wisely) _____ we will have _____.
(20)   (21)

LEARNER LOG Check (✔) *Yes* or *I Need More Practice.*

Lesson	I Can Use . . .	Yes	I Need More Practice
16	Adjectives and Adverbs, Participial Adjectives, Nouns as Adjectives		
17	Gerunds, Verbs + Infinitives; Verbs + Infinitives or Gerunds, Prepositions Followed by Gerunds		
18	Adjectives + Infinitive, *Too/Enough* + Infinitive, Adverbial Infinitives of Purpose: *To/In Order to*		
19	Comparatives: *-er/more/less,* Superlatives		
20	*As . . . as* for Comparisons, Comparative Expressions: *The Same as/ Similar to/Different from/Like/Alike/Unlike*		

PART 1
Advice, Rules, and Obligations:
Should/Ought To/Had Better

PART 2
Be Supposed To

Lesson 21

Journalism: Rules and Ethics

■ CONTENT VOCABULARY

Look at the pictures. Do you know the words?

Mr. President, what is your position on rising health costs?

a journalist/ reporter

an interview

media

Write the new words in your vocabulary journal.

■ THINK ABOUT IT

In your writing journal, write for five minutes about any of these questions: Do you think that journalists always present the truth? Do you think they should write only the truth? What are some rules that journalists should follow?

■ GRAMMAR IN CONTENT

A **Read and listen.**

CD2,TR20

Journalism 101: The School Newspaper

Professor: As you know, this class gives you a chance to work on the school newspaper. We will begin by discussing some basic rules of journalism. First, as a journalist, you **ought to** understand the importance of writing a good article, but you **shouldn't** ever lie or make up a story. Second, when you interview someone for a story, you **had better** not quote the person without getting permission. That is a serious mistake.

Student: **Should** we get that permission before the interview?

Professor: Well, no. First, you **should** get permission to have the interview. Then, during the interview, you **ought to** ask about quoting something specific. Then, you **had better** report accurate information when you write about the interview.

to make up: to create without true facts for support

B **Look at the dialog. The modals and phrasal modals are in bold.**

1. Underline the verbs that follow the modals and phrasal modals.
2. Are there any endings on the verbs? ___ Yes ___ No
3. Here are two sentences with ***do*** as the auxiliary ("helping") verb.
   Does *she **write** every day? No, she **doesn't write** every day.*
   Here are two sentences with modals.
   Should *we **get** permission? You **should get** permission.*
   Do you think a modal is also an auxiliary verb? ___ Yes ___ No

Should/Ought To/Had Better		
Forms		**Examples**
Affirmative Statements		
should *ought to* *had better*	simple verb	You **should get** permission. You **ought to understand** the importance. You **had better ask** permission to quote.

Should/Ought To/Had Better

Forms				Examples
Negative Statements				
should *ought* *had better*	*not*		simple verb	You **shouldn't** ever **lie** or **make up** a story. Journalists **ought not take** money for a story. You **had better not lie**.
Questions				
should	subject		simple verb	**Should** we **get** that permission before the interview?

Notes:

- In general, don't use **ought to** or **had better** for questions.
- *Ought to* is <u>more formal</u> than *should*. *Had better* is <u>stronger</u> than *should*.
- The use of *had better* usually implies negative consequences, for example, *You had better revise this essay.* (meaning: *If you don't, you'll get a bad grade.*)

C Think about the job of journalists and their stories. (Circle) the answer choice with which you agree. Then discuss with your classmates the reasons for your answers.

1. A journalist ((should) / should not) write interesting stories.
2. Newspaper stories (ought to / ought not) be truthful.
3. A newspaper story (should / should not) report only facts.
4. A journalist (had better / had better not) state an opinion in a news story.
5. The newspaper (should / shouldn't) print a story with lies.

D Fill in the blanks with the correct form of *should/had better/ought to* and a verb in the box. Add *not* where needed.

~~follow~~	attack	be	write	use	read

Blogs are a new form of journalism. When you respond to a blog, you

_____*should follow*_____ a few simple rules. First, you _____ other
    (1)   **(2)**

comments before you write yours. You _____ very long pieces, and
                                              (3)

you _____ polite when you state a strong opinion. When you comment
       (4)

on other people's blogs, you _____ impolite language and you
                                     (5)

_____ other bloggers.
    (6)

GRAMMAR IN CONTENT

A **Read and listen.**

CD2,TR21

Final Copy

Pablo: Hey, Khalid, are you ready to put this newspaper together?

Khalid: Well, we're **supposed to** review all of our articles before we complete the final copy.

Pablo: We **were supposed to** do that yesterday. Do you still have an article that needs review?

Khalid: Yeah. I'm sorry. I **was supposed to** complete it yesterday, but I **didn't.** I finished my interview too late to write the article on time.

Julia: **Are** we **supposed to** have the final copy ready by tomorrow?

Khalid: No, we're **supposed to have** everything ready for review, and we **do.**

B **Find the past tense forms of *be supposed to* in the reading. Which of these forms is it? Check all that apply.**

___ *we're supposed to*   ___ *were supposed to*   ___ *was supposed to*

Find the compound sentence with *but*.

a. What is the form of ***be supposed to?*** ___ affirmative ___ negative

b. What is the form of the ***do*** auxiliary? ___ affirmative ___ negative

Be Supposed To	
Forms	**Examples**
Affirmative Statements	
be supposed to + simple verb	We're **supposed to review** all of our articles.
	We **were supposed to do** that yesterday.
	We're **supposed to have** everything ready by tomorrow.
Negative Statements	
be + *not* + *supposed to* + simple verb	We **aren't supposed to make up** stories.
	She **wasn't supposed to do** the interview.
	They **aren't supposed to finish** tomorrow.

Questions

be + subject + *supposed to* + simple verb	**Are** we **supposed to review** the articles?
	Were we **supposed to have** the story ready?
	Is she **supposed to meet** us tomorrow?

Note:

• Use the present tense with *future* time expressions to show the future. For example,

    present   future
    We **are** supposed to go tomorrow.

C **Kim (K) is a journalism major. She is being interviewed by an interviewer (I) from the city newspaper. Fill in the blanks with the correct form of *be supposed to*. Add *not* and/or a pronoun or auxiliary if necessary. (Use the *do* auxiliary in one blank.)**

I: What kind of stories _____*are you supposed to*_____ write?
                                 (1)

K: As a reporter for the school newspaper, I _____ find
                                              (2)
interesting stories about the school, programs, activities, teachers, and
students.

I: _____ state your opinion when you write a story?
          (3)

K: No, I _____ write my own personal opinion. I should try
                (4)
to present the truth.

I: What happened to your friend Bob Cummings? Wasn't he fired?

K: Yes. He broke an important rule. He _____ make up
                                      (5)
any information, but he _____ .
                        (6)

I: Tell me, what _____ learn most recently in your class?
                 (7)

K: We _____ learn the rules of interviewing, and now we
         (8)
_____ be ready for our first interview.
        (9)

I: Oh yes, I know those rules. So, what is the first rule of interviewing?

K: The reporter _____ be late. And if my interview is
                        (10)
tomorrow, I _____ review my questions tonight.
             (11)

I: Well thanks, Kim. I appreciate your time.

D Complete the sentences with the correct form of *be supposed to*. Also use *not* and the correct form of *do* and *be* where needed.

1. I _____ was supposed to _____ finish yesterday, but I _____ didn't _____.

2. The newspaper _____ come out today, but it

   _____.

3. Journalists _____ be honest, but sometimes they

   _____.

4. We _____ have good ethics, and we _____.

5. You _____ do yesterday's interview without permission,

   but you _____.

6. Members of the media _____ give accurate information,

   but sometimes they _____.

7. Your story _____ be without an opinion, and it

   _____.

E Listen to the dialog between Aisha and her professor, and (circle) the correct answer.

CD2,TR22

1. (a.) Aisha was supposed to interview an instructor and students.
   b. Aisha wasn't supposed to interview an instructor and students.

2. a. She was supposed to check the facts before the interview.
   b. She wasn't supposed to check the facts before the interview.

3. a. She was supposed to have all her questions ready, and she did.
   b. She wasn't supposed to have all her questions ready, but she did.

4. a. She was supposed to ask questions with "yes" or "no" answers.
   b. She wasn't supposed to ask questions with "yes" or "no" answers.

5. a. She wasn't supposed to ask for details, but she did.
   b. She was supposed to ask for details, but she didn't.

6. a. She wasn't supposed to disagree, and she didn't.
   b. She wasn't supposed to disagree, but she did.

7. a. She was supposed to ask for permission, but she didn't.
   b. She wasn't supposed to ask for permission, but she did.

F **PAIR WORK** Student A, look at the Journalism I Schedule on the bottom of this page. Student B, look at page 302. Take turns with your partner. Complete the schedule. Use *be supposed to* and ask a question. Your partner will answer. Follow the model.

> Was Li supposed to interview the psychology professor yesterday?

> When is she supposed to interview him?

> I don't think so. She was supposed to *prepare* for the interview yesterday.

> Today.

Student A: Questions

1. Sadie/take photographs of the culture fair/tomorrow?
2. Sadie/lay out the photos/today?
3. Ali/review the articles for spelling and punctuation/today?
4. Ali/edit the final copy of next week's paper/tomorrow?
5. Ali/send next week's paper to the printer/today?

Student A: Journalism I Schedule

	Yesterday	Today	Tomorrow
Li	prepare for interview with psychology professor	interview psychology professor	write story on basketball game
Gerd	review letters from readers	write summary of readers' comments	ask Ali to review summary
Sadie			
Ali			

GRAMMAR AND VOCABULARY Fill in the blanks using *should, should not, ought to, had better, be supposed to,* and the words in the box.

~~journalist~~   ethics   make up   reporter   opinions   blogs   accurate   media

A: Hey, Bruce, did you learn all about good journalism in your class?

B: I sure did. There are some pretty strict rules to follow. For example,

a _____*journalist*_____ (1) _____ (2) be able to write well,

and _____ (3) _____ (4) stories. Also, a

_____ (5) _____ (6) steal another reporter's story. It's

not good _____ (7). A newspaper story _____ (8) be

_____ (9) in order to give readers the correct facts.

A: I know that rule, but we often find _____ (10) in the

_____ (11), even when it _____ (12) be factual news.

B: Right. We talked about that and compared different stories. We also talked

about new forms of journalism like _____ (13). The most important

rule there is: People _____ (14) be fair and polite.

PROJECT Write a letter to a newspaper.

1. Get a copy of the school newspaper or a local city newspaper. Read through some of the articles on the opinion page. Notice the style of the writing.
2. Work with a partner. Choose one of the topics here or another important topic at your school (for example, smoking on campus, dress code, free speech).
3. Discuss the topic and your opinions about the issues. Take a position.
4. Write a letter to your school or city paper. State your position and explain the reasons for your position. Use the grammar from this lesson.
5. In your class, vote on the three best letters.

 INTERNET Use the topic from your Project. Find out about it on the "blogosphere." Enter "blog" and "(your topic)" into a search engine. Take notes on some of the interesting opinions. Report to your class.

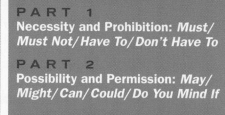

PART 1
Necessity and Prohibition: *Must/
Must Not/Have To/Don't Have To*

PART 2
Possibility and Permission: *May/
Might/Can/Could/Do You Mind If*

Lesson (22)

Accounting:
Money and Taxes

■ CONTENT VOCABULARY

Look at the picture. Do you know the words?

$5,000 + $3,000 = $8,000

a sum

$6,000 − $500

to subtract

taxes = 17% of income − child care expenses

a formula

receipts

April 14

taxes

Write the new words in your vocabulary journal.

■ THINK ABOUT IT

In your writing journal, write for five minutes about any of these questions: Do you or your family have to pay income taxes? How do you figure out your taxes? How often do you have to pay taxes?

■ GRAMMAR IN CONTENT

A **Read and listen.**

CD2,TR23

Accounting Lesson Review

Professor: OK, let's review our lesson on taxes. How do we use the tax formula?

Student 1: First, we **have to add** all of the annual salary. And we **must not forget** about any extra wages or income. Then, we **have to subtract** expenses, like business or medical expenses.

Student 2: We also **have to subtract** the other type of deductions: payroll taxes. The employer takes those from a person's salary.

Student 3: I remember Mr. and Mrs. Brown in our textbook case study. They **had to pay** $5,000 in taxes because it was 17 percent of their annual income after all allowable deductions.

Student 2: OK, but **do** people always **have to send** money to the government? **Must** they always **pay**?

Professor: That's a good question. **Did** the Browns **have to send** a check to the government?

Student 3: No, they **didn't have to send** any money. The government **had to give** the Browns a refund. The sum of the monthly tax deductions taken from their salary was more than the 17 percent they **had to pay**. The formula showed us that.

a deduction: money subtracted

B **Look at the conversation.**

1. Look at the modals and phrasal modals in bold. What is the time reference of

   must? ___ present ___ past

2. What tense is ***have to?*** ___ present ___ past

3. What tense is ***had to?*** ___ present ___ past

4. What phrasal modal do we use for the past form of ***must?*** _____

Function	Form	Examples
Affirmative		
Present or Future Necessity	***have to/must*** + simple verb	We **have to add** the annual salary. We **must subtract** any deductions.
Past Necessity	***had to*** + simple verb	We **had to subtract** deductions. They **had to add** the annual salary.
Negative		
Present Necessity Past Necessity Prohibition	***doesn't/don't have to*** + simple verb ***didn't have to*** + simple verb ***must not*** + simple verb	They **don't have to pay.** They **didn't have to pay.** We **must not forget** about wages.
Questions		
Present Necessity	***do/does*** + subject + ***have to*** + simple verb ***must*** + subject + simple verb	**Do** we **have to send** money today? **Do** we **have to pay** next year? **Must** they always **pay**? **Must** we **pay** next month?
Past Necessity	***did*** + subject + ***have to*** + simple verb	**Did** they **have to send** a check? **Did** they always **have to pay**?

Notes:

- Don't use ***must*** for the function of past necessity:
  Incorrect: ~~I must complete my taxes yesterday.~~   Correct: *I **had to complete** my taxes yesterday.*
- *Must* is stronger and more formal than *have to*.
- **Don't have to** means the subject doesn't need to do something. Example: *You **don't have to** take that class.* **Must not/mustn't** means the subject is not allowed to do something. Example: *You **must not lie** on the tax form.*

C (Circle) **the correct answer. Discuss with your class.**

1. College students ((have to) / don't have to) pay taxes if they work.
2. An accountant (must / doesn't have to) be good with numbers.
3. I (have to / don't have to) pay sales tax when I buy something where I live.
4. My parents (didn't have to / had to) give me money last year.
5. I (had to / didn't have to) pay income taxes last year.
6. I (must / must not / don't have to) keep the receipts when I buy something.

D Listen to the accountant discuss the qualifications for his job, and check the box that expresses what the accountant says about each point.

	must	must not	doesn't have to
speak to the class			
be good at math	✔		
like working with numbers			
work extra hours			
check math			
make mistakes			
take gifts			
speak in front of groups			

E Work with a partner to fill in the blanks with the correct form of *have to* or *must*. Use *not* where needed.

Masami: Hey, Robert, tomorrow is the last day of your accounting class, isn't it?

Robert: That's right. I _____have to_____ finish my final paper tonight. It's
(1)

due early tomorrow morning.

Masami: Do you _____ write many papers for that class?
(2)

Robert: Well, for the midterm we _____ write one five-page
(3)

report on the annual taxes of a company. And we _____
(4)

turn in this paper on accounting ethics tomorrow.

Masami: I wanted to take that class this semester, but I _____
(5)

complete my math requirement first. Now, I can start taking the

accounting classes for my major. So, were the tests difficult?

Robert: Well, you know, I _____ study too hard because my dad
(6)

is an accountant and he taught me a lot.

Masami: Are you going to get a good grade?

Robert: I'm not sure. Professor Lim gave me a deduction for one late

assignment, so I _____ get a good grade on this paper.
(7)

■ **COMMUNICATE**

F **PAIR WORK** Student A, use the information on this page. Student B, turn to page 302. Take turns with your partner. Ask a question about the Accounting 101 syllabus. Your partner will answer. Use *must/have to/must not.*

Do students have to bring their textbooks to every class?

Yes, they do. They have to bring their textbooks and their notebooks to every class. They must not forget them.

Student A:
Questions

1. turn papers in on time?
2. use tax formulas in the papers?
3. underline the title?
4. type the papers?
5. see a tutor about the papers?
6. write an outline?
7. edit for grammar?
8. work with a partner?

Syllabus Information

- textbook and notebook in every class
- calculator in every class
- punctual and regular attendance
- no make-up tests
- no cell phones in class
- participate in class discussions

■ GRAMMAR IN CONTENT

A Read and listen.

CD2,TR25

Accounting Film

Professor:	OK, everybody, we're going to watch a film. You will see Mrs. Ramadji, an accountant, helping Mr. Brown with his taxes.
Student:	**Can** we **take** notes during the film?
Professor:	Of course you **can.**

Mrs. Ramadji:	Well, Mr. Brown, I looked at all your tax forms and your information.
Mr. Brown:	Yes, Mrs. Ramadji, and **can** I **get** a refund?
Mrs. Ramadji:	Well, you **could get** a refund, but I have to figure out a few things. We **might have** a better chance with some deductions. I **couldn't find** any deductions here. Did you use your car for work at all?
Mr. Brown:	Yes, but I **may not have** any receipts for the expenses.
Mrs. Ramadji:	I see. **Could** those receipts **be** at home somewhere?
Mr. Brown:	Um, maybe they are at home. Yeah, it's possible. They **may be** in my home office. **Do you mind if** I call you tonight to tell you?

B (Circle) the correct answer.

1. Mr. Brown (will get / might get) a refund.
2. Mrs. Ramadji (found / didn't find) any deductions.
3. Mr. Brown (doesn't have / might have) some receipts for his car expenses.

May/Might/Can/Could: Possibility

Affirmative

may/might/can/could + simple verb	They **may/might be** at home. You **can/could get** a refund.

Negative

may/might/can/could + *not* + simple verb	I **may/might not have** any receipts. You **can't get** a refund.

Questions

can/could/might + subject + simple verb	**Can/Could/Might** I **get** a refund?

May/Might/Can/Could/Do You Mind If: Permission

Affirmative

may/can + simple verb	You **may/can deduct** child care.

Negative

may/can + *not* + simple verb	You **cannot use** my car. You **may not leave** class early.

Questions

may/might/can/could/do you mind if + subject + simple verb	Very Formal: **May/Might** I **leave** class early? Formal: **Do you mind if** I **leave** class early? Informal: **Can/Could** I **use** your car?

Notes:

- Don't confuse *may be* with *maybe: may be* = verb / *maybe* = adverb
- Don't use *may* for questions about possibility or statements about past possibility.

  Incorrect: ~~*May* you get a refund? No, I already tried, but I *may not.*~~

  Correct: *Can* you get a refund? No, I already tried, but I *couldn't.*

C Listen to the six short dialogs. For each one, check whether the speaker is talking about a possibility or permission.

1. ___ Possibility   ✔ Permission
2. ___ Possibility   ___ Permission
3. ___ Possibility   ___ Permission
4. ___ Possibility   ___ Permission
5. ___ Possibility   ___ Permission
6. ___ Possibility   ___ Permission

D Work with a partner. For each situation, write a question to ask for permission. You want to . . .

1. write a story about your instructor.

   Do you mind if I write a story about you?

2. interview your classmate about his or her country.

   _____

3. move your classmate's backpack to sit down at a desk.

   _____

4. leave class early to go to the doctor.

   _____

5. take a photograph of the school president for the newspaper.

   _____

6. borrow five dollars from your friend.

   _____

E Find the errors and correct them. There are seven errors.

Majid: Did you meet with the career counselor yesterday about your accounting classes?

Jackson: No, she ~~may not~~ *couldn't* see me. She couldn't have enough time.

Majid: May she see you tomorrow?

Jackson: Well, I couldn't see her tomorrow because I have to work after my classes. But I maybe get an appointment for Friday.

Majid: You know, I already talked to my counselor about the accounting major requirements. I got a lot of information.

Jackson: Do you mind I ask you a few questions?

Majid: No, I don't mind. May be I can help you.

F **PAIR WORK** **Work with your partner. Discuss possibility and permission for each situation. Use** *have to/must/can/could/may/might.*

Mary must get $50 to pay for her books. She might borrow it from her parents.

Right, and she can't write a check until she adds $50 to her bank account.

1. Mary has $100 in the bank. She needs $150 for books this semester.
2. Simon wanted to buy a car last year, but he didn't save enough money.
3. If Ruoyi works this summer, she won't have to ask her parents for money.
4. If Clark doesn't get a loan, he won't have enough money for tuition.
5. If Susan writes a good essay for the contest, she will win $1,000 for college costs.
6. Abra tried to register for an accounting class, but she still needs to complete her math requirements.
7. Janek wants to work in the college bank, but they have no openings right now.
8. Pablo can't decide on a major. He likes accounting, but he also likes marketing.

GRAMMAR AND VOCABULARY Fill in the blanks with the correct form of the words from the box or a modal from the lesson.

taxes	subtract	salary	deduction	percent	refund
sum	receipt	formula	income	~~adds~~	

1. When Sarah _____*adds*_____ $250 + $364, she gets this

   _____: $614.

2. Liam _____ get a _____ when he returned his

   accounting book because he didn't have his _____.

3. If you don't work, you don't _____ pay income

   _____.

4. If you _____ pay the full price, you _____ pay 100

   _____.

5. I _____ figure out this accounting problem. I don't know the

   correct _____.

6. Every year Marisa takes a week to work on her _____ taxes.

7. Her _____ is low, so she _____ pay a lot in taxes.

8. You _____ show your formula for the accounting test. If you

   don't, the teacher will give you a _____ in your points.

9. If you _____ taxes from your salary, you will know the amount
   you actually take home.

PROJECT Lia and her parents did not pay their taxes for two years because they didn't have enough money. Now, the government wants them to pay $5,000 plus 7% of all their income for the past two years. They don't have this money. What can they do? Discuss possible solutions in a small group.

 INTERNET Look up "Accounting Major" on a college website. What classes do you *have to* take? What classes *can* you take? Share the information with your class.

Physical Education: Health and Fitness

■ CONTENT VOCABULARY

Look at the pictures. Do you know the words?

stretching

sit-ups

a treadmill

I feel strong and healthy.

CITY GYM

a muscle

a weight

push-ups

a benefit

to exercise/to work out

Write the new words in your vocabulary journal.

■ THINK ABOUT IT

In your writing journal, write for five minutes about any of these questions: How often do you exercise? What kinds of exercise do you like? Do you prefer to exercise indoors or outdoors?

■ GRAMMAR IN CONTENT

A **Read and listen.**

CD2,TR27

Stretching

Professor:	As we discussed in our first class, exercise has many benefits. **Can someone tell us about those benefits, please?**
James:	If I have a good fitness plan, I'll have stronger muscles.
Carol:	When we develop good habits, we can improve our posture, decrease our weight, and increase our self-esteem.
Professor:	That's right. So, we're going to begin our class today with a new stretching exercise. **Will you please pay attention?** First, I'll do the exercise. Now you try it.
Tina:	**Would you mind showing us one more time?** I couldn't see it.
Professor:	Leo, Rob, and Maria, **would you all move to the left?** Thank you. Now, **can you see me**, Tina?
Tina:	Yes, thank you. **Could you please repeat the exercise?** I'll be able to see it.
Professor:	All right. So here it is again, everyone.

self-esteem: a positive feeling about oneself; confidence

posture: how you hold your body when you sit or stand

B **Look at the conversation.**

1. Circle the modals and phrasal modals. Find the verbs after the modals and phrasal modals. Which verb form is different from the others? Write the sentence here.

    _____

2. There are two sentences in the reading that contain ***can.*** One is a request and the other asks about a possibility. Write them here.

    Request: _____

    Possibility: _____

Polite Requests: *Can/Could/Will/Would/Would You Mind?*

Requests	Responses
Polite	**Agree**
Could you (please) repeat the exercise?	Yes, I can./Yes, of course.
Can you (please) tell us about those benefits?	Sure./No problem.
	Refuse
Would you mind showing us one more time (please)?	No, I can't.
Would you (please) all move to the left?	I'm sorry, I can't.
Direct **Will you** (please) pay attention?	

Notes:

- Use a gerund after *would you mind,* for example, *Would you mind closing the door?*
- Make a request more polite by adding *please* and other words, for example,

  Will you pay attention? = very direct. *Would you pay more attention, please?* = more polite

- Don't use *could* to respond to a request unless you mean possibility, for example,

  A: Could you lend me your notes?   *B: I could, but only when I finish with them.*

- Don't use *may* in polite requests.

  Incorrect: ~~*May you help me with this problem?*~~   Correct: *Could you help me with this problem?*

C **Work with a partner. Read the situation. Using an appropriate modal or modal phrase, write a request.**

1. You want to use the treadmill, but someone is using it right now.

   Will you please tell me when you are finished?

2. You want tips from your gym instructor about good stretching exercises.

   _____

3. You want your professor to give you a make-up test.

   _____

4. You were absent yesterday, and your classmate takes good class notes.

   _____

5. You have a difficult writing assignment. You are with a tutor in the Writing Center.

   _____

6. You are at the financial aid office. You don't have any information.

   _____

D (Circle) the correct word for requests and possibility.

1. **A:** ((Will) / Wouldn't) you show us the stretching exercises?
   B: Yes, (can / could) you all see me now?

2. **A:** (Could / Can) you see the instructor when she gave the instructions?
   B: Yes, I (can / could).

3. **A:** (Would / Could) you mind holding my feet while I do my sit-ups?
   B: I'm sorry, I (can't / couldn't). I have to go to class.

4. **A:** (Could / May) you please speak more loudly? I can't hear you.
   B: Sure. (Can / Could) you hear me now?

5. **A:** (Would / Can) I borrow your dictionary?
   B: Well, (can / may) you wait until I finish?

6. **A:** (Can / May) you check my time while I run?
   B: I'm sorry I (couldn't / can't). I don't have a watch.

7. **A:** (Can / Could) Tim run today?
   B: No, he (can't / couldn't). The track is closed.

8. **A:** (Could / Will) you wait for me?
   B: No, I'm sorry, I (can't / couldn't). I'm late for an appointment.

■ **C O M M U N I C A T E**

E **PAIR WORK** Work with a partner. Take turns. Use a modal or phrasal modal and the words to make a request. Use *I* or *you* as the subject. Your partner will answer with a modal or phrasal modal to express affirmative or negative possibility.

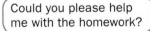 Could you please help me with the homework?

 I'm sorry. I don't understand it either, so I can't help you.

1. help/homework
2. explain/benefits of the treadmill
3. help/work out
4. tell about/fitness assignment

5. give/advice about a fitness plan
6. show/new exercises
7. lend/book
8. ask about/yesterday's class

■ GRAMMAR IN CONTENT

A Read and listen.

CD2,TR28

Fitness Plan

Alisa: Professor, could I speak to you about my fitness plan?

Professor: Sure, Alisa, come in. What are you having trouble with?

Alisa: You gave us a lot of choices, but I don't really like to exercise. I like reading better than exercising. Also, I'm very busy, so I don't have time to exercise.

Professor: I see. Well, **would you prefer to exercise** in the morning **or** in the evening?

Alisa: I **prefer not to exercise.** However, if I have to choose, **I'd prefer to do** it in the morning.

Professor: OK. **Would you rather exercise** at home **or** outside your home?

Alisa: **I'd rather do** something outside, like take a walk, for example, but I don't have time. I need to do something quick.

Professor: Well then, you don't have a lot of choices. You can start with five minutes every morning. So **would you rather do** sit-ups or push-ups?

Alisa: **I'd rather do** sit-ups **than** push-ups.

B Look at the dialog.

1. There are three questions asking about preferences. Write them here.

   _____?

   _____?

   _____?

2. Is ***prefer*** followed by an infinitive or gerund or both?

   ___ infinitive   ___ gerund   ___ both

   Is ***rather*** followed by a base form or gerund or both?

   ___ base form   ___ gerund   ___ both

Preferences: *Like/Would Like/Prefer/Would Prefer/Would Rather*

Questions

Do you Would you	prefer like	to exercise at home or outside of your home? to do sit-ups or push-ups?
Would you rather		exercise at home or outside of your home? do sit-ups or push-ups?

Statements

	like	exercising at home **better than working out** at the gym. to exercise at home.
I	would like	to do sit-ups.
	prefer would prefer	to exercise at home. exercising at home *to working out* at the gym. sit-ups *to* push-ups. not to exercise.
	would rather	exercise at home. do sit-ups **than** push-ups. not do sit-ups.

Notes:

- In general, use a contraction for speaking: *I would = I'd*
- Don't use *to* after *rather*. Incorrect: ~~I'd rather to swim.~~ Correct: *I'd rather swim.* Don't forget *would* before *rather.* Incorrect: ~~I rather exercise.~~ Correct: *I'd rather exercise.*
- After *would rather,* use *or* in questions and *than* in statements, for example, *Would you rather swim or play tennis? I would rather swim than play tennis.*
- When you add *would,* the statement of preference is more polite and more indirect, for example, *I would prefer not to exercise.* (polite, indirect) *I prefer not to exercise.* (direct)
- *Prefer* and *like* can also take gerunds (as well as infinitives). For example, *I prefer swimming to playing tennis. I like hiking in the mountains and biking at the seashore.*

C Complete the sentences with truthful information about your health and fitness. Then write a paragraph in your notebook about your present habits and preferences. Include changes that you would like to make.

1. I prefer _____ to _____.

2. I like _____ better than _____.

3. I would rather _____ than _____.

4. I would prefer not to _____.

D Listen and (circle) the correct answer to the question.

1. a. I'd like to go swimming.
   b. I like to go swimming.

2. a. I like to play tennis.
   b. I'd like to play tennis.

3. a. I would like to hike.
   b. I like hiking.

4. a. I'd rather lift weights than ride a bike.
   b. I'd rather lifting weights than riding a bike.

5. a. No, I prefer to exercise in the evening.
   b. No, I would like to exercise in the morning.

6. a. No, I like to do some push-ups.
   b. No, I'd like to do some push-ups.

E The graph shows fitness choices for college students. Work with a partner to write sentences that explain the choices.

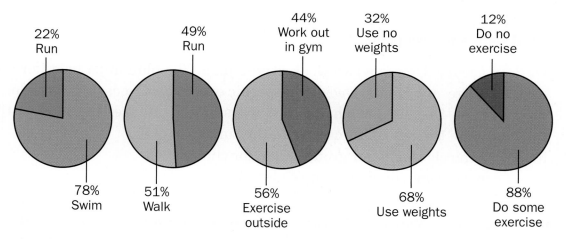

1. _78% of the students would rather swim than run._

2. _____

3. _____

4. _____

5. _____

F PAIR WORK Take turns asking a classmate about his or her preferences. Practice the different forms you have learned in this lesson.

Would you rather swim or run?   I prefer swimming to running.

Connection | Putting It Together

GRAMMAR AND VOCABULARY Write a paragraph about your health and fitness. Discuss your habits for exercise, sleep, and relaxation. State your preferences and explain your habits. Use the vocabulary from the lesson.

PROJECT Create a fitness plan.

1. Work in groups. Create a two-week fitness plan. The plan must be different from your present habits. Decide on specific exercises. Choose times to do the exercises. Discuss sleep habits and ways to relax. Write your plan on the calendar. Use the left column to write the times.
2. Report to the class on your group's plan for changes.
3. If you can, try some of your group's ideas.

Times	Sunday	Monday	Tuesday	Wednesday	Thursday	Friday	Saturday
6:00		walk		walk		walk	

 INTERNET Enter "fitness plan" into a search engine. Get some tips on a personal fitness plan. In your journal, summarize what you learned and state your preferences.

PART 1
Present Perfect: Statements/
Questions/Short Answers

PART 2
Ever/Never/Not Ever

Lesson 24

Nursing I: Basic Skills

■ CONTENT VOCABULARY

Look at the pictures. Do you know the words?

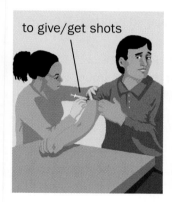

to give/get shots

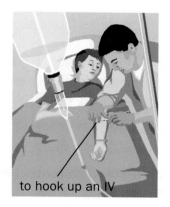

to hook up an IV

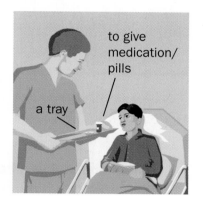

to give medication/pills

a tray

an accident

an ambulance

to give/perform CPR

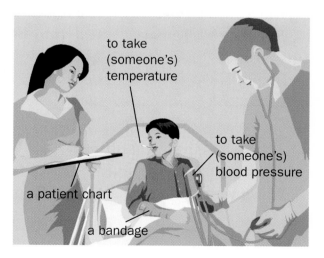

to take (someone's) temperature

to take (someone's) blood pressure

a patient chart

a bandage

Write the new words in your vocabulary journal.

■ THINK ABOUT IT

In your writing journal, write what you know about nursing and hospital care.

■ GRAMMAR IN CONTENT

CD2, TR30

A Read and listen.

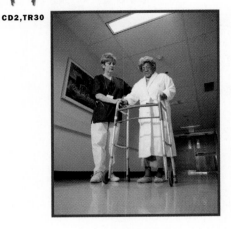

a clinical practice: nursing practice at a hospital

First Experiences

Masami:	Hey Paula, where **have** you **been** all day?
Paula:	I**'ve been** at the hospital.
Masami:	Oh, that's right. Your nursing class has clinical practice every Thursday, doesn't it?
Paula:	Yeah, we**'ve been** to the hospital three times this semester.
Masami:	**Has** it **been** interesting? **Have** you **done** well?
Paula:	I think so. I**'ve taken** patients' blood pressure, and I**'ve given** out medication. I**'ve** also **changed** bandages. I**'ve enjoyed** it.
Masami:	**Has** Alicia **gone** through the same program?
Paula:	Yes, she has, but she**'s been** in a different group. We **haven't had** a chance to work together at the hospital.

B Look at the dialog. The present perfect verb forms are in bold. Fill in the base form and past tense form for the past participle form.

Base Form	Past Tense	Past Participle	Base Form	Past Tense	Past Participle
_____	_____	been	_____	_____	had
_____	_____	gone	_____	_____	changed
_____	_____	done	_____	_____	taken
_____	_____	given	_____	_____	enjoyed

Which verbs have the same form for past tense and past participle?

_____

Present Perfect Tense

Affirmative/Negative Statements

Subject	*Have*	Past Participle	Object
I/You/We/They	have/have not	taken	the patient's blood pressure.
He/She/It	has/has not		
There	has/has not	been	an accident.
	have/have not		serious problems.

Yes/No Questions   Short Answers

Have/ Has	Subject	Past Participle	Object	*Yes/ No*	Subject	*Have/ Has (Not)*
Have	I/you/we/they	enjoyed	the class?	Yes,/ No,	I/you/ we/they	have/haven't.
Has	he/she/it	been	in class?	Yes,/ No,	he/ she/it	has/hasn't.
Has	there	been	an accident?	Yes,/ No,	there	has/hasn't.
Have			any problems?	Yes,/ No,	there	have/haven't.

Wh- Questions

Wh-	*Has/Have*	Subject	Past Participle
Where	has	she	gone?
What	have	they	taken?
How many	have	there	been?

Note:

Use present perfect tense to show (1) completed action sometime in the past, for example, *I have taken that class.* OR (2) action that started sometime in the past, continues to the present, and projects into the future, for example, *I've enjoyed the clinical practice so far.* OR (3) repeated action sometime in the past, for example, *There have been three accidents.*

Common Irregular Verbs		
Base Form	**Past Tense**	**Past Participle**
be	was	been
go	went	gone
do	did	done
have	had	had
take	took	taken
bring	brought	brought
give	gave	given
(mis)understand	(mis)understood	(mis)understood

Note:
- See Appendix 3 for a more complete list of verb forms.

C **Complete the paragraph about Ramon's clinical practice. Use the present perfect form (affirmative or negative) of the verbs in parentheses.**

Ramon (go) ___*has gone*___ to the hospital twice for his class. So far, there
(1)

(not/be) _____ any serious problems for him. Each time, the experience
(2)

(teach) _____ him many important lessons about helping patients. He
(3)

(take) _____ patients' blood pressure and (give) _____
(4)   (5)

them medications, but he (not/hook up) _____ IVs for patients. He (see)
(6)

_____ patients with serious illnesses, and he (feel) _____
(7)   (8)

happy to help them. Some patients (think) _____ of him as an
(9)

experienced nurse, but he (tell) _____ them that he is a college student.
(10)

D **Listen to each conversation. Put a check mark (✔) in the blank for each thing Nadia has done.**

CD2,TR31

1. ✔ taken English composition
2. ___ completed her science classes
3. ___ finished Nursing 51
4. ___ written patient care plans
5. ___ given shots to patients
6. ___ gone to the hospital for clinical practice
7. ___ been at the hospital many times for clinical practice
8. ___ observed the instructor working with patients
9. ___ helped some patients by herself

E PAIR WORK Student A will stay on this page. Student B will turn to page 303. Take turns. Student A will use the words and ask Student B about Basha. Student B will answer by using the schedule. Follow the model.

It's 10:15. Has Basha taken patients' temperature and blood pressure?   Yes, she has.

Student A
Questions about Basha:

1. (10:15 a.m.) take patients' temperature and blood pressure?
2. (11:20 a.m.) give shots to Mr. Barsinian?
3. (12:30 p.m.) bring lunch trays to the patients?
4. (2:00 p.m.) take away lunch trays?
5. (2:15 p.m.) write report on patient care?

Ali's Schedule

6:00 a.m.	prepare medications
7:00 a.m.	check on patients
8:00 a.m.	bring breakfast trays
9:30 a.m.	pick up breakfast trays
10:30 a.m.	write new patient care plans

■ GRAMMAR IN CONTENT

A Read and listen.

CD2,TR32

Communication and Nursing

Professor: If you want to be a nurse, you must work very hard on your English skills. Can you imagine making a mistake with a patient because you misunderstood something?

Student 1: **Have** you **ever made** a mistake like that?

Professor: I don't think so. I've made little mistakes. I've forgotten to check blood pressure a few times, and I've called patients by the wrong name. But **I've never given out** the wrong medicine or **misunderstood** a medical chart.

Student 2: **Have** you **ever mixed up** two patients' charts?

Professor: No, I **haven't ever done** that either.

B Look at the conversation.

Which adverb do we use in negative statements? ___ **ever** ___ **never/not ever**
Which adverb is often used in questions? ___ **ever** ___ **never**

Ever/Never/Not Ever	
Questions	**Have** you *ever* **made** a mistake? **Has** she *ever* **done** that?
Negative Statements	She **has** *never* **made** that kind of mistake. She **hasn't** *ever* **given** the wrong pills.

Notes:
- Place *ever, never,* and *not ever* before the past participle of the verb.
- Don't confuse *ever* with *never/not ever.*
  Incorrect: ~~She has ever taken blood pressure.~~ Correct: She **has** *never* **taken** blood pressure.
  OR She **hasn't** *ever* **taken** blood pressure.

C **Work with a partner. Use the words provided to discuss the student nurse's experience. Write a question with *ever*. Use *never* or *not ever* in your answer and state what the nurse has done after the "but." Follow the model.**

1. (take) patient's blood pressure/patient's temperature

    Question: _Has she ever taken a patient's blood pressure?_

    Answer: _No, she's never taken a patient's blood pressure, but she's taken a patient's temperature._

2. (write) report on the health of a patient/care plan for a patient

    Question: _____

    Answer: _____

    _____

3. (hook up) IV for a patient/computer for a child in the hospital

    Question: _____

    Answer: _____

    _____

4. (misunderstand) a doctor's order/a patient's request

    Question: _____

    Answer: _____

    _____

5. (give) CPR to a patient/a patient shots

    Question: _____

    Answer: _____

    _____

6. (help) a patient in an ambulance/a patient at home

    Question: _____

    Answer: _____

    _____

7. (be afraid) to make a mistake/to make the wrong decision

Question: _____

Answer: _____

_____

D Correct the errors in Masami's nursing journal. There are 12 more errors.

> completed
> I've finally ~~complete~~ my Nursing 101 Clinical Practice. There has
>   ^
>
> being many interesting experiences. My group has went to the hospital
>
> six times, and during that time we have worked with many nice
>
> patients. I taken their blood pressure, giving them their medicine,
>
> and hear their stories. Now, I ask myself: "What I learned in these six
>
> weeks? Have I fell confident as a nurse? Have I been ever afraid
>
> about making mistakes?" I have three thoughts: First, I haven't never
>
> done anything like this for other people. Second, my family has ever
>
> seen me so confident. Third, I have find a new respect for all nurses
>
> because it is not any easy job. I am very proud to be in the program.

E Fill in the blanks using the verbs in the box. Use the correct present perfect form. Add *ever* or *never* when given. Use each word only once.

take	see	explain	warn	choose
tell	~~begin~~	give	write	check

Finally, Maria ___ *has begun* ___ the nursing program at City College,

(1)

and she is very enthusiastic. She (never) _____ anyone's blood

(2)

pressure or _____ medications. However, she _____

(3) (4)

her brother's temperature a few times when he _____ sick with the

(5)

flu. She (not ever) _____ a health care plan or a patient report, but

(6)

she _____ a few of these because her mother is a nurse. Her mother

(7)

_____ the importance of good language skills in nursing. Also, her

(8)

mother _____ Maria many stories about her experiences as a nurse.

(9)

Has her mother (ever) _____ Maria about the difficulty of being a

(10)

nurse? Yes, she has, but Maria _____ this major anyway.

(11)

■ COMMUNICATE

F **PAIR WORK** Use the words and follow the model. Ask your partner a question. Your partner will answer the question and add a sentence with *but.*

Have you ever made a serious mistake?   No, I haven't ever made a serious mistake, but I've made little mistakes. For example, once I . . .

1. make a serious mistake?
2. work in a hospital?
3. meet an unfriendly nurse?
4. feel afraid of getting a shot?
5. need a nurse at home?
6. want to be a nurse?
7. go to the hospital in an ambulance?
8. have a bad accident?

GRAMMAR AND VOCABULARY Work with a partner. Fill in the blanks with the correct present perfect form of the vocabulary.

| give/get shots | misunderstand | call an ambulance |
| hook up an IV | give someone medication | |

1. **A:** Mrs. Wilson might have a fever. _____ you

   _____?

   B: Yes, _____.

2. **A:** _____ you ever _____

   a doctor's order and _____ the wrong _____

   _____?

   B: No, _____.

3. **A:** Flu season is here. The nurses at the College Health Center

   _____ to many instructors and students.

   _____ you _____ your shot?

   B: No, _____.

4. **A:** The patient can't eat solid food, but I don't think you can help him, Stefan.

   _____ you ever _____?

   B: No, _____.

PROJECT In a group, make a list of different problems that nurses might experience. Exchange your list with another group and brainstorm solutions.

 INTERNET Look up a college nursing program online. What courses does a first-year student have to take? What courses has a second-year student completed? Share with your class.

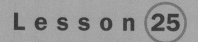
English Composition: The Research Paper

■ CONTENT VOCABULARY

Look at the pictures. Do you know the words?

an outline

the first draft

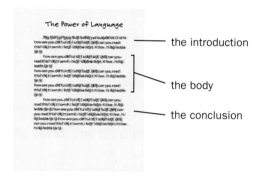

the introduction

the body

the conclusion

the final draft

the writing process

Write the new words in your vocabulary journal.

■ THINK ABOUT IT

In your writing journal, write for five minutes about any of these questions: Have you ever read or written a research paper in your first language? If yes, what was the topic? Do you know the steps normally taken in writing a research paper? What are they?

■ GRAMMAR IN CONTENT

CD2,TR33

A Read and listen.

a **shortage**: an inadequate amount

Office Hour

Professor:	Hi, Lee. Have you **just arrived?** I was worried about being late.
Lee:	No, that's OK. My class finished late today.
Professor:	So, how is your research paper going, Lee? Have you decided on a topic **yet?**
Lee:	Yes, I've **just** decided to write about the nursing shortage. I've **already** looked on the library database and found some useful information.
Professor:	Well, that's a good start. Have you **already** written your first draft?
Lee:	No, I haven't done that **yet**, but I've written my outline.
Professor:	OK, then you've **already** completed three steps in the process. Let's mark those on your checklist.

B The words in bold are time words used with the present perfect tense.

1. Which words do you find in questions? ___ already ___ yet ___ just

2. Which word(s) do you find in negative statements? ___ already ___ yet ___ just

3. Which word(s) do you find in affirmative statements? ___ already ___ yet ___ just

Already/Yet/Just

Affirmative Statements

already	I've *already* written my outline.
just	I've *just* decided to write about the nursing shortage.

Negative Statements

yet	I **haven't done** that *yet.* OR I **haven't** *yet* **done** that.

Questions

already	**Have** you *already* **decided** on a topic?
yet	**Have** you **decided** on a topic *yet?*
just	**Has** he *just* **finished?**

Notes:

- Place *yet* and *already* before the past participle or at the end of the sentence. Place *just* before the past participle.
- Use *just* if the action has been completed very recently.
- Use *already/just* or *yet* to answer questions with present perfect and *ever,* for example, *Have you ever written a research paper? Yes, I've just finished my first one.* OR *No, I haven't written one yet.*
- Don't use *already* or *just* in negative statements or *yet* in affirmative statements.

  Incorrect: ~~I've written my outline yet.~~ ~~I haven't already written my outline.~~

  Correct: *I haven't written my outline yet.* OR *I've written my outline already.*

C **Work in pairs. Write questions using the correct forms of the words provided. Then write appropriate responses.**

1. **A:** you/go/to the library? (already)

   _____ Have you already gone to the library? _____

   B: (yet) _____ No, I haven't gone yet. _____

2. **A:** professor/give/the assignment? (yet)

   _____

   B: (just) _____

3. **A:** the student/write/a good draft? (yet)

   _____

   B: (already) _____

4. **A:** she/finish/her paper? (just)

   _____

   B: (yet) _____

5. **A:** the students/read/their feedback from the professor? (yet)

   _____

   B: (just) _____

6. **A:** Aisha/complete/all the steps on the checklist? (already)

   _____

   B: (yet) _____

D Listen to the short dialogs and (circle) the correct answers.

1. a. She has already started writing.
   (b.) She hasn't started writing yet.

2. a. He hasn't yet been to the library.
   b. He has already done this step.

3. a. He hasn't started his first draft yet.
   b. He has already started his first draft.

4. a. They've already done two peer reviews.
   b. They haven't done any peer reviews.

5. a. She has already finished her final draft.
   b. She hasn't yet finished her final draft.

6. a. He hasn't met with the professor yet.
   b. He has already met with the professor.

7. a. She's already written her introduction.
   b. She's already written her outline.

■ **COMMUNICATE**

E **PAIR WORK** Take turns. Student A, stay on this page. Student B, turn to page 303. Ask your partner about Adrian. Complete Adrian's checklist. Tell your partner about Sam. Use present perfect tense and *already/just/yet.*

Has Adrian chosen his topic yet?

Yes, he has already chosen his topic.

Yes, Adrian has chosen his topic already. Has Sam chosen his topic yet?

Student A
Sam's Checklist

✔ choose topic
✔ check the library database
✔ find three articles
___ write a summary of articles
✔ write an outline
✔ read feedback from the professor
✔ write the first draft
✔ meet with professor
✔ write final draft
___ edit and hand in

Adrian's Checklist

___ choose topic
___ check the library database
___ find three articles
___ write a summary of articles
___ write an outline
___ read feedback from the professor
___ write the first draft
___ meet with professor
___ write final draft
___ edit and hand in

■ GRAMMAR IN CONTENT

CD2,TR35

A Read and listen.

At the Library

Sam: Hey, Adrian, you're revising the first draft of your research paper, aren't you? **How long** have you been here?

Adrian: **I've been** here **since 3:00** this afternoon. I've read the feedback from Professor Johnson, and I've already changed some of the ideas.

Sam: How about your introduction and conclusion? Have you revised those?

Adrian: Not yet. I'm having a difficult time with them. I've worked on the introduction **for an hour** and I still don't have it right. How about you? How much have you done?

Sam: I haven't looked at the draft **since Monday,** and I haven't started my revisions. **Since I got the feedback,** I've had a cold. However, I have thought about the paper **for three days,** and now I understand the problems. Maybe I needed some time away from it.

B Look at the dialog. Find a structurally *similar* expression in bold and write it.

since Friday _____

since 4:30 _____

since she gave the assignment _____

for eight days _____

for five hours _____

Look at the time expressions above. (Circle) the word.

a. Use this word with a specific point in time: **since**   **for**
b. Use this word with a period of time: **since**   **for**

Since/For

Since + specific point in time

Day: *since Monday*	I **haven't looked** at it *since Monday.*
Time: *since 3:00*	They've **been** here *since 3:00.*
Month/Date: *since June/since June 6*	She's **had** the assignment *since June 6.*
Year: *since 2005*	They've **offered** this class *since 2005.*
Event: *since I got the feedback*	*Since* I **got** the feedback, I've **had** a cold.

For + period of time

Days: *for three days*	He **has thought** about it *for three days.*
Hours/Minutes: *for an hour/for 5 minutes*	Marty **has been** in the library *for an hour.*
Months: *for six months*	They **have lived** here *for six months.*
Years: *for one year*	I **have had** this computer *for one year.*

Notes:

- Use *since* or *for* to answer a question with *how long + present perfect,* for example, *How long have you had the assignment? We've had it for two days.*

- In a time clause, use *since* with past tense. Use present perfect in the main clause, for example, *Since* I **came** to this school, I **haven't written** a research paper.

- Don't use *since* when talking about a period of time.
  Incorrect: ~~I've thought about it since three days.~~   Correct: *I've thought about it **for three days.***

C Work with a partner to fill in the blanks with the present perfect form of *choose, take, know,* or *see* and *since* or *for.*

1. **A:** _____ Have _____ you _____ seen _____ Jared?

   B: No, I ___ haven't seen ___ him _____ since _____ Friday.

2. **A:** _____ Maria _____ any English classes yet?

   B: Yes, she _____ two classes _____ she arrived
   here.

3. **A:** How long _____ they _____ about the paper?

   B: They _____ about it _____ a week.

4. **A:** _____ Budi _____ his topic yet?

   B: Well, he _____ _____ two topics

   _____ he got the assignment.

D Write a question beginning with *How long* or *How long has it been.* Complete each sentence about yourself. Use the present perfect form of the verb and *since* or *for* with a time expression. (Use *since* in a time clause if necessary.)

1. **Q:** _How long have you been in this English class?_

   A: (be) I _have been_ in this English class _for six weeks._

2. **Q:** _____

   A: (live) I _____ in my house/apartment

   _____

3. **Q:** _____

   A: (have) I _____ my English dictionary

   _____

4. **Q:** _____

   A: (not/see) I _____ my father

   _____

5. **Q:** _____

   A: (not/write) We _____ a composition

   _____

■ C O M M U N I C A T E

E **PAIR WORK** Take turns with your partner. Use the words below. Ask a question. Begin with *"How long . . .?"* Your partner will answer. Follow the model.

(How long has John had the assignment?)   (He's had it since Tuesday.)

1. John/have/assignment? (Tuesday)
2. students/be/in the library? (2:30)
3. Saskia/live/in Japan? (4 months)
4. Ricardo/be/a tutor? (2 years)
5. Colleen/be interested in/Chinese literature? (she went to China)
6. you/be/in this class? (the first day)
7. the students/use/this book? (the beginning of the class)
8. Mira/know/about the database? (3 weeks)

GRAMMAR AND VOCABULARY Use the correct verb tense for the verb in parentheses. Choose a word from the box to fill in the other blanks.

process	feedback	database
introduction	checklist	conclusion

Tonia's research paper is due in three hours. She (complete)

_____ *has completed* _____ almost everything on her _____.
(1)

She (already/ begin) _____ her paper with
(2)

a good _____. However, she (not/revise/yet)
(3)

_____ her _____. She isn't happy with
(4)   (5)

the last sentence. Also, she (not/edit/yet) _____ her paper to
(6)

check all of the grammar and vocabulary.

She (not/enjoy) _____ every step in this
(7)

_____, but she (learn) _____ a lot. Her
(8)   (9)

favorite steps (be) _____ the _____
(10)   (11)

search and the _____ from her professor. She (appreciate)
(12)

_____ the help from her professor since she (start)
(13)

_____ the paper.
(14)

PROJECT Form teams. Give the other team a vocabulary word and a verb. They should make a sentence with the word and verb in the present perfect. Have them write it on the board and check their work. Then switch roles.

 INTERNET Go to a college library Web page. Look for information about research papers. Share one piece of interesting information with your class.

A Professor Block is helping two students in the Writing Center. Choose the correct word and write it in the blank OR write the correct form of the verb in parentheses. If there is no choice, add a word or words of your own.

Prof: OK. So you're (supposed to/have to) _____ (1) write a research paper and you (would/would rather) _____ (2) like some help. (Has/Have) _____ (3) you both (chose/chosen) _____ (4) a topic already?

S1: (May/Could) _____ (5) you help me with my topic? I (think) _____ (6) about it (for/since) _____ (7) three days. We (supposed to/have to) _____ (8) choose a topic with a strong argument, but I _____ (9) (ever/never) _____ (10) (write) _____ (11) this type of research paper, so I (am/would) _____ (12) rather not (choose/choosing) _____ (13) a difficult topic.

Prof: First, you (ought to/would rather) _____ (14) decide on a topic you're interested in.

S1: Well, one of the topics is taxes, but I (had better/have) _____ (15) not (choose/to choose) _____ (16) that one because I am really not interested in it.

Prof: That's right. Also, you should (to explore/explore) _____ (17) a topic that you _____ (18) (ever/never) _____ (19) (read) _____ (20) about before. If you do that, you'll learn something new.

B Sanji is interviewing the Dean of Nursing for the school newspaper. Choose the correct word OR write the correct form of the verb in parentheses. If there is no choice, add a word or words of your own.

Sanji: Hi, Dean Sanford. I am (supposed to/have to) _____ (1) do an interview for the school newspaper. _____ (2) you answer some questions for me?

Dean: Yes, I (may/can) _____ (3) do that.

Sanji: OK. (will you/could you) _____ (4) speak loudly? I (have) _____ (5) this tape recorder (for/since) _____ (6) a long time, so the sound isn't the best. So, how long _____ (7) you (work) _____ (8) as the Dean of Nursing?

Dean: I (begin) _____ (9) in 2005, so I (be) _____ (10) here (for/since) _____ (11) two years.

Sanji: Before you (take) _____ (12) this position, _____ (13) you (work) _____ (14) as a nurse?

Dean: Yes, I _____ (15). I (work) _____ (16) as a school nurse for 10 years, and then in 1998, I (take) _____ (17) a position at Hilton Hospital. Yes, I (rather/would rather) _____ (18) help nursing students _____ (19) treat patients myself.

LEARNER LOG Check (✔) *Yes* or *I Need More Practice.*

Lesson	I Can Use . . .	Yes	I Need More Practice
21	*Should/Ought To/Had Better, Be Supposed To*		
22	*Must/Must Not/Have To/Don't Have To, May/Might/Can/Could/ Do You Mind If*		
23	*Can/Could/Will/Would/Would You Mind?, Like/Would Like/Prefer/ Would Prefer/Would Rather*		
24	Present Perfect Tense, *Ever/Never/Not Ever*		
25	*Already/Yet/Just, Since/For*		

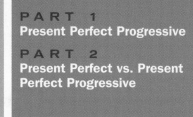

PART 1
Present Perfect Progressive

PART 2
Present Perfect vs. Present
Perfect Progressive

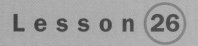

Lesson 26

Sociology:
The Impact of
the Internet

■ CONTENT VOCABULARY

Look at the pictures. Do you know the words?

an online interaction   a personal/face-to-face interaction

Write the new words in your vocabulary journal.

■ THINK ABOUT IT

In your writing journal, write for five minutes about any of these questions: Do you use the Internet? If you do, how long have you been using it? If you do not, why not? In your opinion, how has the Internet changed your life?

■ GRAMMAR IN CONTENT

A **Read and listen.**

CD2,TR36

Internet Use

People **have been using** computers to communicate since 1969. This was the year of the first computer-to-computer message with a network called ARPANET. It took many years after that to develop the Internet, and in the early 1990s people began using e-mail every day. For over 15 years, we **have been sending** e-mail to communicate with our friends and family. In 1992, we also began to buy things over the Internet. Since the 1990s, people **have been purchasing** everything from books to pianos online. In 1996, the first online newspaper appeared. Since that time, we **have been reading** our news, **checking** the weather, and **getting** sports information on the Internet. Since 1995, college professors **have been teaching** classes online, and students **have been doing** research online for a long time. For many years, the Internet **has been affecting** our lives. However, **has** the Internet **been affecting** us in negative ways? What kind of impact **has** the Internet **been having** on our activities and our relationships?

an impact: an influence, effect

a network: system of connected communication lines

B **Look at the reading. The verbs in bold are present perfect progressive tense.**

1. Look at the verbs in bold. How is the present perfect progressive tense formed?

   Fill in the blanks to complete the rule:

   Use the auxiliary: _____ + past participle of *be:* _____ + the _____ ending on the main verb.

2. Which time expressions do you see with the past tense?

   _____ _____

   Which time expressions do you see with the present perfect progressive?

   _____ _____ _____

Present Perfect Progressive Tense

Affirmative/Negative

Subject	*Have*	*Been*	Present Participle	(Object)	(Time Word/Phrase)
I/You/ We/They	have/ have not	been	sending	e-mail	since 1992/since it started. for 15 years. lately/recently. in recent months/years. in the past (two) days.
He/She/ It	has/ has not				

Yes/No Questions   Short Answers

Have/ Has	Subject	*Been*	Present Participle	*Yes/ No*	Subject	*Have/Has* (*not*)
Have	I/you/ we/they	been	working?	Yes,/ No,	I/you/ we/they	have/ haven't.
Has	he/ she/it			Yes,/ No,	he/ she/it	has/ hasn't.

Wh- Questions

Wh-	*Has/ Have*	Subject	*Been*	Present Participle	(Object)
How long What	has have	she they	been	teaching doing?	classes online?

Notes:

- Use the present perfect progressive tense to show continuing action from the past into the present and into the future.
- Use *since* or *for* in a time expression to answer the question *How long*?
  How long **have** you **been using** the Internet? **I've been using** it for 15 years/since the early 1990s.
- Don't use present perfect progressive with a specific point in the past.
  Incorrect: ~~I have been working yesterday.~~   Correct: I **worked** yesterday. OR I **have been working** since yesterday. (if you are still working)

C Use the words given to write a question using present perfect progressive tense. Then write a true answer. Use a time expression when necessary.

1. how long/you/use/the Internet?

   Q: _How long have you been using the Internet?_

   A: _I have been using the Internet for 15 years._

2. how long/your family/use/the Internet?

   Q: _____

   A: _____

3. how/your life/change/recently?

   Q: _____

   A: _____

4. you/get/all your news/from Internet blogs?

   Q: _____

   A: _____

5. what impact/the Internet/have/on your relationships?

   Q: _____

   A: _____

6. use/the Internet/for this class?

   Q: _____

   A: _____

■ COMMUNICATE

D **PAIR WORK** Compare life before the Internet and life since the Internet. Use past tense and present perfect progressive. Use appropriate time expressions.

In the past, teachers wrote notes for students on the blackboard.

Recently, teachers have been giving students information on a website.

■ GRAMMAR IN CONTENT

CD2,TR37

A Read and listen.

Sociology Assignment

Mira: Excuse me, I have an assignment for my sociology class. Can I ask you a few questions about your use of the Internet?

Student: Sure, but I only have a few minutes before my class.

Mira: OK. **Have** you ever **used** the Internet?

Student: Of course I have. **I've been using** it for at least 10 years. **I've found** a lot of good information that way. For the past two weeks, **I've been looking** at college websites because I want to transfer. **I've looked** at 100 different websites.

Mira: So how many hours **have** you **spent** on the Internet in the last two weeks?

Student: Um, let's see, **I've** probably **worked** on this college search for 25 hours. Yeah, **I've been working** on this for about 25 hours.

Mira: And how much time **have** you **spent** with your family and friends during those two weeks? How much interaction **have** you **had** with *them*?

Student: Um, maybe 10 hours.

B Look at the dialog.

Find two verbs with completed action: _____ _____

Find two verbs with continuing action: _____ _____

Present Perfect vs. Present Perfect Progressive	
Present Perfect	**Present Perfect Progressive**
Continuing Action from Past to Present I've **worked** on this **for 25 hours.** They **have lived** there **since 2001.**	Continuing Action from Past to Present I've **been working** on this **for 25 hours.** They **have been living** there **since 2001.**
Completed Action I've **written** an e-mail.	Incomplete Action I've **been writing** an e-mail.
Specific Number (How many?) I've **looked** at 100 different websites.	No Number I've **been looking** at college websites.

Notes:

- There is little difference in meaning between the present perfect and the present perfect progressive with verbs of state (for example, **know, live, feel**) or activity (for example, **walk, use, teach**) with these time expressions: **for, since, lately, recently.**
- There is a difference in meaning with verb phrases of accomplishment (for example, *write a message, go to a chat room, bake a pie*). Compare: *I have written a message.* (completed action) and *I have been writing a message* (incomplete continuing action).
- There is also a difference in these two forms with punctual verbs (for example, *close the door, kick the ball, sneeze*). Compare: *I have closed the door.* (one complete action) and *I have been closing the door* (many repeated actions).

C Use the words given to write a question using present perfect tense. Then write an answer. Use present perfect progressive tense in the answer.

1. send a letter through postal mail (recently)

   Q: _Have you sent a letter through postal mail recently?_

   A: _No, I haven't. I've been sending messages through e-mail. OR Yes, I have. I've been sending letters to my family._

2. talk to your family on the phone (lately)

   Q: _____

   A: _____

3. use the Internet to find information (in the past six months)

   Q: _____

   A: _____

4. buy a newspaper (in the past year)

   Q: _____

   A: _____

5. meet someone in a chat room (lately)

   Q: _____

   A: _____

D Listen to the eight statements and check (✔) "Completed" if the action is completed. Check "Continuing" if the action is continuing.

CD2,TR38

	Completed	Continuing
1.	✔	_____
2.	_____	_____
3.	_____	_____
4.	_____	_____
5.	_____	_____
6.	_____	_____
7.	_____	_____
8.	_____	_____

■ COMMUNICATE

E **PAIR WORK** Use the phrases given below. Take turns with your partner. Ask a question about the impact of the Internet on people. Your partner will answer. Use the present perfect progressive and present perfect. Add information about your personal experience.

Have people been using the Internet more and more?   Yes, I think they have. They've been spending more time on the Internet. I've already spent five hours this week on the Internet.

1. use Internet more than they used to?
2. watch less TV than they did five years ago?
3. talk on the phone less than they did five years ago?
4. spend more time alone than they used to?
5. use the Internet more often than their travel agents for travel plans?
6. shop less in stores than on the Internet?
7. read the newspaper less frequently than they did 15 years ago?
8. enough time in person with your friends?
9. learn more because of the Internet?
10. have less interaction with your family than you did two years ago?

GRAMMAR AND VOCABULARY Review the reading on page 251. Write a paragraph to answer the two questions at the end of the reading. Use your experience to support your ideas.

> The Internet has been having a big impact on people's activities and relationships in recent years. People have been saving a lot of time by using the Internet.

PROJECT Create a survey to find out about Internet use.

1. Form groups of three or four students.
2. In your group, choose one of these age groups for your survey OR your instructor will assign you a group:

   - teenagers and young college students (18–23 years old)
   - young adults (24–35)
   - middle-aged adults (36–64)
   - instructors (any age)
   - seniors (65+)

3. Write questions for your age group about their Internet use. You want to find out about the impact of the Internet on their activities and relationships.
4. Each student from your group should then use the survey to ask at least two people the questions.
5. Share your answers with your group. Summarize your information for the class.

 INTERNET Enter "Internet Use" into a search engine. Find one interesting fact or statistic about the use of the Internet. Bring your information to class and share it with your classmates.

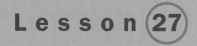
The EMT Major (Emergency Medical Technology)

■ CONTENT VOCABULARY

Look at the pictures. Do you know the words?

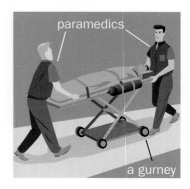

paramedics

a gurney

trauma

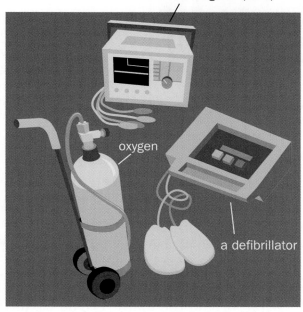

an electrocardiogram (ECG)

oxygen

a defibrillator

equipment

Write the new words in your vocabulary journal.

■ THINK ABOUT IT

In your writing journal, write for five minutes about any of these questions: How are people helped by paramedics? Have you ever been helped by a paramedic? Have you seen someone else being helped by a paramedic? What happened?

■ GRAMMAR IN CONTENT

A Read and listen.

CD2, TR39

A Difficult Career Choice

Becca: So, Brian, have you decided on your major?

Brian: Yeah, I think so. I want to be a paramedic, and EMT **is** now **being offered** as a major. You know, more and more paramedics **are needed** in emergency situations these days, and the EMT college major **has** recently **been created** to fill that need. I can help a lot of people if I complete this major.

Becca: Yeah, that's true. In an emergency situation, a person's life **can be saved** by paramedics. But it's a difficult career. Paramedics work all hours of the day and night, don't they?

Brian: You're right. It's not easy. A lot of bending, kneeling, and heavy lifting **is required**. Paramedics **can be injured** when they lift patients. Also, sometimes they**'re exposed** to disease or violence. But I'm very interested in biology and health, and I want to work in emergency situations to save people.

a disease: serious illness

violence: strong and cruel behavior causing injury or damage

B Look at the dialog. Find the passive voice verbs in bold.

1. What auxiliary verb do we use with the passive voice? _____

2. What form of the main verb do we use? _____

3. Write one passive voice example from the reading for each of these verb tenses.

   simple present: _____

   present progressive: _____

   present perfect: _____

   modal: _____

Forms

Active vs. Passive Voice:

1. The object of an active sentence is the subject of a passive sentence.

2. Use a passive verb:
   be + the past participle.

3. Use *get* + past participle for a less formal way of expressing a past action.

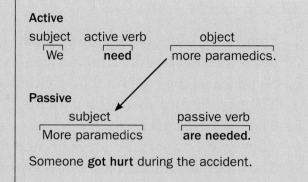

Active

subject	active verb	object
We	need	more paramedics.

Passive

subject	passive verb
More paramedics	are needed.

Someone **got hurt** during the accident.

Notes:

- Don't use passive voice with intransitive verbs.

   Incorrect: ~~The accident was happened at 3:00.~~   Correct: *The accident **happened** at 3:00.*

- In general, don't use *have* in the passive voice.

   Incorrect: ~~An accident was had at 3:00.~~   Correct: *Someone **had** an accident at 3:00.*

Tenses	Active			Passive		
	Subject	**Active Verb**	**Object**	**Subject**	***Be***	**Past Participle**
Simple Present	They	help	the man.	The man	is	helped.
Present Progressive	They	are helping	the man.	The man	is being	helped.
Simple Past	They	helped	the man.	The man	was	helped.
Past Progressive	They	were helping	the man.	The man	was being	helped.
Future	They	will help	the man.	The man	will be	helped.
Present Perfect	They	have helped	the man.	The man	has been	helped.
Modals	They	can help	the man.	The man	can be	helped.

C Read the steps for an EMT call. Then, complete the following paragraph by changing the active voice verbs to the passive voice.

Steps in an EMT call

1. Someone makes an emergency call.
2. EMS (Emergency Medical Services) sends an ambulance to the scene.
3. Sometimes, they also call firefighters and police.
4. The paramedics check the patients.
5. They follow strict rules.
6. They make important decisions and use the necessary equipment.
7. They handle trauma patients very carefully.
8. Sometimes they transport patients to the hospital.

There are several important steps in an EMT call. First, an emergency call _____ (1). Then, an ambulance _____ (2) to the scene. Sometimes, firefighters and police _____ (3). Next, at the scene, the patients _____ (4). Strict rules _____ (5) and important decisions _____ (6). The necessary equipment _____ (7) to save the patient's life. A trauma patient _____ (8) very carefully. Sometimes the patients _____ (9) to the hospital.

D Complete the student answers for an EMT clinical practice. Use the correct form of the passive voice.

1. **Teacher:** Have you checked the patient?

   Student: Yes, _____ *the patient has been checked.* _____

2. **T:** Did you hook up an IV?

   S: Yes, _____ immediately.

3. **T:** How about oxygen? Are you giving her any oxygen?

   S: Yes, one liter _____ right now.

4. **T:** Have you used the defibrillator?

   S: No, _____ yet.

5. **T:** Will you call the doctor if you need advice?

   S: Yes, _____ if _____.

6. **T:** Can you transport the patient to the hospital?

   S: Yes, _____ in the ambulance.

7. **T:** Will you take him to the ambulance when you complete the tests?

   S: Yes, _____ on the stretcher when

   _____ .

■ **COMMUNICATE**

E **GROUP WORK** Work in groups of three. Student A will look at this page. Student B will look at page 304. Student C will look at page 304. Take turns. Ask your partners about what tasks are completed by paramedics at different levels. Fill in the chart for the other two levels. Use the passive voice of the verbs.

Is basic medical care given by a Level II paramedic?

Yes, it is.

Basic medical care is also given by a Level III paramedic.

Student A

	Level I Paramedic	Level II Paramedic	Level III Paramedic
give basic medical care	✔		
check condition of patient	✔		
hook up an IV			
give medication			
manage basic heart problems	✔		
read ECGs			
operate breathing equipment			
give CPR	✔		
use defibrillator			

■ GRAMMAR IN CONTENT

CD2,TR40

A Read and listen.

> **Training Video**
>
> **Instructor:** OK, we just watched a film about paramedics. They **were being called** to the scene of a car accident. Now we're going to make a timeline and discuss their work. So, what time did the call come in, and what happened?
>
> **Student 1:** The call **was received** at 10:00. A car **was hit by a truck.**
>
> **Instructor:** Yes, and who made the call?
>
> **Student 2:** The call **was made by another driver.** She stopped when she saw the accident.
>
> **Instructor:** OK, and at 10:05 the ambulance arrived at the scene. How many paramedics came to the scene? Maria?
>
> **Maria:** Well, the ambulance **was being driven by one paramedic,** and there was another one in the back. Then, a third one **was brought** to the accident **by the fire department.**

B Look at the conversation. The passive verbs are in bold. The agents are also in bold. An "agent" is the performer of the action.

1. Find one sentence with a passive verb and an agent. Write it here:

   _____

2. Change the sentence in question 1 to a sentence with an active verb.

   _____

3. Find one sentence with a passive verb and no agent. Write it here:

   _____

4. Why does sentence 1 have an agent? Why doesn't sentence 3 have an agent? Write a rule:

   _____

Passive Voice with the Agent

Agent

The subject of an active sentence is the agent of a passive sentence.	subject One of the drivers *made* the call. agent The call *was made* **by** one of the drivers.
Use **by** + **noun/pronoun** for the agent. Use the agent to explain **who** or **what** performed the action of the verb.	**What** hit the car? The car was hit **by a truck**.

No Agent

Don't use the agent if (1) the agent is not important (2) the agent is not known (3) the agent is "all people" (4) the agent is obvious	(1) More and more paramedics **are needed**. (2) The call **was received** at 10:00. (3) An IV **is needed** after a serious injury. (4) The paramedics arrived, and the patient **was** immediately **hooked up** to an IV.

Note:
- Don't use the agent if *you* are the obvious agent.
  Incorrect: *I did all the tests. ~~They were completed by me very quickly.~~*
  Correct: *I did all the tests. They were completed by 5:00.*

C **Write the answer in the passive voice. Use the information in parentheses. Add *by* and the agent if necessary.**

1. **A:** How long have they offered the EMT major? (since 2000)

   B: _The EMT major has been offered since 2000._

2. **A:** Who teaches the EMT I class? (Professor Wilcox)

   B: _____

3. **A:** Where do they hold the class? (in the Science Building)

   B: _____

4. **A:** Who takes the class? (beginning students)

   B: _____

5. **A:** How many students are taking the class this semester? (25 students)

   B: _____

6. **A:** Who wrote the textbook? (Michael Fisher)

   B: _____

7. **A:** Does the professor require clinic reports? (yes/every two weeks)

   B: _____

8. **A:** When does the professor collect the clinic reports? (on Fridays)

   B: _____

D Listen and check (✔) the statements that are true.

1. ✔ The call was made at 10:07.

2. ___ The call was made by Lucy Mason.

3. ___ The ambulance was sent by Lucy Mason.

4. ___ A drunk driver caused the accident.

5. ___ The driver was being asked questions by the paramedics.

6. ___ The necessary equipment was used by the EMT team.

7. ___ A patient's arms were cut.

8. ___ A patient's legs were bandaged by the paramedic.

9. ___ A patient was given oxygen by one of the paramedics.

10. ___ The doctor gave orders to transport the two patients to the hospital.

E Correct the errors in the EMT student's report on Dr. Cowley. There are six more. The first one has been done for you.

know

All paramedics should ~~be known~~ about Dr. R. Adams Cowley. He is respect for his hard work in EMT. One of the first air medical systems started by Dr. Cowley. The idea of "the golden hour" was also developed. The "golden hour" is the first hour after a serious injury is happened. Lives can be saved by someone during this hour. Since Dr. Cowley was died in 1991, he has been regarded by everyone as the father of EMT.

F **PAIR WORK** Each of you will have information about an EMT case study. Student A will look at this page. Student B will look at page 305. Take turns. Use the words given to ask the questions. Use the case study information to answer the questions. Use passive voice when it's appropriate.

Who made the call?　　　The call was made by Jin Chang.

Student A: Case Study Information

Mr. Bill Simon made a call at 2:31 PM.
Patricia Andrade took the call.
She called the ambulance and the fire department at 2:35 PM.
The paramedics arrived at the house at 2:50.
A neighbor was giving Mr. Gomez CPR when they arrived.
Another neighbor was helping Mrs. Gomez.
The paramedics gave Mr. Gomez an IV.
The paramedics used the ECG to check his heart.
The paramedics took Mr. Gomez to the hospital.

Student A: Questions to ask Student B

1. who/make/call?
2. what time/make/call?
3. who/take/call?
4. Alan Thompson/call/ambulance?
5. paramedics/send/to a house?
6. what/Jenny Nelson/doing/when paramedics arrive?
7. paramedics/do/any tests/on Jenny?
8. paramedics/ask/Jenny/any questions?
9. paramedics/take/Jenny/to the hospital?

GRAMMAR AND VOCABULARY Fill in the blanks with a word from the list OR the passive form of the verb in parentheses.

| paramedics | defibrillator | equipment | trauma | ECG | oxygen |

When an emergency call (receive) ____is received____ (1), an EMT team (send) _____ (2) to the scene. The _____ (3) on the team (train) _____ (4) to follow important steps and use the necessary _____ (5). For example, if a patient cannot breathe, CPR (perform) _____ (6) immediately. In that situation, the paramedic may also give the patient _____ (7). If the patient is having heart problems, an _____ (8) may (do) _____ (9). When the heart problem is more serious, the _____ (10) will (use) a _____ (11). If there is a _____ (12) patient, the patient must not (move) _____ (13) until tests can (give) _____ (14).

PROJECT Write and perform an EMT skit.

1. Divide into groups of three or four students.
2. Each group will write a short skit. The skit should show an emergency call and a response with paramedics, for example, a fire, a car accident, a home injury, an illness. Include the times and events as they happen. Use the passive voice where appropriate.
3. Practice your skit.
4. Perform your skit for the class.

 INTERNET Enter "EMT major" into a search engine. Read and answer these questions: What is required? What is taught? Take notes. Write a short report of your findings. Use the passive voice as often as it is appropriate.

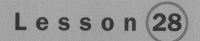
Literature:
Jane Austen's
Pride and Prejudice

■ CONTENT VOCABULARY

Look at the pictures. Do you know the words?

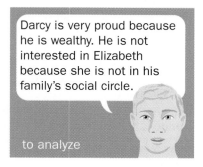

Darcy is very proud because he is wealthy. He is not interested in Elizabeth because she is not in his family's social circle.

to analyze

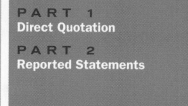

a novel   characters

We learn about Elizabeth's prejudice when the housekeeper says, "He is never rude. He is always polite to me."

a quotation

She is not pretty enough to interest me, and her family is not wealthy.

He is so rude.

pride (proud)   prejudice

Write the new words in your vocabulary journal.

■ THINK ABOUT IT

In your writing journal, write for five minutes about any of these questions: Have you ever read a novel (in any language)? Who were the characters in the novel? What do people say when they are proud? How might prejudice cause problems at the beginning of a relationship?

■ **GRAMMAR IN CONTENT**

A **Read and listen.**

CD2,TR42

Literature Quiz

Question: We have been reading and discussing *Pride and Prejudice* by Jane Austen. Explain the meaning of the title. Discuss the characters, using at least two quotations from the novel.

Student Answer: Elizabeth and Darcy first meet at a party, where they show their prejudice. Darcy's friend Bingley wants Darcy to dance with Elizabeth. **"Why don't you ask her?"** he suggests. **"I'd rather not,"** Darcy says, **"because she is not pretty enough to interest me."** Elizabeth hears him when he says this. **"How rude he is,"** she says to her friend. They each have a strong opinion about the other, without knowing very much. Also, Elizabeth and Darcy are both proud. For example, Elizabeth will not forgive Darcy because he has hurt her pride. She says, **"I could easily forgive HIS pride if he had not hurt mine."**

rude: impolite

B **Look at the sentences in bold.**

1. Circle the quotation marks.

2. Are the punctuation marks (for example, comma, period) inside or outside the quotation marks?

___ inside ___ outside

3. Write the sentence with the phrase that identifies the speaker in the middle of the quotation rather than at the beginning or the end:

_____

Direct Quotation

Rules	Examples
Use quotation marks to show direct speech or thought. Use an identifying phrase, for example, *Darcy says,* to identify the speaker or thinker.	Darcy says, "**She is not pretty enough to interest me.**" "**He is so proud,**" Elizabeth thought.
Place the sentence punctuation (for example, period, comma) of a direct quotation **inside** the quotation marks.	"**How rude he is,**" she says to her friend. "**Why don't you ask her?**" he suggests.
Use a comma if the identifying phrase comes at the beginning or end of the sentence. Use two commas if the phrase comes in the middle of the sentence.	She says, "**I could easily forgive HIS pride if he had not hurt mine.**" "**I'd rather not,**" Darcy says, "**because she is not pretty enough to interest me.**"

Note:

A variety of identifying verbs are used for direct quotations: *say, answer, laugh, reply, argue, suggest, insist, think,* and so forth. Example: *"He is so proud,"* ***Elizabeth thought.***

C **Read the conversation between Mr. Darcy and his friend, Bingley, at the dance. Add the necessary punctuation for the direct quotations. The first one is done for you.**

"Come, Darcy," said Bingley. I hate to see you standing by yourself. It's so much better to dance.

I won't answered his friend. I hate to dance unless I know my partner.

Let me introduce you to one of Jane's sisters. She is very pretty Bingley quickly suggested. He pointed to Elizabeth Bennett. Darcy turned to look at Elizabeth, caught her eye, then turned away. She is not pretty enough to tempt me he said coldly. Elizabeth heard Mr. Darcy say this. How rude he is Elizabeth thought.

CD2, TR43

D **By the end of the novel, Elizabeth and Mr. Darcy fall in love. Listen to the conversation between Elizabeth and Mr. Darcy. You will hear each statement twice. Write the statement as a direct quotation. Also, identify the speaker in the parentheses: *E* for Elizabeth, *D* for Darcy.**

1. (   ) _____

2. (   ) _____

3. (   ) _____

4. (   ) _____

5. (   ) _____

6. (   ) _____

7. (   ) _____

E Using the quotations from exercise D, write a conversation between Elizabeth and Mr. Darcy. Choose from the following identifying phrases. Start a new paragraph when the speaker changes.

| he answered | Elizabeth said | she said warmly | |
| Darcy said | he told her | he replied | she continued |

"I must thank you for your kindness to my sister," Elizabeth said. _____

_____

_____

_____

_____

_____

_____

■ **C O M M U N I C A T E**

F **WRITE** Write the story of the beginning of a relationship. Use at least three direct quotations in your story.

When I first met my friend Colleen, I didn't like her. She didn't smile very much and she always wanted to study. One day, I asked her, "Do you want to go get some coffee?"

"No, thanks," she said, "I have to study." I was upset. Later she said, "Excuse me for being so rude. I was in a hurry, but I have some free time now if you'd still like to talk."

■ GRAMMAR IN CONTENT

CD2,TR44

A **Read and listen.**

Preparing for the Test

Professor: During the next two days, you will review *Pride and Prejudice*. The study guide will help you prepare for the test questions. I'm going to choose from the topics in your study guide. Two of the questions will be about character and two will be about plot. On Monday, you need to be here on time. You can use your notes and your books during the test.

(Later, on the telephone)

Sarah: I missed class today. What did Professor Salinas say about our test?

Maria: **He said that** we **would** review the novel in the next two days. **He** also **said that** he **was going to** choose from the topics in our study guide. **He told us that** two of the questions **would** be about character and two of them **would** be about plot. Then, he **told us** that we **needed** to be there on time on Monday. Oh, and **he said** we **could** use our notes and our books during the test.

B **Look at the conversation.**

Maria reports the speech of the professor. Find her reported statements for the direct speech. Write them here.

1. "During the next two days, you will review *Pride and Prejudice*."

   _____

2. "You can use your notes and your books during the test."

   _____

3. "I'm going to choose from the topics in your study guide."

   _____

Rules	Examples
1. Use a reporting **verb** to report direct speech, for example, *said, told, complained, insisted,* etc. A noun clause follows the verb: (*that*) + subject + verb + (object)	*that* subj verb object He **said that** we would review the novel. subj verb He **said she** was hoping for some good writing.
2. Use a pronoun after the verb *tell.*	He **told us** that two of the questions would be about character.
3. If the reporting verb is in the **present tense,** the noun clause verb is also in the **present tense.** If the reporting verb is in the **past tense,** the noun clause verb changes to the **past form.**	<u>Present</u> "How rude Darcy **is,**" Elizabeth **says.** Elizabeth **says** that Darcy **is** rude. <u>Past</u> "How rude Darcy **is,**" Elizabeth **said.** Elizabeth **said** that Darcy **was** rude.
4. Only the following three modals change to their historical past forms in the noun clause: *will* → *would* *can* → *could* *may* → *might*	"We **can** use our books during the test," he said. He said that we **could** use our books during the test.
5. Change the object or subject pronoun *you* in the reported statement when necessary: you → I/me (sing.)/we/us (plural)	"I'm hoping for some good writing from (you)." He said he was hoping for some good writing from (us). "(You) should stay for the lecture," said John. John said that (we) should stay for the lecture.
6. Change these adverbs in the reported statement when necessary: here → there now → then	"You need to be (here) on time." He said that we needed to be (there) on time.

C **Read the excerpt from the novel. Then rewrite it on the lines below. Use reported statements. Combine sentences when possible.**

> Mrs. Reynolds, Mr. Darcy's housekeeper, began to speak to Elizabeth's aunt and uncle, the Gardiners, about Mr. Darcy. "Mr. Darcy is not here much during the year," she said.
>
> "But when Mr. Darcy marries, you will see more of him," Mr. Gardiner replied. Mrs. Reynolds looked worried when she heard this.
>
> "Yes, sir, but I do not know when that will be. I do not know anyone good enough for him," she said. Mr. and Mrs. Gardiner smiled at the housekeeper's pride in Mr. Darcy.
>
> "He is never rude. He is always polite to me. Some people call him proud, but I don't agree. He is the best landlord, and the best master," Mrs. Reynolds said proudly.
>
> This was praise that disagreed with Elizabeth's own ideas. She had long believed that he was not a good-tempered man. She longed to hear more.

Mrs. Reynolds, Mr. Darcy's housekeeper, began to speak to Elizabeth's aunt and uncle, the Gardiners, about Mr. Darcy. _Mrs. Reynolds said that Mr. Darcy was not there much during the year._

_____

_____

_____

_____

_____

_____

_____

_____

_____

_____

_____

_____

_____

_____

_____

D **Read the class discussion. Then fill in the blanks in Nancy's journal.**

Class Discussion

Professor: Which character in the novel shows more pride?

Nancy: Darcy is definitely the proud one. He is very proud at the beginning when he won't dance with Elizabeth.

Peter: I don't agree. Elizabeth shows her pride when she can't forgive Darcy.

Professor: Now remember, you need to analyze each character very carefully. Elizabeth is proud, but her prejudice is really a bigger problem. When she hears negative stories about Darcy, she believes them.

Nancy: Yes, it takes her a long time to see Darcy clearly. It really doesn't happen until the end of the novel.

Nancy's Journal

Today we discussed the British novel <u>Pride and Prejudice</u>. It was a lively

discussion. The professor wanted us to think about the pride of the two

characters. First, I said that Darcy ___was___ the prouder character. I
(1)

said that he _____ very proud at the beginning when he _____
(2)   (3)

dance with Elizabeth. Peter answered that he _____ agree. He
(4)

argued that Elizabeth _____ her pride when she _____ forgive
(5)   (6)

Darcy. Then the professor told _____ that _____
(7)   (8)

_____ to analyze each character carefully. He said that Elizabeth
(9)

_____ proud but that her prejudice _____ really a bigger
(10)   (11)

problem. He said that when Elizabeth _____ negative stories about
(12)

Darcy, she _____ them. I understood the professor's ideas. I agreed
(13)

that it _____ Elizabeth a long time to see Darcy clearly.
(14)

E (Circle) **the correct verb.**

Professor Salinas ((said) / told) that next Friday we were going to have a
(1)
test on the novel *Pride and Prejudice.* He (said / told) us that we had to know the
(2)
important characters in the story. He also (said / told) that he was going to give us a
(3)
quotation and we would have to identify the character who spoke those words.

Later, he (said / told) that we could get an "A" on the test if we wrote a clear,
(4)
well-written deep analysis. When Marcus asked about this, he (said / told) us
(5)
that an example question would be, "Who had more pride, Darcy or Elizabeth?"

He (said / told) that Darcy showed his pride when he didn't want to dance with
(6)
Elizabeth because she wasn't pretty enough. He also (said / told) us that Elizabeth's
(7)
prejudice prevented her from seeing Darcy's positive characteristics. He (said / told)
(8)
that this was an example of a deep analysis.

■ **COMMUNICATE**

F **PAIR WORK** **Who are you proud of? Tell your partner about this person. Your
partner will take notes. Then your partner will report your statements to the class.**

I am very proud of my sister.
She has a good job, and she
is a good mother.

He said he was very proud of his sister.
He told me she had a good job, and he
also said that she was a good mother.

GRAMMAR AND VOCABULARY Read the excerpt from *Pride and Prejudice*. Add the correct punctuation.

> We have both changed she smiled. We are both more kind, more understanding of each other.
>
> You know he nodded I was upset when you refused me last spring. At first, I was angry. Then I realized you were right about me. That's why I wrote you that letter. Did it make you think better of me? he asked.
>
> It did she replied. It helped remove my prejudice about you. But please don't worry any more she said. Think only of pleasing past memories.
>
> I had too much pride he said. I was rude and spoiled. I cared for no one beyond my family circle he continued and I thought less of others. You helped me to see that part of myself.

PROJECT Analyze a quotation.

1. Form groups and discuss one of the following Jane Austen quotations:

   "Happiness in marriage is entirely a matter of chance."
   "I do not want people to be agreeable as it saves me the trouble of liking them."
   "A large income is the best recipe for happiness I ever heard of."
   "One half of the world cannot understand the pleasures of the other."

2. When you are finished, take turns repeating what various group members said during the discussion.

3. Each member of the group will write a summary of the discussion, using direct quotations and reported statements.

 INTERNET Enter "reviews of *Pride and Prejudice*" into a search engine. Find quotations about a movie based on the novel. Report to your class. Use direct quotation and reported statements.

PART 1
Yes/No Reported Questions:
Present

PART 2
Wh- Reported Questions:
Present

L e s s o n ㉙

Psychology:
Research Methods

■ CONTENT VOCABULARY

Look at the pictures. Do you know the words?

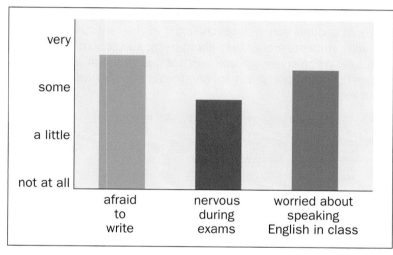

data

	Yes	NO
1. Students tell you can?	☐	☐
2. Students tell you?	☐	☐
3. Students tell you can?	☐	☐
4. Students tell you pants?	☐	☐

Write the new words in your vocabulary journal.

■ THINK ABOUT IT

In your writing journal, write for five minutes about any of these questions: Have you ever answered a formal survey or questionnaire? What is the purpose of surveys and questionnaires? What are some questions that you might find on a survey or questionnaire?

■ GRAMMAR IN CONTENT

A Read and listen.

CD2,TR45

The Work of Psychologists

Psychology is the study of human emotion and behavior. Psychologists investigate the feelings, thoughts, and actions of ordinary people. There are many questions that psychologists try to answer to reach a deeper understanding of these areas. For example, they ask **if experience affects behavior.**

Some of us might wonder **if it is possible to be scientific about emotions or thoughts.** However, scientific methods are used by psychologists in their research on these topics. Two common methods are questionnaires and surveys. For instance, in one survey, a psychologist might ask **if people are happy.** In another survey, a psychologist might want to know **if language students feel anxiety** about using a second or foreign language. When enough people answer questions on a survey or questionnaire, psychologists can then make generalizations about the data.

to investigate: to look at carefully

anxiety: a feeling of nervousness, worry, or fear

B The bold sentences in the reading report *yes/no* questions. What are the questions? Write the four questions here.

1. _Does experience affect behavior?_

2. _____

3. _____

4. _____

Yes/No Reported Questions: Present Tense	
Steps in Reporting a *Yes/No* Question	**Example**
1. Use a reporting phrase. 2. Add *if, whether,* or *whether or not* after the reporting phrase. 3. Change the *yes/no* question to a statement. Add the statement after *if/whether/whether or not.*	*Yes/No Question: Are people happy?* **Psychologists want to know** Psychologists want to know **if** Psychologists want to know **whether** Psychologists want to know **whether or not** Psychologists want to know if **people are happy.**

Notes:

- Use the simple present or present progressive tense in the reporting phrase to introduce *yes/no* questions about general truth or facts. The reported *yes/no* questions are in the simple present tense, for example, *The survey **is asking** if students **are** anxious.*
- In reported questions, sentence word order (subject-verb-object) is used.
- Use reporting verbs such as *ask, wonder, explore, want to know, want to find out* to report questions from academic **texts** such as surveys or questionnaires or academic **activity** such as research.

C **Part 1: Read the summary of Cathy and Amanda's research and their data.**

> We had to conduct a survey for our Research Methods class. We wrote six questions to ask students about their language learning attitudes. We collected the data and summarized the results. We found some interesting results. 67% of the students like working in groups, and only 40% of the students are afraid to ask questions in class. 80% of the students feel comfortable in the Writing Center, but only 50% of the students are interested in the assigned readings.

Part 2: What are their research questions? Using Cathy and Amanda's summary, you can figure out their questions. First, write each question as a reported question. Then write the survey question itself.

1. a. _The research is asking if students like working in groups._

   b. Survey question: _Do you like working in groups?_

2. a. _____

   b. Survey question: _____

3. a. _____

   b. Survey question: _____

4. a. _____

   b. Survey question: _____

D Fill in the blanks with a reported question. Use the question in parentheses.

In every field of study, there are important and difficult questions to think about. For example, historians ask ("Do present events correspond to past events?") *whether present events correspond to past events*, and geographers want to know
(1)

("Are the maps accurate?") _____. Philosophers
(2)

ask ("Can we define beauty?") _____, and
(3)

poets ask ("Is love eternal?") _____. In
(4)

psychology, research methods help psychologists to investigate questions about thoughts, emotions, and behavior. When they want to find out ("Does environment affect emotions?") _____, they will design a
(5)

questionnaire to get some of the data. For example, a survey might ask ("Do you feel depressed in the evenings?") _____.
(6)

Psychologists often want to find out ("Does the mind affect the body?")

_____, so, for example, a questionnaire
(7)

will ask ("Do you get headaches when you experience stress?")

_____.
(8)

■ COMMUNICATE

E **PAIR WORK** With a partner, create a simple survey. Have your classmates take the survey. Summarize the results in a report. Here are some questions you might use in your survey:

1. Do you worry about speaking in class?

2. Are you confident about your writing?

3. Does grammar make you nervous?

4. Are you afraid of writing essays?

5. Can you relax during a conversation?

■ GRAMMAR IN CONTENT

CD2, TR46

A Read and listen.

The Writing Center

Tutor: How can I help you?

Yves: I have this difficult writing assignment and I don't understand it.

Tutor: OK. Well, let's look at it and figure out **what your professor is asking.** Can you find the questions in the prompt?

Yves: Yes, there are four questions.

Tutor: OK. What are they?

Yves: "How do language students feel when they write?" "Why do they get nervous?" "What can they do to relax?" "How do *you* feel when *you* write?"

Tutor: OK, so your professor is asking **how language students feel when they write.** She's also asking **why they get nervous,** and she wants to know **what they can do to relax.** First, she wants you to think about language students in general, right? Then, she wants to know **how *you* feel when *you* write.**

Yves: Yes, I see. Thank you very much. That's very helpful.

Tutor: You're welcome.

B The five reported *wh-* questions in the dialog are in bold. Figure out the *wh-* question for each reported question and write it here.

1. _____   2. _____

3. _____   4. _____

5. _____

Wh- Reported Questions: Present Tense

Wh- Questions: *Why* do students get nervous?/*Who* is anxious?

Steps in Reporting a *Wh-* Question	Example
1. Use a reporting phrase.	*Your professor is asking*
2. Add a *wh-* question word.	*Your professor is asking **why***
3. Use sentence word order after the *wh-* word.	***Your professor is asking why ~~do~~ students get nervous.***
OR	
If the *wh-* word is the subject, don't change anything after the reporting phrase.	*(Question: **Who is anxious?**)* The professor wants to know **who is anxious**.

Note:

Use simple present or present progressive tense in the reporting phrase to introduce *wh-* questions about general truth or facts. The reported *wh-* questions are in the simple present tense. Example: *The survey is asking why students get anxious.*

C **Complete each conversation about the study guide for an Introduction to Psychology class. Use a reported question.**

1. **A:** Can you help me with question #1? ("What is psychology?")

   B: Sure, let's see, question #1 is asking

   what psychology is .

2. **A:** Do you understand question #2? ("Why do psychologists use surveys?")

   B: Yes, I do. Question #2 is asking

   _____ .

3. **A:** Can you help me with the next one? ("What kind of data do psychologists use?")

   B: Sure. This one asks

   _____ .

4. **A:** What is question #4 asking? ("Who participates in surveys?")

   B: The question is asking

   _____ .

CD2, TR47

D **Jeff is conducting a survey for his class. He asks Monique to answer some questions. Listen to their dialog. Then check (✔) statements that report the research questions.**

1. ___ Jeff wants to know where Monique is going.

2. ___ Jeff wants to know if she has time to answer questions.

3. ___ Monique wants to know why Jeff is doing the survey.

4. ___ Jeff wants to find out how many classes Monique is taking.

5. ___ Jeff is asking how many hours she works.

6. ___ Jeff wants to find out what kinds of situations cause stress for her.

■ **COMMUNICATE**

E **GROUP WORK** In a group of three students, take turns and follow these steps:
Student A: Using the cue, ask a question of Student B.
Student C: Ask Student B about the question.
Student B: Report the question to Student C. Then, answer the question.
All three students should take notes on the questions and answers.

Where do psychologists work?   What is she asking?

 She is asking where psychologists work. I think they work in their offices and outside of their offices with people.

1. where/psychologists/work?
2. what kind of issues/child psychologists/interested in?
3. which areas of psychology/use/surveys?
4. how/social psychologists/learn about/people's behavior?
5. educational psychologists/ask questions about/learning?
6. what kinds of books/psychologists/write?
7. what kind of data/psychologists/collect?
8. psychotherapy/research method?

F **Write some of the results of your discussion in exercise E and use some reported *wh-* questions.**

GRAMMAR AND VOCABULARY Read the assignment below. Write a summary to explain what the assignment is asking and what the instructor wants to know. Use the vocabulary and grammar from the lesson.

Assignment: Write a composition about the following topic. Use the results of your survey in the essay.

There are many students of English all over the world. Why do these students want to learn English? What is their motivation? Are they motivated to learn English for their jobs? Do they want to communicate when they travel?

What is *your* motivation to learn English? How do *you* feel about the English language? What do you like or dislike about studying English?

PROJECT **Conduct a student survey.**

1. Work in pairs. Write a survey for students in your English class or another English class. Ask this research question: *How do you feel about learning English?* Write five–ten questions you would like to ask in your survey. Here are some possible areas of focus: *shyness, motivation, fear about grades, correction,* or *confidence.*
2. Use reported questions to tell the class about your survey. Ask your classmates for suggestions and improvements.
3. You and your partner should each do the survey with at least five students.
4. With your partner, write a summary of your survey results. In the summary, explain the purpose of your survey. Then report each question and the data you have for that question. Use reported questions in your summary.

 INTERNET Enter this phrase into a search engine: "psychology and questionnaires." Choose a questionnaire. What is the questionnaire asking? Report to your class on some of the questions being asked.

PART 1
Past Review: Simple Past,
Past Progressive, *Used To/Would*

PART 2
Present Review: Simple Present,
Present Progressive, Present
Perfect, Present Perfect
Progressive

PART 3
Future Review: Simple Future,
Future Progressive

Lesson (30)

Communication Studies: The History of Communication

■ CONTENT VOCABULARY

Look at the pictures. Do you know the words?

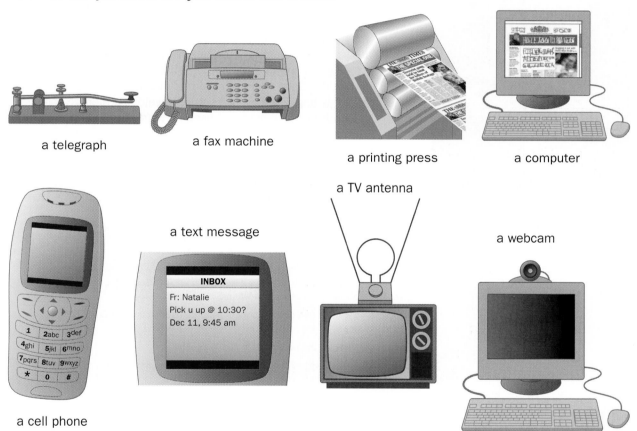

a telegraph

a fax machine

a printing press

a computer

a TV antenna

a text message

INBOX
Fr: Natalie
Pick u up @ 10:30?
Dec 11, 9:45 am

a webcam

a cell phone

Write the new words in your vocabulary journal.

■ THINK ABOUT IT

In your writing journal, write for five minutes about any of these questions: How did people communicate before the invention of cell phones, fax machines, radio, and television? How are phones used today? How were they used 50 years ago? How many different forms of communication did you use last week?

■ GRAMMAR IN CONTENT

A Read and listen.

CD2,TR48

Early Communication

Long before we **had** computers, telephones, or fax machines, humans **used** a variety of methods to communicate. One of the earliest forms of nonverbal communication **was** cave drawings. People **used to tell** the stories of their hunts, battles, family, and culture by using pictures and symbols. Communication **was** also **used** for practical purposes. In many areas, such as Africa, tropical America, and Asia, if people **wanted** to communicate over long distances, they **beat** on drums and **sent** smoke signals. They **would tell** other tribes about important events, and they **would warn** other groups of danger.

Later, communication methods **advanced** when the first writing systems **began** to develop. Between 3500 and 2900 BCE, **while** the Sumerians **were** already **using** the cuneiform system of writing, the Egyptians **were developing** hieroglyphic writing. Both of these systems **used** pictographs—symbols or pictures to communicate an idea, object, activity, place, or event. During that time, people **weren't writing** with a phonetic alphabet. Then, around 1200–1000 BCE, the Phoenicians **developed** a syllabary. Later, the Greeks **used** this syllabary to develop the first alphabet. This **led** to the alphabet used in the Western world today.

cuneiform writing: characters formed by the arrangement of small wedge-shaped elements pressed into clay tablets and used in ancient Sumerian, Akkadian, Assyrian, Babylonian, and Persian writing

hieroglyphic writing: a set of symbols or pictures used in ancient Egypt to represent ideas

phonetic: related to the sounds of words in speech

syllabary: a set of written characters for a language; each character represents a syllable

B Look at the reading.

1. Find a verb that shows ongoing action in the past: _____

2. Find a verb that shows completed action in the past: _____

3. Find two verbs that describe past habitual activity: _____ _____

Simple Past Tense and Past Progressive Tense

Form	Simple Past	Past Progressive
Affirmative	They **drew** pictures in caves.	While they **were drawing** pictures, others were using symbols.
Negative	They **didn't use** words in their messages.	During that time, people **weren't using** words.
Yes/No Questions	**Did** they **use** symbols?	**Were** the Sumerians **using** the cuneiform system at that time?
Wh- Questions	Who **wrote** the first book?	What **were** they **communicating** about in their messages?

Notes:

- Use the simple past tense for completed actions/events in the past. Use the past progressive for continuing actions/events in the past.
- Add *-d* or *-ed* to regular past tense verbs in affirmative statements. Use the past form of **be** with the *-ing* form of the verb for past progressive. Use **while** with the past progressive to show ongoing activity.
- Irregular verbs do not have the *-d/-ed* ending in the past tense. See Appendix 3 for irregular verb forms.
- See Lessons 7, 8, 9, and 12 for more information on the past and past progressive tenses.

Used To/Would

Form	Used To	Would
Affirmative	People **used to draw** on caves.	The pictures **would tell** stories.
Negative	They **didn't use to write**.	They **wouldn't write** words on caves.
Yes/No Questions	**Did** they **use to get** messages?	**Would** they **wait** for an answer?
Wh- Questions	What **did** they **use to do** at school?	How **would** they **communicate**?

Notes:

- *Used to* and *would* suggest a past habit no longer true in the present.
- See Lesson 8 for more information on **used to** and **would**.

C Use the verbs in parentheses. Fill in the blanks with the simple past, past progressive, *used to,* or *would.*

Before the invention of the printing press, telegraph, and telephone,

people (find) _____*found*_____ effective methods for communicating news and
(1)

important messages. They (send) _____ messages using homing
(2)

pigeons, mirrors, smoke, and human messengers. For example, in 776 BCE, while

the citizens of Athens (wait) _____ to hear about the winners of the
(3)

Olympic Games, homing pigeons (fly) _____ from Olympia with the
(4)

news. In 37 BCE, while the Roman Emperor Tiberius (rule) _____ his
(5)

empire from the Isle of Capri, he (need) _____ a way to communicate
(6)

with the mainland. Every day, he (send) _____ urgent messages by
(7)

"heliograph"—messages by mirror. The mirror was used to flash a code using light.

Later, in the fifteenth century, while the colonists (settle) _____
(8)

America, the Native Americans (find) _____ effective ways to
(9)

communicate with each other. When they (hear) _____ of a coming
(10)

attack, they (make) _____ smoke patterns to send coded messages.
(11)

Still later, in 1860, in the United States, 83 people (ride) _____ horses
(12)

night and day, through rain and snow, for the Pony Express to achieve the first fast

mail delivery from Missouri to California.

D **Fill in the blanks with the simple past, past progressive, *used to*, or *would*.**

Before the telephone, people (communicate) _communicated_ by telegraph.
(1)

Samuel Morse (get) _____ the idea for the telegraph during a trip on
(2)

the ocean. While he (sail) _____, he (talk) _____ to some
(3) (4)

passengers about the electromagnet. The electromagnet (look) _____
(5)

like a horseshoe with wire around it. Electricity (travel) _____ through
(6)

the wire. While Morse (tell) _____ them about it, he suddenly (have)
(7)

_____ an idea. Later, he (try) _____ out his idea, and it
(8) (9)

(work) _____. Electricity (travel) _____ a short distance,
(10) (11)

but under the right conditions it also (travel) _____ a long distance.
(12)

■ COMMUNICATE

E **PAIR WORK** Student A stays on this page. Student B turns to page 305. Use the words on the timeline. Take turns with your partner. Ask and answer questions about communication history. Use the information on the timeline and the model conversation.

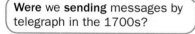

Were we **sending** messages by telegraph in the 1700s?

No, we **sent** telegraphs for the first time in 1830. Before that, people **used to send** messages by mail.

Student A's Timeline

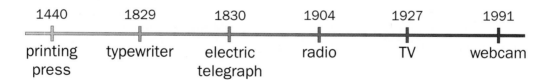

1440	1829	1830	1904	1927	1991
printing press	typewriter	electric telegraph	radio	TV	webcam

Questions to ask Student B

1. Prehistoric times: Write messages on papyrus?
2. 400 BCE: Write messages on paper?
3. 14 BCE: Romans use postal service to send messages?
4. The 1900s: speak to each other on the telephone?
5. The 1960s: Make calls on cell phones?

■ GRAMMAR IN CONTENT

A Read and listen.

CD2,TR49

In-Class Essay

Question: How **has** communication **changed** since the invention of the telephone? **Do** people **communicate** differently because of the technology? **Are** people **experiencing** any negative impacts of technology on communication?

Student Response: There **have been** significant changes in communication since the invention of the telephone. The speed of communication **has been increasing** with every invention. In the past, it took days or months to communicate a message over long distances, but today it **takes** less than a minute to call someone on a phone, send a text message to a friend, or get the news on TV and online. Technology **makes** it possible for us to communicate faster and more efficiently. However, there **are** some negative impacts of this high speed and efficiency. Because technology **gives** us easier ways to reach each other, we **are becoming** less patient, more impolite, and more dangerous. High school students **are sending** text messages to their friends during class. Drivers **are not paying** attention because they**'re talking** on their phones. People **are shouting** into their phones while they **are standing** in line at the grocery store.

B Find one example in the reading of each of the following:

1. Present perfect *wh-* question: _____

2. Simple present *yes/no* question: _____

3. Present progressive *yes/no* question: _____

4. Present perfect affirmative statement: _____

Simple Present and Present Progressive

Form	Simple Present	Present Progressive
Affirmative	It **takes** less than a minute.	We **are becoming** less patient.
Negative	The cell phone **doesn't work.**	Drivers **aren't paying** attention.
Yes/No Questions	**Do** drivers **pay** attention?	**Is** the driver **paying** attention?
Wh- Questions	**Where does** a cell phone **work** best?	**Who is talking** on the phone?

Notes:

- Use simple present tense for habits and general truth. Use present progressive for continuing actions/events and temporary situations in the present.
- Remember the **-s** ending after *he/she/it* in the simple present tense. Use the present tense of *be* with the *-ing* form of the verb for present progressive.
- See Lessons 1, 5, and 12 for more information on the simple present and present progressive tenses.

Present Perfect and Present Perfect Progressive

Form	Present Perfect	Present Perfect Progressive
Affirmative	There **have been** changes.	The speed **has been increasing.**
Negative	The technology **hasn't slowed.**	Callers **haven't been thinking.**
Yes/No Questions	**Has** the technology **changed?**	**Have** people **been calling** more?
Wh- Questions	How **has** it **improved?**	Who **has been thinking** about this?

Notes:

- Use the present perfect for actions completed sometime in the past. Use the present perfect progressive for actions beginning in the past and continuing into the present and possibly into the future.
- Use *have/has* + past participle for present perfect. Use *have/has* + *been* + verb + *-ing* for present perfect progressive.
- See Lessons 24, 25, and 26 for more information on the present perfect and present perfect progressive tenses.

C Fill in the blanks in the following interview with the correct form of the simple present, present progressive, present perfect, or present perfect progressive.

1. (have)　　**A:** Excuse me, _____ you _____ time to answer some questions?

　　　　　　B: Well, I _____ about ten minutes.

2. (own)　　**A:** _____ you _____ a cell phone?

　　　　　　B: Yes, I _____ one since 2005.

3. (use)　　**A:** How often _____ you _____ your cell phone?

　　　　　　B: Hmmm. Let's see, I _____ it about five times a day.

4. (use/drive)　**A:** _____ you ever _____ your cell phone while driving?

　　　　　　B: Yes, sometimes I _____ it while I _____, but I

　　　　　　_____ never _____ it for text messaging in that situation.

4. (drive/see)　**A:** That's good to hear.

　　　　　　B: However, once, while I _____, I _____ a driver in the next car text messaging on a cell phone.

D Two college students did a research study on cell phone use for their Communication Studies class. Listen to the results from their research. Choose the best meaning for each statement you hear.

CD2,TR50

1. a. 75% of the people are not using cell phones.
   b. 75% of the people are not using home telephones.

2. a. 90% of the people usually use their cell phones while they're driving.
   b. 90% of the people used their cell phones at least once while they were driving.

3. a. 89% of the people used a cell phone five years ago.
   b. 89% of the people didn't use a cell phone five years ago.

4. a. 68% of the people said cell phones are not having a negative impact.
   b. 32% of the people said cell phones are not having a negative impact.

5. a. 43% of the people have been using cell phones every day for their jobs.
   b. 57% of the people use their cell phones every day for their jobs.

■ COMMUNICATE

E **PAIR WORK** With a partner, discuss each of the changes in the technology of communication. Answer these questions.

1. How has the new technology changed communication?
2. How do people behave differently because of the method of communication?
3. Are people (you) experiencing any negative impacts from this technology?

Past	Present
telephone	→ cell phone
TV antenna	→ webcam
letters	→ e-mail
printing press	→ online newspaper
records/tapes/CDs	→ music downloads to digital music player

Cell phones have made life so much easier. But people are using their cell phones too much. People make calls whenever they feel like it. Yesterday, while I was sitting on the bus, a man was shouting into his phone next to me.

PART THREE | **Future Review: Simple Future, Future Progressive**

■ GRAMMAR IN CONTENT

A **Read and listen.**

CD2,TR51

Future Change

Professor: We've been learning about the history of communication. Now, we**'re going to think** about the future. Here's the question. How much change **will** we **see** in the next 20 years?

Student 1: Well, we've seen the size of phones get smaller. They**'re** probably **going to get** even smaller and more efficient.

Student 2: We'll probably **be** able to read a whole book on one piece of memory paper.

Student 3: Do you want to know what I think? By 2020, we **will be talking** to our friends without speaking. There **will be** a computer chip in our brains.

B **Look at the conversation. Underline three predictions about future communication.**

Simple Future and Future Progressive

Form	Simple Future	Future Progressive
Affirmative	Life **is going to change.** Life **will change.**	By 2020, we **are going to (will) be communicating** very differently.
Negative	It **isn't going to be** different. It **won't be** different.	We **are not going to (will not) be holding** cell phones.
Yes/No Questions	**Is** life **going to be** different? **Will** life **be** different?	**Are** we **going to be writing?** **Will** we **be writing?**
Wh- Questions	What **is going to change?** What **will change?**	How **are** we **going to be living?** How **will** we **be living?**

Note:

See Lessons 10 and 11 for more information on the future tense.

C Read the predictions. Write **A** if you agree. Write **D** if you disagree. Discuss with your class.

1. ___ Cell phones will be smaller in the future.

2. ___ People will use computer chips in their brains to communicate.

3. ___ TVs are going to be as flat as paper.

4. ___ We will communicate just by thinking.

5. ___ It will be more difficult to communicate in the future.

6. ___ We are going to communicate less in the future.

CD2,TR52

D Listen to the communication student's oral presentation about communication in the future. Check the statement (✔) if it correctly states the information in the presentation. Then discuss these ideas with your classmates.

1. ___ The technology of communication is going to change our lives.

2. ___ Technology will make communication more efficient in the future.

3. ___ We will communicate more in the future.

4. ___ We are going to use a glove phone to carry a computer.

5. ___ We will wear a glove in order to carry a phone.

6. ___ The glove phone will be a phone.

7. ___ We will not have to carry a cell phone.

8. ___ The "hug hat" is going to hug us when we feel lonely.

9. ___ If we are busy, the hat will help us to remember things.

10. ___ In the future, there will be no communication problems based on different languages.

■ COMMUNICATE

E **WRITE** Write one to two paragraphs about the development of your English communication skills. Compare the past and present. Make predictions about the future.

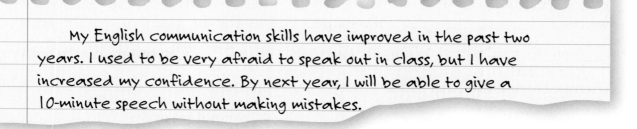

My English communication skills have improved in the past two years. I used to be very afraid to speak out in class, but I have increased my confidence. By next year, I will be able to give a 10-minute speech without making mistakes.

GRAMMAR AND VOCABULARY With a partner, fill in the blanks with the correct verb tense of the verb in parentheses or a vocabulary item from the list.

webcam	fax machine	cell phone
telegraph	printing press	text messages

Today in Communication Studies class, while we (discuss) __were discussing__ (1) the history of communication, I (think) _____ (2) about all of the interesting changes. For example, people (begin) _____ (3) reading newspapers when the _____ (4) (be) _____ (5) invented. Today we (read) _____ (6) newspapers online. For the past two years, I (send) _____ (7) e-mails and _____ (8) to communicate with my friends. During the 13th century, people (not/communicate) _____ (9) this way because they (not/have) _____ (10) computers or _____ (11). Before the _____ (12) and the _____ (13), people (send) _____ (14) very few messages across long distances because it (take) _____ (15) so long. Finally, in the past, I (talk) _____ (16) to my mother on the telephone and I (hear) _____ (17) her voice. Now I use a _____ (18) when I (talk) _____ (19) to my mother.

PROJECT Write and perform a communications technology skit.

1. In groups of three, choose one of the following: text message, fax machine, cell phone, e-mail, webcam, or digital music player.
2. Create a skit about two people from the past meeting a person from the present. The person from the present must teach the people from the past about communication in the present, explaining their present method of communication and comparing it to past methods.
3. Perform your skit for the class.

 INTERNET Enter "history of communication" into a search engine. Find three interesting facts not mentioned in this lesson. Report to your class.

A Read the conversation between two students. Fill in the blank with the correct tense of the verb in parentheses OR choose from the two words in parentheses. Fill in the blank by reporting the question in parentheses where a question is provided.

Pam: Hi, Carol. I (not/see) _____*haven't seen*_____ you (since/for) _____ last
(1)   (2)

week. (work) _____ on your research project?
(3)

Carol: Yes, I (look) _____ at the data from my survey on writing anxiety.
(4)

Pam: What (explore) _____ in your research?
(5)

Carol: I (ask) _____ ("Why does writing produce so much anxiety?")
(6)

_____ and ("Do certain situations
(7)

cause writing anxiety?") _____.
(8)

Pam: (find) _____ anything interesting yet?
(9)

Carol: Well, I (give) _____ the survey to 50 college students, and so
(10)

far I (receive) _____ 34 completed surveys. Also, I (interview)
(11)

_____ 10 of the students from that group. Most of them
(12)

(said/told) _____ ("I get anxious when I have to write.")
(13)

_____. They also (said/told)
(14)

_____ ("In-class timed essay tests make me very nervous.")
(15)

_____. One student (said/
(16)

told) _____ me ("I always feel nervous during essay tests.")
(17)

_____. While she (say/tell)
(18)

_____ me this, she (begin) _____ to shake.
(19)   (20)

B Andrew is being interviewed for medical school by Mr. Evans. Fill in the blanks with the correct tense of the verb or choose from the words in parentheses. Use passive voice if necessary.

Mr. E: Andrew, what kind of experience (have) _____ in hospital
(1)

emergency situations?

A: Well, I (hire) _____ to work at Washington Hospital in 2005 as
(2)

an EMT in the emergency room. I (work) _____ there (since/for)
(3)

_____ two years while I (complete) _____ my degree.
(4)   (5)

That experience (teach) _____ me a lot about trauma medicine.
(6)

Before that, while I (complete) _____ my EMT courses, I (assist)
(7)

_____ as a Level I paramedic on emergency calls. When a call
(8)

(receive) _____, I (ride) _____ in the ambulance and (help)
(9)   (10)

_____ at the scene of the emergency. That experience (prepare)
(11)

_____ me for the position at the hospital.
(12)

Mr. E: And what kind of research (do) _____ so far?
(13)

A: Well, while I (finish) _____ my last year in college, I (do)
(14)

_____ research on the types of cancers that affect children.
(15)

I (present) _____ three papers at conferences, and one of my
(16)

papers (publish) _____ by a medical journal.
(17)

Mr. E: Yes, I (read) _____ your papers. You (do) _____ some very
(18)   (19)

good work. If you (accept) _____ here, (continue) _____
(20)   (21)

that research?

A: Yes, I (study) _____ the specific causes of early childhood cancers.
(22)

LEARNER LOG Check (✔) *Yes* or *I Need More Practice.*

Lesson	I Can Use . . .	Yes	I Need More Practice
26	Present Perfect Progressive, Present Perfect vs. Present Perfect Progressive		
27	Passive Voice: Forms & Tenses, Passive Voice with the Agent, Passive with *Get & Have*		
28	Direct Quotation, Reported Statements		
29	*Yes/No* Reported Questions, *Wh-* Reported Questions		
30	Past (Progressive) Tense, *Used To/Would,* Present (Progressive) Tense, Present Perfect (Progressive) Tense, Future (Progressive) Tense		

APPENDIX 1 | Activities for Student B

LESSON 2, PART 1, EXERCISE E (p. 14)

Student B

Course #	Class	Days	Time	Location	Instructor
2137		MW			Reed
	Engl 200		10:00–10:50am		
2245		TTh	1:00–2:20pm	C-217	
3186		TTh		C-165	Jackson
3278			7:00–8:50pm	R-354	Oleksy

LESSON 10, PART 3, EXERCISE E (p. 101)

Student B

FIELD TRIP SCHEDULE

7:00	meet in the parking lot	2:30	
8:00	group will pack vans	3:00	
9:00	vans will leave school	5:00	
12:00	lunch in Sedona	6:00	

LESSON 13, PART 2, EXERCISE F (p. 131)

EXPORTS	INDIA	ITALY	CHINA	BRAZIL	U.S.	NIGERIA
		69 million			190 million	
	350 million		30 million	2 billion		0
		47 million			5 billion	

EXPORTS	INDIA	ITALY	CHINA	BRAZIL	U.S.	NIGERIA
	220 million		43 million		280 million	
		170 million		2 billion		23 billion
	340 million				1.82 billion	

Amounts in U.S. dollars. (Estimates based on past years.)

LESSON 14, PART 2, EXERCISE E (p. 138)

Student B Questions

1. servings/bag of pasta
2. carbohydrates/pasta
3. sugar/ice cream
4. calories/a bowl of oatmeal
5. grams of fat/toast with peanut butter

Student B Nutrition Chart		
Food	**Serving**	**Nutrition**
cheeseburger	one	13 grams of fat
apple	one	81 calories
brown rice	$\frac{1}{2}$ cup	2.5 grams of protein
cheddar cheese	one slice	1 gram of sugar
carrot juice	one cup	Vitamin A, B, C

LESSON 14, PART 3, EXERCISE E (p. 141)

Jenny	Breakfast	Snack	Lunch	Dinner	Snack
Monday	oatmeal with apples and milk/orange juice	apple/nuts	tofu/broccoli/ brown rice/salad	fish/ vegetables/ potatoes/pie	popcorn with olive oil
Tuesday	1 egg/whole grain toast/ 1/2 grapefruit	1 orange	cheese on whole wheat bread with lettuce & tomato	whole wheat pasta/ meatballs/ salad/apple	raisins and almonds
Wednesday	green tea/ 1 tsp. honey/ 1 bran muffin	1 banana 1 cup of yogurt	quinoa (grain) with onions and tomatoes	chicken/mixed vegetables/ rice	strawberries with honey

LESSON 18, PART 2, EXERCISE E (p. 180)

Student B Questions
1. warm/Mars?
2. water/Earth?
3. oxygen/Mars?
4. cool/Venus?
5. gravity/Earth?

Student B Information

	Average Temperature	Oxygen/ Atmosphere	Gravity	Other
Mars				
Venus				
Earth				
Uranus	−212°C (↓)	no oxygen (↓)	86% of Earth (↓)	no solid core
Jupiter	−150°C (↓)	no oxygen (↓)	can't move (↑)	

Key: (↑) = too much   (↓) = too little/not enough   (*) = OK/enough

LESSON 21, PART 2, EXERCISE F (p. 209)

Student B: Questions
1. Li/interview the psychology professor/yesterday?
2. Gerd/ask Ali to review the summary/yesterday?
3. Li/write story on the basketball game/today?
4. Gerd/review letters from readers/today?

Student B: Journalism I Schedule

	Yesterday	Today	Tomorrow
Li			
Gerd			
Sadie	take photographs of the culture fair	pick up photographs	lay out photos for next week
Ali	review articles for spelling and punctuation	edit final copy of next week's paper	send next week's paper to printer

LESSON 22, PART 1, EXERCISE F (p. 215)

Student B:

Questions

1. have textbook in class?
2. attend class every day?
3. check homework in a group?
4. turn off cell phones?
5. make up a test if you miss it?
6. ask questions during class?
7. bring the syllabus to class every day?
8. use a calculator in class?

Syllabus Information

- show tax formulas
- no late papers
- edit carefully
- no handwritten papers
- meet with a tutor about the paper

LESSON 24, PART 1, EXERCISE E (p. 233)

Student A
Questions about Basha:
1. (10:30 a.m.) prepare medications?
2. (11:20 a.m.) check on patients?
3. (12:30 p.m.) bring breakfast trays?
4. (2:00 p.m.) pick up breakfast trays?
5. (2:15 p.m.) write report on patient care?

Basha's Schedule

10:30 a.m.	take patients' temperature and blood pressure
11:30 a.m.	give shots to Mr. Barsinian
12:00 p.m.	bring lunch trays to the patients
1:30 p.m.	take away lunch trays
2:30 p.m.	write new patient care plans

LESSON 25, PART 1, EXERCISE E (p. 242)

Student B

Sam's Checklist	Adrian's Checklist
___ choose topic	___ choose topic
___ check the library database	✔ check the library database
___ find three articles	✔ find three articles
___ write a summary of articles	___ write a summary of articles
___ write an outline	✔ write an outline
___ read feedback from the professor	___ read feedback from the professor
___ write the first draft	___ write the first draft
___ meet with professor	✔ meet with professor
___ write final draft	___ write final draft
___ edit and hand in	___ edit and hand in

LESSON 27, PART 1, EXERCISE E (p. 261)

Student B

	Level I Paramedic	Level II Paramedic	Level III Paramedic
give basic medical care		✔	
check condition of patient		✔	
hook up an IV		✔	
give medication			
manage basic heart problems		✔	
read ECGs			
operate breathing equipment		✔	
give CPR		✔	
use defibrillator		✔	

Student C

	Level I Paramedic	Level II Paramedic	Level III Paramedic
give basic medical care			✔
check condition of patient			✔
hook up an IV			✔
give medication			✔
manage basic heart problems			✔
read ECGs			✔
operate breathing equipment			✔
give CPR			✔
use defibrillator			✔

LESSON 27, PART 2, EXERCISE F (p. 265)

Student B: Case Study Information

Jin Chang made a call at 6:11 PM from Number 53 Elementary School.
Alan Thompson took the call.
He called an ambulance at 6:15 and sent the paramedics to the school.
The paramedics arrived at the school at 2:50.
The school nurse was bandaging Jenny Nelson's arm when they arrived.
Another student was holding Jenny's hand to make her feel better.
The paramedics did some tests on Jenny.
The paramedics asked Jenny some questions about the pain.
The paramedics took Jenny to the hospital.

Student B: Questions to Ask Student A

1. who/make/call?
2. what time/make/call?
3. who/take/call?
4. call/ambulance?
5. what time/call /the Fire Department?
6. when/paramedics/arrive?
7. what/Mr. Gomez/doing/when/you/arrive?
8. paramedics/take/anyone/to the hospital?

LESSON 30, PART 1, EXERCISE E (p. 289)

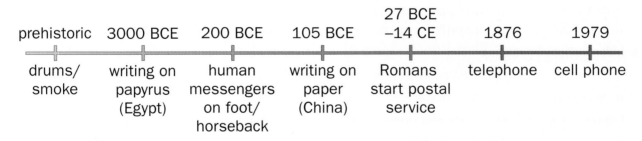

1. 1700s: Send messages by telegraph?
2. 1435: Use printing press to print books?
3. 1906: Watch the news on TV?
4. 1867: Type letters?
5. 1860: Listen to radio?

■ **Adjective** An adjective describes a noun. Example: *That's a **small** desk.*

■ **Adverb** An adverb describes the verb of a sentence or an adjective. Examples: *He is **very** smart. I run **quickly**.*

■ **Adverb of Frequency** An adverb of frequency tells how often an action happens. Example: *I **always** go to the library after class.*

■ **Affirmative** An affirmative means *yes*.

■ **Article** An article (*a, an,* and *the*) comes before a noun. Example: *I have **a** book and **an** eraser.*

■ **Base Form** The base form of a verb has no tense. It has no ending (*-s* or *-ed*). Examples: ***be, go, eat, take, write***

■ **Clause** A clause is a group of words that has a subject and a verb. Example: ***Harry likes** college.*

■ **Comparative Form** A comparative form of an adjective or adverb is used to compare two things. Example: *I am **taller** than you.*

■ **Consonant** The following letters are consonants: ***b, c, d, f, g, h, j, k, l, m, n, p, q, r, s, t, v, w, x, y, z.***

■ **Contraction** A contraction is made up of two words put together with an apostrophe. Example: ***She's** my friend.* (She is = she's)

■ **Count Noun** Count nouns are nouns that we can count. They have a singular and a plural form. Examples: ***book – books, nurse – nurses***

■ **Frequency Expressions** Frequency expressions answer *How often* questions. Examples: ***once a week, three times a week, every day***

■ **Imperative** An imperative sentence gives a command or instructions. An imperative sentence usually omits the word *you*. Example: ***Open** the door.*

■ **Information Questions** Questions that ask *what, when, who, how,* or *which*.

■ **Intransitive** Intransitive verbs do not have an object.

■ **Irregular Verbs** See Appendix 3.

■ **Linking Verb** A linking verb connects the subject of a sentence to a noun, adjective, or prepositional phrase.

■ **Modal** Some examples of modal verbs are ***can, could, should, will, would, must.***

■ **Negative** Means *no*.

■ **Noncount Noun** A noncount noun is a noun that we don't count. It has no plural form. Examples: ***water, money, rice***

■ **Noun** A noun is a word for a person, a place, or a thing. Nouns can be singular (only one) or plural (more than one).

■ **Object** The object of the sentence follows the verb. It receives the action of the verb. Example: *Kat wrote a **paragraph**.*

■ **Object Pronoun** Use object pronouns (*me, you, him, her, it, us, them*) after the verb or preposition. Example: *Kat wore **it**.*

- **Phrasal Verb** A verb followed by a particle, such as *point out, think over,* and *turn in.*
- **Plural** Plural means more than one. A plural noun usually ends with *-s* or *-es*. Examples: *The books are heavy. The buses are not running.*
- **Possessive Form** The possessive form of a noun has an apostrophe: *the teacher's class, Jupiter's moons.* Possessive pronouns *(my, mine, our, ours, his, her, hers, their, theirs, its, your, yours)* do not use an apostrophe.
- **Preposition** A preposition is a short, connecting word. Examples: *about, above, across, after, around, as, at, away, before, behind, below, by, down, for, from, in, into, like, of, on, out, over, to, under, up, with*
- **Punctuation (. , ' ?)** Punctuation marks are used to make writing clear (for example: periods, commas, apostrophes, question marks).
- **Regular Verb** A regular verb forms its past tense with *-d* or *-ed*. Example: *He lived in Mexico.*
- **Sentence** A sentence is a group of words that contains a subject and a verb and expresses a complete thought.
- **Singular** Means one.
- **Stative Verb** Stative verbs have no action. They do not often take the progressive form. Examples: *love, like, think, own, understand, want*
- **Subject** The subject of the sentence tells who or what the sentence is about. Example: *The water does not taste good.*
- **Subject Pronoun** Use subject pronouns (*I, you, he, she, it, we, they*) in place of a subject noun. Example: *They* (= *the books*) *are on the desk.*
- **Tense** A verb has tense. Tense shows when the action of the sentence happened.

   Simple Present: *She occasionally reads before bed.*

   Present Progressive: *He is thinking about it now.*

   Simple Past: *I talked to him yesterday.*
- **Transitive** Transitive verbs have an object.
- **Verb** Verbs are words of action or state. Example: *I go to work every day. Joe stays at home.*
- **Verb of Perception** Verbs related to the senses, such as *look, see, watch, hear, listen, taste, smell,* and *feel.*
- **Yes/No Questions** Yes/No questions ask for a *yes* or *no* answer. Example: *Is she from Mexico? Yes, she is.*

The following chart gives the past and past participles of some common verbs. You must memorize these forms, because they are irregular.

Base Form	Past Tense	Past Participle
be	was, were	been
begin	began	begun
bite	bit	bitten
break	broke	broken
bring	brought	brought
build	built	built
buy	bought	bought
catch	caught	caught
choose	chose	chosen
come	came	come
cost	cost	cost
cut	cut	cut
do	did	done
draw	drew	drawn
drink	drank	drunk
eat	ate	eaten
feel	felt	felt
find	found	found
give	gave	given
go	went	gone
grow	grew	grown
hide	hid	hidden
have	had	had
hear	heard	heard
keep	kept	kept
know	knew	known
make	made	made
pay	paid	paid
read	read	read
say	said	said
see	saw	seen
speak	spoke	spoken
take	took	taken
teach	taught	taught
tell	told	told
think	thought	thought
write	wrote	written

Review: Lessons 1–5
(pages 49–50)

A.

1. do
2. have
3. come
4. is sleeping
5. am making
6. needs
7. is
8. am writing
9. is
10. isn't
11. is
12. am writing
13. seems
14. have
15. don't
16. do
17. aren't
18. are
19. Ask
20. do you take
21. work
22. spends
23. does she like
24. looks
25. happy
26. pick
27. Does
28. cry
29. leave
30. ever
31. does she
32. leave
33. sometimes
34. cries
35. pick

B.

1. is working
2. has
3. receives
4. give
5. feels
6. helps
7. tutors
8. arrives
9. leaves
10. does she arrive
11. is
12. become
13. aren't
14. themselves

Review: Lessons 6–10
(pages 103–104)

A.

1. did
2. choose
3. decided
4. spent
5. looked him up
6. found
7. read
8. checked
9. out
10. wanted
11. taking
12. went over
13. thought
14. decided
15. be
16. was thinking
17. looked up
18. is
19. figure out
20. was
21. used to
22. would
23. would

B.

1. Didn't
2. sleep
3. went
4. slept
5. was sneezing
6. caught
7. were hiking
8. did
9. hike
10. was raining
11. began
12. were going
13. put
14. got
15. did
16. do
17. finished
18. were studying
19. wrote
20. arrived
21. made
22. had
23. cooked
24. went
25. slept

Review: Lessons 11–15
(pages 153–154)

A.

1. will/'ll discuss
2. begin
3. will explain
4. will give
5. a little
6. information
7. a few
8. ideas
9. will listen
10. a few
11. beliefs
12. give
13. a few
14. will see
15. finish
16. will have
17. will give
18. some
19. Many

20. very
21. believe
22. has
23. wishes
24. dreams
25. other
26. think
27. bodies
28. other
29. too little
30. information

B.
1. Have
2. seen
3. heard
4. continues
5. many
6. the
7. will have
8. the
9. most of the
10. will be fighting
11. are
12. the
13. the
14. Do
15. think
16. do
17. believe
18. is
19. A lot of
20. believe
21. an
22. the
23. the
24. think
25. will experience
26. another

Review: Lessons 16–20
(pages 201–202)

A.
1. interested
2. five-year-old
3. famous
4. hard
5. to discover
6. spending
7. fascinating
8. to teach
9. too busy
10. to give
11. frustrating
12. to look
13. to use
14. tall enough
15. to reach
16. quickly
17. to stand
18. surprised
19. to see
20. complete
21. disappointing
22. slowly
23. smiling
24. taking
25. telling
26. to give
27. frequent

B.
1. to decide
2. less
3. than
4. reading
5. as
6. as
7. more
8. than
9. as
10. to participate
11. to receive
12. less
13. same as
14. similar
15. different
16. simply

17. better
18. enough
19. to pay
20. wisely
21. enough

Review: Lessons 21–25
(pages 247–248)

A.
1. supposed
2. would
3. Have
4. chosen
5. Could
6. have been thinking
7. for
8. have to
9. have
10. never
11. written
12. would
13. choose
14. ought to
15. had better
16. choose
17. explore
18. have
19. never
20. read

B.
1. supposed to
2. Could
3. can
4. Could
5. have had
6. for
7. have
8. been working
9. began
10. have been
11. for
12. took
13. had
14. ever worked
15. had
16. worked
17. took

18. would rather
19. than

**Review: Lessons 26–30
(pages 297–298)**

A.
1. haven't seen
2. since
3. Have you been working
4. have been looking
5. have you explored
6. am asking
7. why writing produces
   so much anxiety
8. whether/if certain
   situations cause
   writing anxiety
9. Have you found

10. have given
11. have received
12. have interviewed
13. have said
14. that they get anxious
    when they had to write
15. said that
16. in-class timed essay tests
    made them very nervous
17. told
18. he always felt nervous
    during essay tests
19. was telling
20. began

B.
1. have you had
2. was hired
3. worked

4. for
5. was completing
6. taught
7. was completing
8. was assisting
9. was received
10. would ride
11. help
12. prepared
13. have you done
14. was finishing
15. did
16. presented
17. was published
18. have read
19. did
20. are accepted
21. will you continue
22. will study

Words in blue are part of the Content Vocabulary section at the start of each lesson.
Words in black are words glossed with the readings in each lesson.
Words in **bold** are words from the Academic Word List.

Index

Credits

Illustrators

Amy Cartwright/illustrationOnLine.com: pp. 1 (bottom 2), 11, 21, 31, 42–43, 51 (top 2), 133, 143, 150, 267.

InContext Publishing Partners: pp. 51, 185, 257, 273.

Alan King/illustrationOnLine.com: pp. 81, 84–86.

Precision Graphics: pp. 1 (top 2), 5, 8, 10, 14, 18, 25, 29, 34, 39, 47, 51 (bottom 2), 59–60, 69, 78, 80, 87, 89–90, 101–102, 105 (right), 113 (bottom), 121, 127, 130, 142, 151, 164, 171, 174, 191, 227, 236, 239, 256, 270, 274, 276–277, 279, 285, 289, 295, 299, 305.

David Preiss/Munro Campagna.com: pp. 61–62, 66, 71, 91.

Scott Wakefield/Gwen Walters Artist Representative: pp. 105 (top and bottom left), 113 (top), 115, 175.

Claudia Wolf/contactjupiter.com: pp. 123, 155, 165, 193, 203, 211, 221, 229, 249.

Photo Credits

Page 2: © Photos.com/RF **page 5:** © Ken Chernus/Photodisc Red/Getty/RF **page 12:** © Ingram Publishing/Getty/RF **page 15:** © Douglas Dobbins/America 24-7/Getty **page 22:** © Keith Brofsky/Photodisc Green/Getty/RF **page 25:** © Denny Ellis/Alamy **page 26:** © Jutta Klee/Stone/Getty **page 28:** © IndexOpen/RF **page 31: (Left to Right):** © IndexOpen/RF, © Tim Laman/National Geographic/Getty/RF, © Flying Colours/Photographer's Choice/Getty/RF, © IndexOpen/RF, © IndexOpen/RF **page 32:** © David Ellis/Digital Vision/Getty/RF **page 35:** © Sean Justice/The Image Bank/Getty **page 40:** © Jason Dewey/The Image Bank/Getty **page 44:** © Photodisc Green/Getty/RF **page 52:** © Bruce Ayres/Stone/Getty **page 55:** © Ian Shaw/Stone/Getty **page 58:** © Image Source Pink/Image Source/Getty/RF **page 72:** © Getty Images **page 76:** © Getty Images **page 82:** © NASA/Photonica/Getty **page 87:** © AP Photo/Zia Mazhar **page 92:** © Greg Gilman/Alamy **page 96:** © Danita Delimont/Alamy **page 98:** © Ilan Rosen/Alamy **page 99:** © RubberBall/Alamy **page 106:** © World Perspectives/Stone/Getty **page 109:** © The Photolibrary Wales/Alamy **page 112:** © AP Photo/NASA **page 116:** © Glen Allison/Stone/Getty **page 119:** © Frans Lemmens/Photographer's Choice/Getty **page 124:** © AP Photo/Jalil Bounhar **page 128:** © Jens Buettner/epa/Corbis **page 131 (All Photos):** © Photos.com/RF **page 134:** © STOCK4B/Getty/RF **page 136:** © MyPyramid.gov/RF **page 139:** © David Buffington/Photodisc Green/Getty/RF **page 144:** © Aura/Taxi Japan/Getty **page 145:** © Natalie Kauffman/First Light/Getty **page 147:** © Amy Neunsinger/The Image Bank/Getty **page 149:** © Christopher Bissell/Stone/Getty **page 156:** © Stock Connection Blue/Alamy

page 159: © Comstock Images/Alamy **page 161:** © John-Francis Bourke/Photographer's Choice/Getty **page 166:** © ML Harris/Iconica/Getty/RF **page 168:** © Susan Chiang/Photodisc Blue/Getty/RF **page 172:** © Juan Silva/Photodisc Red/Getty/RF **page 176:** © AP Photo/NASA **page 178:** © Derek Berwin/Riser/Getty **page 181:** © AP Photo/NASA **page 186:** © Image courtesy of The Advertising Archives **page 189:** © Image courtesy of The Advertising Archives **page 194:** © Photos.com/RF **page 197:** © Photos.com/RF **page 204:** © Mark Pierce/Alamy **page 206:** © PhotoAlto/Alamy **page 212:** © CuboImages srl/Alamy **page 216:** © Thomas Fricke/First Light/Getty **page 222:** © Photos.com/RF **page 225:** © Photos.com/RF **page 230:** © IndexOpen/RF **page 234:** © Custom Medical Stock Photo/Alamy **page 240:** © Manfred Rutz/Taxi/Getty **page 243:** © Michael Blann/Digital Vision/Getty/RF **page 250:** © IndexOpen/RF **page 253:** © IndexOpen/RF **page 258:** © Photos.com/RF **page 262:** © Getty Images/Taxi **page 268:** © Working Title Films/ZUMA/Corbis **page 271:** © Blend Images/Alamy **page 278:** © BananaStock/Alamy **page 281:** © Photofusion Picture Library/Alamy **page 286:** © LHB Photo/Alamy **page 288:** © Hulton Archive/Stringer/Getty **page 290:** © Ilene MacDonald/Alamy **page 293:** © Digital Vision/Getty/RF